Public W
Private Faith

DATE DUE

John Bealle

Public Worship, Private Faith

SACRED HARP

AND

AMERICAN

FOLKSONG

The University of Georgia Press

Athens and London

© 1997 by the University of Georgia Press
Athens, Georgia 30602
All rights reserved
Designed by Betty Palmer McDaniel
Set in 10/14 Sabon with Nicholas Cochin
by G & S Typesetters, Inc.
Printed and bound by Braun-Brumfield, Inc.
The paper in this book meets the guidelines for
permanence and durability of the Committee on
Production Guidelines for Book Longevity of the
Council on Library Resources.

Printed in the United States of America

01   00   99   98   97   C   5   4   3   2   1
01   00   99   98   97   P   5   4   3   2   1

Library of Congress Cataloging in Publication Data
Bealle, John.
Public worship, private faith : sacred harp and American
folksong / John Bealle.
p.   cm.
ISBN 0-8203-1921-X (alk. paper).
—ISBN 0-8203-1988-0 (pbk. : alk. paper)
1. Shape note singing—History and criticism.   2. Hymns,
English—Southern States—History and criticism.
ML3188.B43   1997
782.27′0975—dc21   97-19852
MN
British Library Cataloging in Publication Data available

FOR
Harry Gammerdinger
(1956–1990)

a gracious friend, a quintessential folklorist

No vain Discourse shall fill our Tongue,
Nor Trifles vex our Ear;
Infinite Grace shall be our Song,
And God rejoice to hear.
—ISAAC WATTS

Contents

CONTENTS

Introduction

With a little effort, almost any American today could make his or her way to a distinctive traditional musical event that participants call a "Sacred Harp singing." There, set apart in so many ways from the furious pace of contemporary life, one might well be swept up by a glorious unaccompanied vocal music, extracted from the pages of a unique book of nineteenth-century lineage, *The Sacred Harp*.

Too few do, of course: Sacred Harp singings are customarily peopled by a loyal and talented band of singers, most from the southeastern United States, some from large "singing families" whose involvement spans many generations. It is entirely common for singers to shape their lives around this indescribable expression of faith, praise, and ecstacy. As one singer, Leonard Lacy, once put it: "I wish I could just tell people how I feel about it. But when I get to talking about it, it thrills me so much, I'm so emotional, I can't say what I'd like to say. I've often wondered why I was that way—as much as I love Sacred Harp—I've sung it and taught it—why I can't get up in front of a congregation and talk about it. But I can't. But I love it. I love to sing it" (Brice and Petry 1984). This, in a nutshell, is what Sacred Harp singing is about.

Others, however, find Sacred Harp by way of what might well qualify as the "vain Discourse" of American culture. Indeed, Sacred Harp singing is a substantial living tradition with unbroken links to the eighteenth century and to America's earliest native composers. At the turn of the nineteenth century, its cause was advanced by a clever pedagogical innovation, "shape note" musical notation. By midcentury, it had been expelled from mainstream American musical discourse by an aggressive reform movement. During this period, *The Sacred Harp* (1844) itself was compiled in Hamilton, Georgia, employing the shape note system and drawing from the most popular tunes of the period. As shape note tunebooks fell into decline elsewhere, Sacred Harp singing took root in the American South and was aligned with the most tradition-minded people of the region. There, it is often said, the singing tradition weathered every storm of modernization, seemingly growing more resilient with each assault. This story has been told and retold, nowhere more eloquently than in Buell Cobb's book *The Sacred Harp: A Tradition and Its Music* (1978). As I discuss in chapter 4, Cobb's timely exposition is set squarely on the seam that binds insider experience to outsider understanding. Nearly two decades in print, his concise work shows little sign of wear as the definitive introduction to Sacred Harp singing.

But the story does not end there. In the 1920s, the singing tradition was "discovered" as folksong and, through printed and other media, adopted into the emerging taxonomy of American musical culture. To a large degree, traditional practice persisted unaffected by these events, yet countless Americans outside the singing tradition were reintroduced to the shape note idiom through the discourse of American culture. Some, particularly in the post–World War II decades, were motivated to participate in the singing tradition precisely because of its interaction with the compelling attractions of the folksong idea. It is this process—and all of the broader issues of cultural taxonomy, modernization, and the varieties of religious exercise—that are the concerns of my book. My purpose is not so much to recount Sacred Harp history or to provide a comprehensive overview of the tradition—although certainly some of that will be necessary. Rather, I mean to examine particular defining events in the dramatic encounter of Sacred Harp tradition with American public culture. Fundamental to this exercise will be to call into question the status of Sacred Harp as folksong. "Why folksong?" I ask, and, with that, I hope to discover the meaning of folksong through Sacred Harp as much as the reverse.

I have organized my book in four chapters, each of which addresses what I consider an essential component of any musical form that has entered the canon of American folksong. The first reviews the conditions that long ago predisposed the treatment of the singing tradition as folksong. It is an old argument, here newly situated in a single locale, and with attention to the social, political, and theological context that motivated musical reform and exiled the shape note idiom to the margins of American musical culture. The second chapter dissects the rhetoric of culture writing in which the idea of Sacred Harp singing as folksong was developed. With the third chapter, I turn to the singing tradition itself. In particular, I review traditional writing practices, spanning the tenure of Sacred Harp singing, with an eye to the way traditional writers in various periods situated their tradition in the spectrum of American musical culture. Of preeminent concern in this is the degree to which the recent Sacred Harp revival, originating in large part from the folksong idea, was anticipated, guided, encouraged, or resisted by traditional singers. These three chapters are prerequisite to the fourth, where I turn at last to this self-described and self-conscious "Sacred Harp revival" that has so flourished since the 1980s.

Although this book is ostensibly and thoroughly concerned with Sacred Harp and American culture, I have insisted upon framing it within the scope of a less salient yet no less important theme, "public worship, private faith." This is because Sacred Harp singings, aside from their historical importance or their musical qualities, are fundamentally nondenominational religious exercises. Together, singers strive to attain praise of the highest order without confronting or compromising the ecclesiastical or personal sources of religious faith.

Yet this is not a book about the ways singers experience singing. Rather, I attend to the cultural and historical conditions that foster these experiences. This is not only a deferential gesture to traditional values but also a methodological imperative. In this regard, I take folksong revival not as a cultural movement but as a site of encounter, one of many through which traditional discourses engage those discourses that have assumed the character and status of the cultural mainstream. As a consequence, my argument runs, this is also a site of historical convergence, with the possibility of rediscovering the fundamental character of traditional discourses. It is from this point of departure that I revisit the various encounters of Sacred Harp and American folksong.

This book has incurred a wholesome indebtedness to many benefactors. Libraries have provided essential primary materials: the hymnbook and tunebook collection at the Southern Baptist Theological Seminary, nineteenth-century newspapers and other local materials in the Cincinnati Historical Society, and the libraries of the University of Cincinnati. Foremost, the Sacred Harp Foundation allowed me generous access to their headquarters library where singers have deposited materials.

Day in and day out, the most constant resource has been the Hamilton County Public Library (Ohio), available to any citizen for no more than the effort of applying for a library card. It is a paragon of effective public service and intellectual breadth, delivering materials of the most extraordinary depth and diversity to the far reaches of the community. I owe a particular word of thanks to the staff at the Clifton branch, all of whom have been genuine allies to my cause.

During this book's lengthy incubation, when all seemed incoherent, I drank heartily from many inspiring conversations with singers and scholars. Those who granted lengthy interviews included Boston composer Bruce Randall, Chicago composer and writer Ted Johnson, Cincinnati singer Faye Bresler (now of Boston), revival spiritual scholar Ellen Jane Porter, Hugh McElrath of the Southern Baptist Theological Seminary, and Peter W. Williams of Miami University. Joey Brackner, Joyce Cauthen, and others in the Alabama public folklore community provided advice and materials on demand. John H. McDowell of Indiana University has remained a steadfast and able mentor, periodically fending off those demons who might impede free scholarly practice. Janet Herman, Ted Mercer, Nancy Michael, and Jeff Todd Titon each brought essential insights to issues that were difficult to untangle. Joel Cohen, John Garst, Richard Hulan, Warren Steel, Keith Willard, Karen Willard, and so many others on the "fasola" electronic mail conference kept up an invigorating discussion and with it a lively interest in many issues related to this book. Singers in the local Cincinnati singing group, including Jim and Linda Coppock, Christine Cox, Bobbie Goodell, Billie Gray, Debbie Hall, Michael Hieber,

Jodi Liss, Claire Outten, Rich Overturf, Tineke and John Stevens, and Steve Tossey provided a nourishing mix of inspiration and encouragement. John Bayer Jr. of Dayton, Ohio, sent me countless historical materials, cassette tapes, and photocopies of tunebooks and enriched my understanding of how the hymns we were singing were emblems of the most profound Christian faith.

Still, the greatest contributions have come from the longtime custodians of the Sacred Harp singing tradition, of whom generosity is always too modest an attribute. Of them, Hugh McGraw has been inexhaustible in his support. Like so many others, he has devoted his life to *The Sacred Harp* and continues to provide time and resources to anyone who gives the faintest glimmer of hope that their work might benefit the book and its singers. I am certain that the manner and motive of his generosity had as much influence over me as anything he said or did.

I could not have done any of this without the support of all of my families. My parents, Ann and Rufus Bealle of Tuscaloosa, Alabama, have stood behind my work and are proud to see it come to fruition in this form. My wife's family, the Clarks, have given encouragement at various stages; the Rev. Robert Clark became a tenacious proofreader in the home stretch. My daughter Josie was born somewhere in chapter 2 and added a multitude of smiles and tears to an otherwise solitary task. My wife, Eloise Clark, has shared with me a personal investment in Sacred Harp, having learned to sing in Chapel Hill, North Carolina, in the group Dan Patterson founded. Only recently have we learned that her grandmother, Dora Brake, studied shape note singing under J. H. Ruebush at Shenandoah Institute in Dayton, Virginia, around 1920, and sang from shape note books in her region of West Virginia until they were replaced, only after considerable resistance, with round notes. While these events may have precipitated Eloise's genuine interest in my work, the sacrifice it has entailed has been all her own. In this, she has embraced this book, and the relentless burdens that accompany it, as an essential part of our life together. No writer could ask for more.

Public Worship,
Private Faith

Chapter 1

TIMOTHY MASON IN CINCINNATI:
MUSIC REFORM ON THE
URBAN FRONTIER

In 1802 there appeared a curious book. Compiled by William Little and William Smith, *The Easy Instructor* was in many ways like other collections of music popular at the time.[1] It contained predominantly American compositions, reflecting the vigorous musical activity that had arisen during the Revolution when the rate of immigration was low and patriotic sentiment was high. It had a visible pedagogical element—it was an instructor—indicating its intended use in singing schools, which had been the mainstay of musical culture in eighteenth-century New England.

But in one respect *The Easy Instructor* was different from its predecessors, for it introduced Americans to an unusual pedagogical system. Specifically, the book rendered its musical notation in what would come to be called "shape notes" or, because their inventors sought to protect them legally, "patent notes." In this type of notation, each tone in the musical scale was given a corresponding shape to aid singers in note reading. This was an ingenious device, as some musicologists have noted: "The clear advantages of the shape note system are almost immediately apparent. Providing an individual shape for each syllable enables anyone, after a modicum of attention to the matter, to name the proper syllables of any piece of music instantaneously. One of the genuine difficulties in ordinary solmization is that . . . the student must make continual mental computations. With shape notes, this is completely avoided" (Lowens and Britton 1953, 31–32).

The response to this system was astounding. For the next half century, shape notes dominated the music publishing business to the extent that some publishers, fearing a possible loss of sales, would sometimes refuse to print music in any other manner. And singing school teachers, who promoted sales of their own books, adopted the Little and Smith system or developed alternative systems of shape notes for their compilations. As time went on, shape note composers and arrangers articulated an increasingly coherent vernacular aesthetic, so that shape notes themselves came to be associated with the unique style of vocal music popular at the time (Stanislaw 1976, 53, 89).

Almost as soon as it achieved popularity, however, the shape note system came under assault. Touting European pedagogical methods and compositional styles, influential American musicians such as Lowell Mason (1792–1872) and Thomas Hastings (1784–1872) criticized shape notes and American composition style as "unscientific." An aggressive campaign against shape notes and singing schools was launched, drawing alliances from churches, public schools, and budding music academies. Consequently, in predominant strains of American culture today, even among those people who enjoy singing hymns, shape notes and the music they represent are practically unheard of. "Ordinary solmization" has prevailed. Among some predisposed not to follow prevailing cultural trends, however, the system has maintained its vigor. A few books in the shape note tradition, notably *The Sacred Harp* (1844), have enjoyed continuous use since they first were introduced.

SHAPE NOTES AS FOLK MUSIC

Clearly, there is nothing inherently unscientific about shape notes. Yet because of the cultural dynamics at work in nineteenth-century America, shape note singing fell into relative decline. Much of this oft-told story was outlined in George Pullen Jackson's extensive writings spanning the period from 1926 until his death in 1953, particularly in *White Spirituals in the Southern Uplands* (1933). In this work, he sought to outline a historical account of the living singing traditions of the Upland South that were not known to many Americans at the time. In this region, conditions had prevailed that nurtured the shape note and old hymn singing culture just as it was in decline elsewhere. Jackson "discovered" these singing traditions and became their tireless champion, devoting much of his life to their study while he taught German at Vanderbilt University in Nashville, Tennessee.

The decline of the four-shape or fasola tunebook, as his account so often went, largely resulted from a deliberate movement to suppress this music in favor of a style thought by reformers to be more refined. Nowadays this story is a stock component of American music history, and Jackson's account of it is sometimes only a footnote. He surely wrote more passionately than others, and he labeled as "Better Music Boosters" those who promoted music education, "scientific" harmony, music printing in round notes, a preference for European composers, and the use of choirs of trained singers—all of this with the effect of driving shape notes, the singing school, and the independent tunebook out of meaningful public discourse.

The disdain for native works was even incorporated in the shape note tunebooks themselves: In the 1802 *Easy Instructor* there were 100 American and 5 European compositions; by 1831 the ratio had shifted to 27 American and 126 European compositions (Lowens and Britton 1953, 55). By the end of the nineteenth century, followers of gospel song had further eroded support for the older styles, leaving a limited following in certain areas of the American South. The "fasola folk," as Jackson called them, embodied the antithesis of these various modernizing forces.

These and other factors influenced the formation of a coherent vernacular musical idiom around shape note notation itself. This process began, some say, with William Smith's deliberate Americanist inclinations and his insistence on American tunes in the earliest editions of *The Easy Instructor*, when prevailing opinion might just as well have led him to do otherwise (Lowens and Britton 1953, 40). As the variety of options in education and the arts grew in urban centers, singing schools began losing their cultural footing among the elite. But their popularity was sustained in rural areas, and very soon the shape note system itself was linked to the tastes of country people (Stanislaw 1976, 50). Increasingly, shape note tunebooks were incorporating vernacular musical forms into their system—secular melodies, melodies from folk hymnody, and popular revival choruses. Most books underscored this "eclectic" quality, using phrases in their titles that referred to tunes "in general use," "a pleasing selection," or "many of the most popular" (Stanislaw 1976, 51). "Early in the shape-note movement," concluded Richard Stanislaw, "a number of influences began to force the notational style into an inescapable association with certain groups of people and a sociological-geographical-musical style" (1976, 46). As the books traveled south, the music they contained—Yankee anthems and fuging tunes, popular psalm tunes, and folk hymns—coalesced into what came to be called the southern folk hymnody tradition.

It was not until the 1920s that George Pullen Jackson, largely because of his training in German Romanticism, rather instantly identified the rural shape note singing movement as "folk music." By this time, music reform had vastly amplified the vernacular qualities of tunebook culture. Where the reform deliberately imitated European style, the shape note tradition arose on American soil and eventually employed melodies that circulated in oral tradition until first printed by tunebook compilers. Where reformers employed formal urban institutions, the shape note tradition was informal, rural, and communal. Where formal choirs mirrored genteel society with the rigorously premeditated performances of a directed choir, Jackson recognized the "democratic song-form" of shape note traditions. Consequently, he effortlessly likened the shape note idiom to other musical forms that were being identified at the time as having innate folk qualities.

But his efforts were not merely historical and scholarly. Like many folk-song scholars of the time, Jackson was a personal champion of the neglected idiom. He lamented the decline of the oblong nineteenth-century books printed in shape notes, especially those older ones that, like Little and Smith's *Easy Instructor,* used only four shapes. Where many gospel music composers and compilers had adopted seven-shape systems, proponents of four-shape books more often clung to the older musical idiom. Moreover, it was the four-shape book whose decline was most severe: of thirty-eight four-shape books published between 1798 and 1855, only one, Jackson noted, retained its wide use into the 1930s: *The Sacred Harp*.[2]

As the preeminent survivor of the reform movement, *The Sacred Harp* became something of an overdetermined cultural symbol, representing America's "musical ancestors." It also absorbed meaning from its designation as folksong, taking on affiliations with other forms in the American folksong canon. Again and again—in magazine articles, scholarly journals, newspapers, concert programs, folk festival performances, and sound recordings—this descriptive apparatus affirmed a cultural taxonomy or classification that designated shape notes and Sacred Harp as folk music. But the folksong label did more than this: it affixed to the music particular institutions, regions, or people as "natural"—sometimes in such a way that impeded discussion of the system as a serious competitor to what was taken as conventional musical practice. Taxonomy begat ontology.

Sacred Harp singers themselves had little to do with this. As Buell Cobb noted, most traditional singers "have never been fond of the term 'folk music' when applied to their singing" (Cobb 1978, 30). On the other hand, Sacred Harp's status as folksong has had much to do with its post–World War II expansion into new areas as a part of the so-called Sacred Harp revival. In this, a widely dispersed "folksong revival" following, predisposed to the forms, styles, and institutions of American folksong, approached the music precisely from the vantage of American musical taxonomy. Yet folksong revival initially consisted not in participation in Sacred Harp singing but in its own institutions—with performance practices and stock sentiments that were somehow meant to approximate traditional practice. This arrangement of parallel performance institutions prevailed until the 1970s, when meaningful dialogue began to resolve performance differences and attract widespread coparticipation. By so many accounts, this process was not at all superficial, but engaged new singers in a spiritual encounter that no folksong revival experience had theretofore provided.

It is the development of this dialogue—whereby Sacred Harp traditions rapidly absorbed folksong revival participation on terms widely acceptable to many traditional singers—that is the ultimate concern of my book. But there were many steps leading to the peculiar social and cultural dispositions that emerged as a "tradition" and a "revival." So I will begin at what some say is the beginning—when a faction of New England Puritans sought to reintroduce note reading into church music.

REGULAR SINGING AMONG THE PURITANS

It is often considered ironic that shape note singing, so widely perceived as antique, actually emerged from a progressive movement. This observation is usually sufficient to underscore the fact that nothing is inherently "folk" about the music—that its vernacular qualities were inherited from the cultural dynamics that evolved around it. Indeed, nearly a century before Little and Smith introduced shape notes, there arose in New England a movement to teach "Regular Singing," or note reading, to the singing public. This was necessary, the homilies said, because music in the churches was in a state of horrible neglect. By the practice called the "Common Way" or the "Old Way," church deacons "lined out" psalms, reading lines aloud, and congregations responded by singing a familiar melody from a repertoire that had reportedly dwindled to a few tunes. Some congregations "set the tunes" using straightforward melodies from the Bay Psalm Book (1640), of which the ninth edition (1698) had introduced printed music. The tunes for this edition were taken from John Playford's *Introduction to the Skill of Musick* (eleventh edition, 1687) and printed in two parts with the letters F, S, L, or M beneath the notes as "fasola" notation. Other congregations sang from the more challenging Ainsworth Psalter (1690), but declining skills limited the appeal of this book.

To remedy this circumstance, reformers urged the sanctioning of a loosely formed institution, the New England singing school. Its purpose was to teach music reading and thereby promote Regular Singing, deriving its pedagogical theory from Johan H. Alsted's *Encyclopedia* (1630). Initial support came primarily from a group of Harvard-trained clergymen, who introduced music instruction in the curriculum there under the auspices of mathematics and physics (Buechner 1960, 63; Hall 1968, 155). Ultimately, the influence on church music was magnified by the effects of establishing this new social institution—the singing school—near to but not exactly within the orb of orthodoxy.

The Regular Singing movement established its theological grounding in musical discourses by Puritan clergy in the 1720s (Irwin 1978). Thomas Symmes's *The Reasonableness of Regular Singing* (1720) actually appealed to traditional sentiments, reminding readers that early Puritans had used notes for psalm singing. Mankind, Symmes said, was authored by God as a rational being with an obligation to "shew yourselves Men" (Isa. 46:8) before God. Symmes noted that music instruction was among the duties of levitical priests in Jerusalem (1 Chron. 15:22), and he interpreted the Pauline charge to "sing with understanding" (1 Cor. 14:15) to obligate God's people to learn the skills of proper singing. Cotton Mather's *Accomplished Singer* (1721) was indebted to Pietism and concentrated on the inward spiritual effects on the singer. Any Christian, wrote Mather "that Lives unto GOD, and is no Stranger to the Sentiments of Piety, may in that way [by singing] reach the True sense of the Lively Oracles and . . . he will have within him, an Exposition far more Valuable, than any of the Commentators, (truly Commentators!) who are Alienated from the Life of GOD, can help him to" (quoted in Irwin 1978, 188). More than in Symmes's or Mather's discourses, Thomas Walter's *Sweet Psalmist of Israel* (1722) departed from Puritan orthodoxy by postulating a natural theology of music. By the sheer beauty articulated through its physical and mathematical principles, music was said to have the power to dispel evil influences. For Walter, the passions were not automatically inclined toward sin but were "subservient to the same designs of religion and devotion" as intellect and will (quoted in Irwin 1978, 185).

Although some historians have regarded these documents as having been incendiary, there is reason to suspect that they actually sought to resituate note-reading within the bounds of Puritan orthodoxy. For example, noting Cotton Mather's claim that Puritan music had "degenerated" from some previous higher standard, Alan Buechner has argued that reformers actually sought to restimulate traditional practice. Buechner assembled earlier manuscripts and found evidence of a once lively Puritan musical culture characterized by dogged determination in maintaining good singing, respect for the relative difficulty of some musical pieces as a gauge of declining skills, and a sense of overall community status measured by the combined musical skills of its members (Buechner 1960, 8–21).

The taproot of orthodoxy in these documents is even more evident when one considers the range of other theological reforms confronting Puritans in the early eighteenth century. There was apparently general agreement that an "extraordinary dullness in religion" had settled over New England's churches, and the various solutions brought forth after 1720 were not always modest. For example, this impulse to revitalize religion led Solomon Stoddard of Northampton in a different direction—toward liberalized conversion, and Stoddardeanism swept over the Connecticut Valley bringing new members into the church in theretofore unimaginable numbers. And in Boston, a flirtation with Arminianism began in the 1720s—raising moral choice, and thus the possibility of human perfectibility, as a means to salvation, in place of God's inscrutable sovereignty. But among these camps, battle lines had not yet been clearly drawn. And none of the theological camps, not even the Boston rationalists, aligned themselves with Regular Singing: in 1720, Thomas Walter himself took on Arminianism with a vehement defense of strict Calvinism (Wright 1955, 19–21).

Even in matters of church polity, Regular Singing initially presented mild reforms compared with the rise of itinerancy and lay exhorters, both of which challenged the authority of established clergy. Still, there is evidence that the Regular Singing reformers provoked a conservative backlash in their methods. Music historian Gilbert Chase has espoused this view, arguing that followers of the Common Way "simply wished to be left alone," whereas Regular Singing proponents aggressively promoted "the Only True Way of Singing the Songs of the Lord" (1987, chap. 2). Surely an aggravating circumstance was the appointment of deacons: over the years, community standing had come to displace musical ability as the prevailing qualification (Buechner 1960, 22). This meant that even the mildest complaints over declining musicals skills had the effect of an affront to the social hierarchy.

To make matters worse, Regular Singers took few pains to avoid confrontation. They appealed explicitly to young singers, who could learn music more easily than their seniors and were "more free from prejudice" (Buechner 1960, 109–15). Singing psalms, they also argued, would deflect the young from the temptations of idle and foolish secular music, which at that time was substantial, and redirect their natural mirth toward Scripture. While evidence abounds of its successful appeal to youth, Regular Singing soon came under attack precisely on account of its association with "youthful mirth." Positions on both sides became entrenched, with lasting effects. As Buechner concluded, "The decision to make the younger generation the standard-bearers of reform set a precedent which largely determined the character of the later-day singing school as an institution devoted to the education of youth through music" (1960, 115).

If affiliations with youth suggested a progressive atmosphere, so also did the rationalist underpinnings of the movement. The Regular Singing discourses had the effect of resolving, in music, the Puritan belief in God's sovereignty with new understandings of the natural world brought on by the Enlightenment. Walter even assured readers that he could provide the "physical and mathematical" roots of harmony (quoted in Buechner 1960, 96). Defending it against charges of blasphemy and popishness, Symmes wrote: "Have we any reason to expect to be inspired with the gift of singing any more than that of *reading?*" Instruction manuals were soon assembled, emphasizing logical methods "whereby even Children, or People of the meanest Capacities, may come to Sing . . . by Rule" (quoted in Chase 1987, 33). In 1721, two manuals appeared that had no competitors until the 1750s: Thomas Walter's *Grounds and Rules of Music, Explained,* printed with bar lines in three parts, and John Tuft's *Introduction to the Singing of Psalm-Tunes,* printed with "fasola" letter notation.

Armed with the self-assurance of rationalist thought, Regular Singers could then engage the practices of the Common Way as quaint and antique. Chase has argued persuasively that the odd consequence of this posture was to establish Regular Singers as proto-folklorists. To emphasize the rational character of note-reading skills, they were apt to contrast their enlightened following with the "Country People" who clung to the Common Way (1987, 22, quoting Walter). It was also common to contrast the printed musical text of psalters and instruction books with the ornamented and unstable musical practice of the Common Way, which Walter called the "Uncertain and doubtful Conveyance of *Oral Tradition*" (quoted in Chase 1987, 28). Both sides, moreover, seized on the fluidity of secular tradition and attempted to associate the other with its "airy and vain" song-tunes (Chase 1987, 23; Buechner 1960, 43). But since reformers were more apt to harbor hostility than nostalgia for these "Oral Traditions," Chase stops short of suggesting that the social dynamics of folksong had fully developed at this date (1987, 30).

Surely the Regular Singers' affections would have been more forthcoming had their adversaries been more fully subdued. But apparently the genuine integrity of the Common Way was maintained throughout the reign of singing schools: nostalgic calls for the revival of the music of the Common Way did not appear until century's end. The social standing of the deacons undoubtedly played a major role in its longevity, but the Common Way of singing seems not to have engendered the kind of loyalty to style to sustain it as a freestanding musical tradition. In contrast, in Scotland, "lining out" had been reluctantly accepted as an ordinance of the Westminster Assembly (London, 1644), and its lengthy tenure had garnered such loyalty, in the face of attacks against it, to become "a vital and intrinsic element of demotic psalmody." In contrast, evidence suggests that in New England, with a century less longevity than in Scotland, it was primarily an ad hoc expedient, developed to accommodate singing where illiteracy prevailed (Buechner 1960, 54; Chase 1987, 27).

In sum, the effect of the Regular Singing discourses was cautiously progressive but not reactionary: Regular Singers meant not to stamp out an impious fashion but to sanction a new institution—the singing school—that would help restore quality in singing. It was left to individual congregations to decide whether to adopt the new practice. In 1736, the First Church of Windsor, Connecticut, held a protracted meeting to decide by vote whether, "respecting that part of publick Worship called Singing," to adopt "Singing by Rule" or "singing the way that Deacon Marshall usually sung in his lifetime commonly called the 'Old Way'" (Earle 1891, 210). In other churches, however, members were fined for making public complaints about singing (Earle 1891, 260). Facing congregational resistance may have slowed the progress of Regular Singing, but in the democratic and parliamentary process of deciding the matter, it also reinforced the sense of congregational autonomy that was so important to colonial churches (Buechner 1960, 124).

WATTS IN AMERICA

With the spread of public singing schools, the institutional nucleus of the movement gradually expanded outside the churches. Even parish-sponsored schools, which enjoyed some measure of official sanction, were often initiated by those in a congregation who were the most progressive. Other schools were promoted directly by teachers, who appealed to the most ambitious singers to subscribe by placing advertisements in local newspapers. Whereas the Common Way had evolved within congregations as an integral feature of worship, Regular Singing worked from the outside, designed to improve worship indirectly by developing musical skill. It was supported from the beginning by a following with specialized skills, conscious of their overall status as a movement and of the character of Regular Singing as a distinct musical style. But the popularity of Regular Singing, eventually widespread in eighteenth-century New England, obscured its shaky institutional foundation. Indeed, it never gained any permanent stronghold beyond what immediate popular support would provide. This fact is underscored by accounts depicting singing teachers who achieved considerable musical influence and generous and heartfelt popularity, yet who died in poverty. Already, Regular Singing had the makings of a "tradition," a curious structure separated from the prevailing nucleus of cultural authority.

The adoption of Regular Singing proceeded slowly at first, following the stock of skilled teachers from its roots in the Boston area. On the whole it was a Congregationalist enterprise, and only after it was well established throughout New England did it make inroads into other churches. In fact, throughout nearly the same period of the expansion of Regular Singing, young singers from some congregations were calling for new hymn and psalm collections by Isaac Watts or by Tate and Brady, which featured bold innovations in religious poetry but contained no music (see, e.g., Earle 1891, 191).

Initially, Watts had little success in America. Eastern cities had local printings of *Psalms of David Imitated* (orig. 1719) and *Hymns and Spiritual Songs* (orig. 1707) by midcentury. But sales were not strong, and there was widespread and outspoken resistance to Watts's imitations and hymns (Benson [1915] 1962, 186). Benjamin Franklin's 1729 edition of the Psalms, issued without prior demand, languished unsold on the shelves for years. This was not for lack of initiative: Watts wooed American support by dedicating Psalm 107 to New England and even sent *Psalms of David Imitated* to Cotton Mather for his approval. Around 1740 regularly reprinted editions began appearing in New England and in Philadelphia; Benson reported the Philadelphia sequence as 1740, 1741, 1753?, 1757, 1760, 1778, and 1781 (Benson 1903, 18).

In its essence, religious poetry struck at the core of what worship music was about, and for some it was a far greater threat than Regular Singing. If it was controversial to sanction a singing school or a meeting of Regular Singers outside the church, it could be more divisive to try to introduce the religious poetry of Watts into worship in a congregation or parish that had accepted established psalmody as Scripture. Consequently, resistance from singers slowed the adoption of Watts throughout the eighteenth century. For example, in the 1760s, the parish of Spencer, Massachusetts, agonized over the adoption of Tate and Brady, Watts's *Psalms and Hymns,* or the Bay Psalm Book before finally deciding by vote in favor of Watts (Benson [1915] 1962, 165). Even in 1758, Boston's Old South Church, where Billings would later teach, went to extremes to avoid Watts by commissioning a revision of the Bay Psalm Book, with an appendix of hymns, from Thomas Prince. At Boston's West Church, where the outspoken liberal Jonathan Mayhew was installed in 1747, Tate and Brady prevailed throughout his tenure to 1767. The church seated a choir around 1754, yet did not allow hymns until 1783. Brattle Street Church, also frequented later by Billings, rejected Watts in 1739 and then adopted Tate and Brady, with an appendix of Watts's hymns, in 1753. Soon after, this combination was bound with Bayley's *Essex Harmony* or Billings's *Psalm Singer's As-*

sistant, and it was through these tunebooks that Watts gained acceptance in some parishes. Soon enough, composers for Regular Singers embraced Watts enthusiastically by giving many new musical settings to his tunes. Surely the publication of Samuel Holyoke's *Columbian Repository* (1800) marked Watts's secure acceptance among Regular Singers: it contained musical settings in four parts for all of Watts's *Psalms of David Imitated* and *Hymns and Spiritual Songs* in one volume (Benson [1915] 1962, 172–73).

Of the various objectionable features, Watts's zealous allusions to the British sovereign and state were among the most serious. This visible feature of Watts became intolerable with the onset of the Revolution, and in 1781 a group was convened by John Mycall in Newburyport to prepare an American edition with the purpose of "getting King George well out of King David's Psalms" (Benson 1903, 20). Perhaps the altered title will suffice as an illustration of the dramatic and extensive changes that were exacted in this first American revision of Watts's psalms. Where Watts himself had proclaimed,

> Power and government from God alone. Apply'd to the Glorious Revolution by King WILLIAM, or the Happy Accession of King GEORGE to the Throne.

Mycall revised the title to read,

> Applied to the glorious revolution in *America, July 4th 1776.*

Benson recorded reprints of Mycall's Watts beginning in 1787 and running to 1812, establishing evidence of its continued popularity (1903, 21).

Oddly enough, in 1784, only three years after the Mycall edition, the General Association of Connecticut authorized a revision by Joel Barlow, again to address the matter of Watts's "local appropriations." Where Mycall had merely reapplied them to New England, the General Association sought in this revision to remove them altogether. Barlow's Watts appeared the following year and had a modest run of success. Despite the tangible chasm that separated Mycall's Watts from Barlow's, we might well mark the Barlow edition as a watershed. With it, a once-controversial work was now authorized by the Connecticut General Assembly, indicating that much in it was being resolved by and assimilated into orthodox thought. Nothing of this sort was happening among Regular Singers, who, we will see, were farthest from the gravitational pull of orthodoxy at precisely this point in time.

Still, the Barlow editions were meeting with popular resistance of a sort that bears examination. Weighing the evidence, Benson concluded that there was considerable dissatisfaction with Barlow's textual alterations not on the basis of patriotism but on his having "exalted himself at the expense of Dr. Watts" (1903, 80). What he did, in fact, was to make stylistic adjustments other than those called for by the General Assembly, then attach an "indiscriminate" mixture of his own and Watts's hymns (Mycall had included only psalms), and then, finally, affix his name, "by Joel Barlow," prominently on the cover. Still, self-exultation seems on the surface an odd complaint, since every editor, even Watts himself, had taken the wildest liberties with the fixed and readily identifiable psalm texts that stood before all in the King James Bible. But it is not: Barlow had exceeded what by then had been well established as the ontological domain of the text, the logos within which an "imitation" might be assembled without the imposition of human disturbance—"vain Discourse," as Watts himself put it. By such reasoning, one could, as Timothy Dwight soon did, extend the sincerest reverence toward Dr. Watts even while exacting extensive alterations on Watts's texts. Such an understanding governed shape note tunebook revision throughout the nineteenth and twentieth centuries.

By 1790 success for Barlow's Watts had ended in New England, for no subsequent reprints appeared there. Its demise was hastened by a trip abroad, which brought Barlow irreversible disrepute among Connecticut Federalists on account of his association with French "infidels." Very soon, historians elevated the significance of Barlow's democratic leanings such that any other cause for the demise of his Watts edition was neglected; in fact, it was precisely to assess this claim that Benson so carefully assembled evidence of prior resistance. In any case, both kinds of misgivings in some proportion motivated the General Assembly to authorize a second revision, this time by Timothy Dwight, then president of Yale and leader of a burgeoning conservative Federalist movement. After being withheld pending further revision, Dwight's Watts was published in 1801. Despite Dwight's name prominently included in the title, despite alteration and composition in equal or greater measure to Barlow, Dwight's Watts was adopted by Connecticut churches and was used for years (Benson 1903, 75, 83; see also Silverman 1969, 101, Tyler 1895, 98n. 5, and Chase 1987, 39–40).

Although the political schism that divided Dwight and Barlow was centered in Connecticut, its westward migration with Lyman Beecher would eventually influence the Regular Singing movement. I will return to this point later. For now, we might only marvel at the authorization of hymnody by the General Assembly and the extraordinary extent to which Watts was assimilated, in Connecticut at least, into an increasingly hardening orthodoxy. But, according to Benson, this was not ironic: the General Assembly was notably unmoved by the agitation against Barlow and the solicitous reverence for Watts himself. Instead, it had discovered the power that controlling the content of hymnody brought (1903, 84).

We might also note that as "Watts" spread so pervasively across America during the nineteenth century, he did so in the various guises that revisers made for him. In fact, outside New England, even Barlow's Watts continued to be reprinted, extensively so in the early 1800s. When hymnbook and tunebook compilers began drawing together general collections of hymns and psalms, they took texts from many sources. For example, *The Sacred Harp* twice employs the Watts quatrain that reads,

> Behold the love, the generous love,
> That holy David shows;
> Behold his kind compassion move,
> To his afflicted foes.

The third line indicates that the passage, taken (according to J. S. James) from the hymnbook *Mercer's Cluster*, was originally Barlow's:

WATTS: "Hark, how his sounding bowels move"
BARLOW: "Behold his kind compassion move"
DWIGHT: "Mark how his tender bowels move"

It is unlikely that Barlow's transgressions or Dwight's admonitions had any effect on Jesse Mercer's printing of the text in south Georgia; perhaps, on the other hand, Barlow's language did. In any case, too little is said of the rich ambiguity that underlies the attribution of a text to "Watts."

REGULAR SINGING AND THE GREAT AWAKENING

Watts's innovations in hymnody and in the "imitation" of psalms, however, had another sphere of influence and popularity. Whereas Regular Singing articulated the practice of Calvinist piety among saints and cultivated beauty as a moral influence, hymnody found its surest appeal among evangelicals, for whom tangible conversion was the centerpiece of Christian experience. The primary difference seems mostly to have been practice: where Regular Singing nurtured order and beauty, the poetry of the eighteenth-century hymn lent itself to spontaneous bursts of emotion. In its vivid articulation of the imperatives of the New Birth, the hymn appealed to evangelicals as "the language of the regenerate soul, the inevitable burst of praise issuing from redeemed intelligent creatures to their Creator" (Marini 1982, 157).

The influential Edwardean revivals, which introduced evangelical religion in New England beginning in 1734, left a curious record on the subject of music. Revivalism began in the Connecticut Valley when Jonathan Edwards, grandson of Solomon Stoddard, preached a series of influential sermons on the miraculous gift of salvation. But they were soon amplified to the status of "Great Awakening" in 1740 with the tour of fiery preaching by George Whitefield (Goen 1962, 7–9). Some have suggested that there was a general lack of concern with music among the revivalists, who were more interested in the spontaneity of conversion. Regarding their position on Regular Singing, Irwin noted that opposition to revivals came from both Old Calvinists and liberal ministers, some of whom had been advocates of regular singing (1978, 192). And on Watts: Whitefield apparently admired Watts moreso than the Wesleys, and Edwards gave his approval upon learning that congregations had begun to sing Watts in his absence (Benson [1915] 1962, 163; Buechner 1960, 331).

But neither championed any musical cause with conviction, and White-field, George Pullen Jackson took care to remind us, "roamed the colonies off and on for twenty years" before feeling the need, in 1753, to edit his own hymnbook (Jackson 1943, 23). And Buechner, measuring the evidence on the Edwardean revivals, concluded that the revivals did little to advance the cause of Regular Singing and were more in keeping, in their nature, with the spirit of the Common Way (1960, 330–35). He cited a description by Charles Chauncy of typically enthusiastic singing during a conversion, and by example he concluded that "only by the wildest stretch of the imagination" could the singing of the revivals be called "regular" (1960, 334).[3]

On the whole, the exact locus of Regular Singing on New England's turbulent theological map of 1720–1750 is difficult to pin down. It has been estimated, partly on the basis of an observation by Ezra Stiles, that in 1743 there were four hundred ministers in New England (Goen 1962, 32–35). As a result of the revivals, these had coalesced into three distinct camps of approximately equal numbers. One group, consisting of followers of George Whitefield and James Davenport, was the "New Lights"—proponents of revivalism, lay preaching, itinerancy, dramatic conversion, intolerant judgment of the "unconverted," and emotional manifestations of the Holy Spirit. A second group—tending toward rational theology and modest Arminianism based in morality—opposed revivals and became known as "Old Lights." Of this group, Charles Chauncy and Jonathan Mayhew, who led the way eventually to Unitarianism, were the most outspoken proponents. A third group was the Edwardeans, conservative New Lights—those who adopted the principles of revivalism but drew back from the divisive extremes that evolved from them. But none of these groups established a unilateral position on Regular Singing, nor was there any inherent reason for them to have done so.

It may be that cataloging the locations of parish-sponsored singing schools according to the political and theological leanings of the resident minister and congregation would reveal more distinct patterns of the acceptance of the movement by the various ecclesiastical factions. Still, as things stand, it seems safe to identify several tendencies, some of which would later become important. (1) There is little evidence that Regular Singing was a concern of the first group, the "New Lights." Accounts of the revivals of the Great Awakening, moreover, seem to describe events that were inherently unaccommodating to the performance practices of Regular Singing. (2) Among the rationalists, Regular Singers would enjoy long-standing support, particularly around Boston during the Revolution when the philosophy of the European Enlightenment fueled the cause of freedom. (3) Conservative Edwardeans may have supported the movement at the outset, but later generations—from Timothy Dwight to Lyman Beecher—would author an increasingly narrow secular morality with an eventually unswerving hostility to the singing school movement. Ultimately they would take control of the prevailing historical record, and the Regular Singing movement's finest hour would be deemed the "dark age" of American music.

THE "DARK AGE" AND THE FLOWERING OF AMERICAN COMPOSITION

After 1750, the adoption of more ambitious American and British tunebooks in the colonies dramatically advanced the development of New England musical culture. James Lyon's *Urania* was published by subscription in Philadelphia in 1761, accompanying a modest effort by Presbyterians to introduce Regular Singing there. The book anticipated in size (198 pages) and content (a variety of musical styles) the format of the American tunebook that would soon come to prevail (McKay and Crawford 1975, 21–22; Benson [1915] 1962, 184–85). Following this, American editions of William Tans'ur's *Royal Melody Compleat* and Aaron Williams's *Universal Psalmodist* (issued together beginning in 1767 under the title *The American Harmony*) introduced such choral forms as canons, fuging tunes, anthems, and occasional pieces.

According to Buechner, it was the lasting influence of these musical forms that precipitated the call by Regular Singers for the right to form choirs (1960, 127). The first church to reseat its Regular Singers together into a choir was Boston's First Church, in 1761 with Chauncy as minister, but the movement spread quickly throughout New England (Buechner

1960, 264 and table 5).[4] Support for the Common Way of singing was still considerable at this time, particularly among the deacons, and some churches provided equal time for Regular Singing and Common Way singing as a compromise. But the formation of choirs, even as part-time enterprises, allowed congregations to hear Regular Singers at their best, and this apparently swayed many to their side. As choirs grew in size, segregated seating became a problem, sometimes displacing prominent church members from their designated seats. Many churches responded by relocating the choir to the gallery—a place of modest status. Still, the combination of building alteration and social dislocation was divisive, exacerbating old social tensions between Regular Singers and prominent members of the congregations.

The year 1770, with the publication of Billings's *New-England Psalm Singer,* marked the beginning of the period of intense native composition and of the popularity of fuging tunes. Following Billings's example, singing school teachers aspired to increasing independence in musical careers, supplementing school subscription income by publishing their compositions and instruction manuals. Along with singing schools and music publication, singing societies and singing lectures provided singing teachers direct access to their public. A vibrant musical culture developed around New England choral music—a definitive "Golden Age," as Buechner put it, in the history of American music. Later, when shape note notation was developed and the movement spread south and west, the style and repertory of music and the singing school pedagogy of the "Golden Age" were retained as a definitive component.

But Buechner's salutary term was employed only with tragic irony. In fact, by the turn of the century, the influence of this musical culture began to meet with a powerful resistance, ultimately diverting it to the margins of American music. The earliest historians of American choral music, notably Nathaniel Gould in 1853, wrote with considerable hostility to this age, calling it the "Dark Age" of American music. According to Gould himself, this dialectic began taking shape around 1770, with a shift of focus in the singing schools. They became frivolous secular affairs, he said: "We are aware that classing them as amusements seems rather extravagant; but we have reason to fear, from the *kind* of music practiced, and the demeanor at the schools, that they could be considered as little else" (1853, 78). It is from this dialectic that the music ultimately began to be molded by the social dynamics of folksong.

From the beginning, of course, proponents of Regular Singing had anticipated the type of criticism Gould described, and they had proceeded much in spite of it. In fact, in the 1720s, both Regular Singers and proponents of the Common Way found ample cause to associate the other's "*kind* of music practiced" with frivolous airs. But the historical discourse that Gould espoused seized on the social atmosphere of singing schools and the sprightly character of the new musical forms as proof that the Regular Singing movement fostered moral corruption. How did this suddenly become so effective and so one-sided?

According to one theory, by 1800, the climate for all public institutions had changed dramatically since the inception of singing schools. Formal schooling, for example, once comprised but a small part of Puritan education, supported by a "web of connections between family, church, and community" (Demos 1970, 144). Singing schools, which, after all, had been devised to teach psalm singing, had little necessity of doctrinal control at the outset. As the singing school grew to become the province of independent teachers and general cultural life, as public institutions of all sorts absorbed the burdens that informal community had once borne, the once-large moral province of informal Puritan community became strained. Increasing doctrinal expectations were placed on public institutions that once had little moral authority.

All of this was amplified by the schism in Puritan orthodoxy, which placed complex doctrinal conflicts upon an institution, the singing school, that had never been designed to resolve them. On the one hand, Regular Singing thrived on the emerging religious toleration in New England that, responding to pressures at home and abroad, had advanced by the mid-eighteenth century to a state that had been unimaginable a century earlier (Wright 1955, 223–40). But toleration also opened the door to doctrinal confrontation and, in theory, favored neither Arminians nor evangelicals. But the Arminians became its chief benefactors, and conservatives responded with creeds and confessions designed to require Christians to "think alike upon religious subjects." This was an ironic reversal, for evangelicals had veered perilously close to a theology of "means," and Arminians were warning, in response, to "keep close to the Bible" and not to be "wise above what is written." Proponents of psalmody had long followed this close-to-Scripture principle for different reasons, of course. Consequently, singing schools became, more by default than by design, institutions of doctrinal tolerance.

The argument that singing schools were respectable activities caught suddenly in theological crossfire is augmented by the view of Percy Scholes (1934), who was among the first to aggressively seek the historical recovery of Puritan secular musical life. Scholes argued that because of theological upheavals, Puritan musical culture was put in jeopardy with conservative factions in the churches. Consequently, like the vivid secular musical world Scholes described, singing schools were likely to have changed far less than the critical atmosphere around them. Instead, at this point, particularly in the writings of Joseph Bellamy and Samuel Hopkins, conservative Congregationalists began to rehistoricize their culture, inventing a past of deeply rooted "puritanical" distaste for worldly pleasures, particularly music (1934, 358–60; cf. Valeri 1994, esp. 49, 62–63, 116). It is on this foundation, we can infer, that later historians such as Gould built their case for the "Dark Ages."

If the prevailing historical record was tainted by prejudice, surely something could be learned from Regular Singers themselves and their own accounts of the demeanor of the schools? Indeed, what seems so distinctive in later accounts of singing schools was the absence of the moral purpose that originally inspired the movement. Accounts from diaries of those who participated in the singing school movement, even at century's end, describe the most wholesome recreation, and an innocent lack of concern with the moral controversy that surrounded it. Buechner quoted three of these, of whom one was fifteen-year-old Elizabeth Fuller. In 1791, for example, she wrote: "Leonard Woods here all this forenoon, brought Holyoke's Singing Book, left it here" (quoted in Buechner 1960, 178). Nineteen-year-old Caleb Jackson wrote in 1805: "I made 5 shoes and Samuel 4 and we went to Singing School in the evening. There were about 20 of us to sing and 14 or 15 spectators from Old Rowley and Byefield" (quoted in Buechner 1960, 180). Such accounts were common and suggested to Buechner that Regular Singing had been rather fully integrated into New England life as a traditional form of wholesome recreation for young people.

Possibly the most extensive personal reflection on singing schools was made by Buechner's third subject, William Bentley, a Unitarian minister from Salem, Massachusetts, and an avid patron of music. Bentley diligently maintained a diary covering 1784–1819 and containing many references indicating his support for singing schools. Bentley's record is important because he bore no hostility toward singing schools, yet he was a minister, sensitive to their moral dimensions. Generally Bentley was tolerant of the views of the widest diversity of musical factions—e.g., instruments in churches, public exhibitions of music, singing societies, European or American compositions, preference for old tunes, and the approaches of Billings, Law, Holyoke, and others. He had considerable empathy for the struggles of singing teachers and great respect for those whose efforts were genuine—particularly Samuel Holyoke, who "had done more for psalmody than any man of the present generation & has been poorly rewarded" (Bentley 3:414, 9 February 1809). Of Billings, he recorded what is apparently the lone surviving private obituary, including this comment: "Many who have imitated have excelled him, but none of them had better original powers" (2:350–51, 28 September 1800; see McKay and Crawford 1975, 186). Once, in a letter, Bentley composed a lengthy history of psalmody, recognizing each phase and approach without apparent favoritism or prejudice (2:371, 3 April 1801).

So it is surely significant that over the thirty-five years Bentley recorded his observations, only a few times did he comment on the moral atmosphere of singing schools—and this in a way that was considerably less resolute than the commentary of reformers. More often, he gave detailed accounts of subscriptions, sometimes with a complete list of names and ages, and also his impressions on the quality of the singing. When he found cause to complain, most often it was of those who fostered ill feeling toward some musical style without offering anything better. Bentley generally took care to position himself outside the growing hostility toward singing schools. His record stands as evidence that the shifting status of singing schools and American composition was precipitated less by the behavior of their proponents and more by the ever widening chasm that befell New England Congregationalism.

Bentley came closest to condemning singing schools in 1791 when a female singer in his choir "violated her chastity." By Bentley's and apparently others' reasoning, she brought disrepute not only to herself but to the other female singers and to singing schools as a whole. "The invectives against Singing Schools as corrupting Morals have been frequent," Bentley was compelled by the incident to write (1:261, 22 May 1791). Whereas Bentley was unequivocal about the gravity of the offense, however, he put himself at a distance from the force of the "invectives." The following January he had apparently forgotten the matter and "went about to induce parents to send their young children to the Singing school" (1:338, 9 January 1792). Despite Bentley's unwillingness to endorse the censure of the singing school, we can rightly marvel at how thoroughly it had become a gendered institution, susceptible to the moral incontinence associated with Puritan femininity.[5] Singing schools, as Bentley insisted, may not have been institutions of immorality, but they had also not become instruments of moral control.

This is not to say that singing teachers themselves were silent on the matter of decorum in their schools. But scholars have often read "rules for decorum" as an indication of their prevailing lack of control. McKay and Crawford have even suggested that Billings's "Rules for regulating a Singing-School" (1778) might have served as a preemptive tactic, establishing explicit disapproval on matters of which he may have had little genuine concern (1975, 39). Whether or not Billings was sincere is not clear—he was certainly capable of both motives. In his choice of scriptural quotation on the title page of *The New-England Psalm Singer* (1770), he neglected an easy opportunity to admonish readers to sing out of sober Christian duty (McKay and Crawford 1975, 42). Instead, even at age twenty-four, in this his first publication, he unabashedly recalled the oft-quoted James 5:13: "Is any merry? Let him sing psalms."

The earliest complaints about singing schools so often mentioned Billings—and conflated the character of singing schools with that of his music—that one wonders whether their target was Billings rather than the schools. When in 1782 Andrew Law reissued his *Select Harmony,* all six Billings compositions from the previous edition were removed. The overall character of the revision, however, consisted of a substantial reduction in plain tunes (25 to 14) and an increase in the kinds of compositions— fuging tunes, tunes with extensions, set pieces, and anthems (40 to 45)— that Billings had cultivated (Crawford 1968, 18–20). Law's slight of Billings in this edition so long preceded other evidence of shifting tastes that McKay and Crawford wondered if "some event that occurred between 1779 and 1881" had precipitated Law's change of heart (1975, 137). By this time, of course, Billings had gained his ascendancy in New England musical culture, but he also had accumulated a considerable record of intemperances of opinion, even on theological matters. McKay and Crawford suggested that the genius of his achievement was in seizing upon the exuberance of American independence asserted and won, taking perilous liberties with conventions of poetry, music, theology, and the social world. Indeed, throughout his career, Billings protected the core of his work with many preemptive gestures to orthodoxy, such as by buttressing outspoken religious satire with scriptural references. So it is hardly surprising that he might have raised the hackles of orthodox thinkers and that his eccentricity might have tainted the reputation of the overall musical culture he championed.

On the other hand, neither did his detractors cling to the church. With telling irony, even while outspoken in his contempt for Billings, Andrew Law may have been among the first teachers to divorce singing schools from their ecclesiastical moorings. In 1796, Bentley reported on Law's attempts to introduce singing in Salem as a Liberal Art:

> Mr. Law has now formed his Music School from the object of particular singing for religious societies, to the mere teaching of the art, which is a commendable exchange. Singing has never been taught in New England as a Liberal Art, in public schools, but by private tuition. Our Song Singers are generally self taught & sing best alone. By learning music upon a large scale, real advantages are to be hoped. Mr. Law has not the extent of the plan. But he teaches the Rules

without regard to performance in the churches, tho' by Psalmody only. (2:192, 2 August 1796)

Neither could have known the degrees by which the "large scale" would expand and prevail in the nineteenth century nor the degree to which "religious societies" would retain their influence. To Bentley, this shift would nourish the flowering of musical culture. But the loss of ecclesiastical attachment lightened the movement's moral burdens far less than it would seem, yet left it without the moral agency that the churches provided. It may be that this "commendable exchange" was an ominous event, one which saw the innocent and complacent singing school movement on the eve of its apocalypse.

"ANCIENT HARMONY" AND THE CLIMATE OF REFORM

As the century drew to a close, rumblings began to be heard of another coherent music reform movement. In 1791, Samuel Holyoke had complained that fugues produced only a "trifling effect," serving to "confound the sense, and render the performance a mere jargon of words" (1791:4, quoted in McKay and Crawford 1975, 6). Andrew Law was apparently the first to explicitly attack composers on the basis of American nationality. In the 1782 edition of *Select Harmony,* he had championed the compositions of Martin Madan, an Anglican clergyman (Crawford 1968, 18). But by 1793, he was commenting, more explicitly, that "a considerable part of American composition is in reality faulty" (Law 1793, 5, quoted in Crawford 1968, 105). By Gould's account, trifling compositions and irreverent schools were symptoms of the overall deplorable state of musical culture.

By the turn of the century, a more substantial reactionary movement began to turn the tide of popular sentiment. In the beginning of Samuel Gilman's vivid *Memories of a New England Village Choir,* set at about this time, the choir was enjoying the most popular American tunes— "Russia" (1786), "Northfield" (1800), "New Jerusalem" (1796), and most anything by Billings—singing primarily from the collection *Village Harmony* (orig. 1795). Once, during a brief period when the leader's post was vacant, a new singer arrived from another choir, eager to impose his views on this happy band. Gilman, who had no predisposition at all against the substance of the newcomer's ideas, was distressed by the strength of his intolerance. In the narrative, Gilman assigned him the pseudonym "Mr. Forehead":

> It seems that . . . he had occasionally assisted in the choir of some congregation, into which had been introduced a new and purer taste for sacred music than generally prevailed through the rest of the country. In that choir, as he informed me, no tunes of American origin were ever permitted to gain entrance. Fugues there were a loathing and detestation. None but the slow, grand, and simple airs which our forefathers sang, found any indulgence. Mr. Forehead assured me that no other music was worth hearing, and what seemed to weigh particularly with him was the circumstance; that the slow music in question was beginning to be in fashion. (Gilman [1829] 1984, 60)

Gilman's narrative, of course, was built upon the tragic decline of his own contented choir. Over the course of the narrative Gilman strove in vain to dispel polemics with tolerance and reconciliation, but the group was subjected to discord too poisonous to deflect. When Gilman returned after a period away, he found the once flourishing singing-pews empty, "too desolate and dusty to be occupied."

The "fashion" of slow music was the "Ancient Harmony" movement that Richard Crawford has documented (1990). This was the direct precursor to the more imposing "Better Music" movement that shaped American musical culture throughout the nineteenth century. Citing Gould, Crawford pinpointed the origins of the movement in two locales around 1804. There, musical societies with "formidable prestige" were formed, allied to the Federalist Party sufficiently to raise accusations of political motivation (Crawford 1990, 233; Gould 1853, 69). One of these sites was Salem, where Bentley preached—and Bentley has little enough to say about it (and mostly negative) to raise questions of the sense of destiny that Gould, in his history, assigned to the movement. "Much is said of Church Music," Bentley complained in 1807, "& an attempt is made to put a stop to the many ridiculous publications which are offered to the world" (3:322, 4 October). Later he commented that in some musical societies in Salem, "no talents are displayed & perhaps only some few prejudices indulged" (4:124, 11 October 1812).

The essential ingredient that the "Ancient Harmony" movement added to the brew of discontent was to introduce an identifiable alternative to the prevailing style of music. To whatever extent Federalist ties or realignment with British culture served as motives, they were enveloped in a tangible veneer of antiquarianism—the idea that ancient tunes were more genuine in spirit than newfangled ones associated with recent eccentric composers like Billings. Still, this was built on a foundation of ideology sufficiently discernible that even antiquarianism met with resistance. Tunebooks such as the Worcester Collection and the Norfolk Collection, issued under collective authorship (rather than by individual compilers), reintroduced old tunes—but Gould reported that they were considered "subversive" by many in the singing public (1853, 70). In Gilman's narrative, only after those who favored fugues had resigned from the choir did the remaining choristers abandon *Village Harmony:* "It was resolved among those who remained behind, to perform no other music than such as we deemed the most genuine, and an express was sent off by first opportunity to purchase thirty copies of the lately published ******* Collection" (Gilman [1829] 1984, 83).

Ostensibly, all that was won was the ascendancy of a musical style. Along with it, however, "Ancient Harmony" proponents gained moral control over an essential feature of New England public life. And just as the shift in musical taste toward European styles became the clarion call "Better Music," so also did the moral machinery carved out of New England theological strife prepare the foundation for Lyman Beecher's definitive influence in the West and ultimately on American public culture. But the turn-of-the-century upheaval in choral music actually followed many other courses. In closing, Crawford added that the urgency to "draw American taste into a European orbit" penetrated a diversity of approaches to reform, not all aligned with the movement for "ancient harmony."

American composers like Samuel Holyoke and Timothy Olmsted sought to master the "Methodist" style of Martin Madan and other mid-eighteenth-century Englishmen. English-born compilers like John Aitken, Benjamin Carr, and John Cole, all involved in music publishing as well as compiling, helped to keep American singers south of New England abreast of the music considered fashionable by English Protestants of the 1780s and 1790s. An independent-minded connoisseur of psalmody like Andrew Law sought to lead Americans into the Promised Land of refined European-style musical taste by means of his own brand of shape notation. And men like Amos Albee, Zedekiah Sanger, and Oliver Shaw embraced a kind of new eclecticism, in which European music was balanced with American—not the traditional American styles of Billings, Read, and Swan, but a style forged under the influence of English psalmody, more subdued, dignified, and "grammatical." (Crawford 1990, 245)

Still, the effects of these efforts were more uniform than their manner suggested. If their immediate results were imperfect and uneven, they still succeeded overall in "shifting the grounds of the appeal from personal taste to theological consensus" (Crawford 1990, 246).

As we look for the origins of American folksong in this transitional decade, we find only perplexing ironies, a picture out of sync with the American musical taxonomy that would come to prevail over much of the nineteenth and twentieth centuries. Clearly, reformers such as Law sought and briefly attained the benefits of the "theological consensus" that emerged from the post-Revolutionary struggle for doctrinal preeminence. But in only a generation, even their ideas would be too severe for the bland extraction that came to prevail. When the next generation of reformers took up their work, the explicit discourse of "Ancient Music" and the books that articulated it were themselves out of fashion. In their place, a powerful moral code was evolved, a millennial rhetoric that extracted its provisional "theological consensus." Through this narrow moral vision of America, American composers themselves were excluded. Ultimately, reformers turned to the rhetoric of progress, abandoning antiquarianism to adopt the cause of "scientific" harmony. "Public" institutions, such as common schools, were linked with increasing exclusivity to a unified "mainstream," pressing excluded discourses to the emerging margins of American culture (Bailyn 1960, 100).

The reform movement might have been restricted to the East had there not been a determined effort to extend the movement to the West. Astute members of the clergy predicted that the West, with its exploding population, would become decisive in the nation's affairs. Consequently, extensive evangelical efforts were launched by the Protestant churches to conquer this nineteenth-century "New Jerusalem," resulting, it is commonly concluded, in the overwhelming Protestant character of nineteenth-century America. With Puritan-style theocracy precluded by the Bill of Rights, reformers turned to a common secular morality—a "civil religion" detached from its ecclesiastical moorings—to extend the reach of Protestantism into the secular mainstream.

Music reform was an explicit part of this movement, in part, because it had played so pivotal a role in New England public culture. In the West, Cincinnati was a key site for the reform movement. Ironically, this was not so much because Cincinnati was the site of a vibrant musical culture as it was because key cultural resources—common school pedagogy, the western printing trade, and frontier Presbyterianism—were controlled from this urban center. These were brought under the influence of the evangelical minister Lyman Beecher and others in his milieu. Indeed, the initial successes in music reform came during a crucial period during 1835 after Beecher had sent to Boston for Timothy Mason (1801–1861), Lowell Mason's younger brother. In the West, the Masons' music reform agenda was brought into alignment not with political and religious factions but with generic urban institutions—a kind of urban archetype—that would be replicated again and again, regardless of the locale or the character of the population, as cities sprang up over the frontier.

VERNACULAR SINGING IN SOUTHWEST OHIO

Those gentlemen and ladies who feel disposed to Patronize a SINGING SCHOOL will please to convene at the court house tomorrow night, as it is proposed to have singing. They will please bring their books with them.

Advertisement, Cincinnati, Ohio, December 27, 1800

Levi McLean advertises his singing school, $1. for thirteen nights, or $2. per quarter; subscribers to find own wood and candles.

Advertisement, Cincinnati, Ohio, 1801

SACRED MUSIC.—The season for singing schools being at hand, those who are fond of a good style of music, are reminded, that the 'WESTERN LYRE,' (in *patent notes*) can be had of the compiler and publisher, in any quantity.

This being a work avowedly intended to introduce a favorable change in the singing, where patent notes prevail, *Teachers*, with *Ministers* and *leading* members of different churches, are requested to give it an examination; for it is through their influence, *mainly*, that speedy success is looked for.

Already, the work has been introduced into many neighborhoods to great effect; and from present appearances, will meet a much more extensive circulation this fall and winter.

W. L. CHAPPELL, Publisher
141 Main Street, Cincinnati
Cincinnati Journal, 11 October 1833

As settlers poured into Ohio in the early nineteenth century, the colonial singing school came with them. In frontier urban centers like Cincinnati, whose population grew from 2,540 in 1810 to 24,831 in 1830, the singing traditions of its eastern transplants became a part of local life. As early as 1805, *The Easy Instructor* was advertised in Cincinnati newspapers and in 1811 was said by the Chillicothe, Ohio, *Supporter* to be "much approved of in Kentucky and Ohio" (Hamm 1958, 294). An 1817 book order from Cincinnati booksellers Phillips and Speer called for seventy-two copies of *The Easy Instructor,* three times the number requested of any other single publication (Sutton 1961, 48–49). After the original publisher began licensing reprints of the book, publisher J. Pace, in 1819, even issued an edition from Cincinnati (Lowens and Britton 1953, 43).

But evidence of singing in Cincinnati comes primarily from advertise-ments and book sale statistics, not, as was more common in New England, from written accounts of public singing events. Mrs. Trollope, who in 1832 took care to assess religion and the arts in Cincinnati, did not men-tion it (Trollope 1949). Descriptions of city life such as *Cincinnati in 1826* did not include singing in assessments of the "Fine Arts" or the "State of Society" or even in sections on churches. Included were "public balls, as-semblies, and cotillion parties" and an "increasing fondness for the Stage" (Drake and Mansfield 1827, 90). Even those predisposed to look for sing-ing found little to their liking. Writer and missionary Timothy Flint, arriv-ing in Cincinnati in November 1815, found "the taste, the singing and the selections that prevailed here, to the last degree bad" (Kirkpatrick [1911] 1968, 78).

Other researches into southwest Ohio confirm this view. Harry R. Ste-vens, who surveyed newspapers and other accounts of early-nineteenth-century Cincinnati life, could report extensively on concert life, cotillions, dancing schools, and secular folk music (Stevens 1943, 1947, 1948, 1952). But he concluded that "the singing school, an institution often re-garded as an important feature of frontier life, seems to have had a minor place in Cincinnati" (Stevens 1948, 135). We must conclude that, popular or not, singing schools in southwest Ohio were not part of the emerging municipal discourse, as they had been in the East.

This is not to say that singing schools were nonexistent in the West, but they did not leave a record of having established a musical culture. Even the most enthusiastic singing teachers often did not promote their work as a profession. Most depended on other income, although some worked ex-tensively as composers and music teachers. This relatively diminished sense of professionalism may have also limited the visibility of the singing school in comparison with other urban cultural institutions. Nonetheless, in the area surrounding Cincinnati, singing schools were observed in Ken-tucky as early as 1792 (Graham 1971, 77). In 1794 singing teacher and composer Lucius Chapin (1760–1842) crossed the Allegheny Mountains and taught in southern Ohio, southern Indiana, and northern Kentucky. Chapin was trained in the method developed by New England composer Andrew Law (1749–1821), and he promoted Law's books, pedagogy, and unusual notation (shapes without the musical staff) until his death. In 1819 Chapin taught a singing school in Chillicothe, and one of his students in the school later wrote Andrew Law: "About 18 months ago Mr. Chapin taught in this town the Harmonic Companion [compiled by Andrew Law] and at the close of his schools was able to afford the best Music we had ever heard. But the use of it in the church was opposed by those who understood it not, and were incapable of relishing its excellence" (quoted in Scholten 1976, 71).

Beginning around 1800, Chapin commissioned his best students as teachers to hold schools of their own under his supervision (Hamm 1960, 93). As it turned out, Chapin did not always find enthusiasm for Law's method in the Ohio River valley and at one point concluded, "Teaching sacred Music properly is an unprofitable business." Indeed, Chapin's successes were infrequent in his senior years, a condition he attributed to the "ignorance & vice" that prevailed "amidst all the means of improvement" (quoted in Hamm 1960, 93).

Thus it comes as some surprise that between 1813 and 1850, Cincinnati served as a major publishing center for patent note books (Hamm 1958). Many of the books printed in Cincinnati were popular elsewhere, so the city's reputation as a shape note publishing hub may have been a consequence merely of its status as the then-preeminent urban center in the West. The list of tunebooks published in Cincinnati is impressive—it includes *The Missouri Harmony, The Western Lyre,* and even an edition of *The Easy Instructor* among a dozen or so—but looking for a local compiler/teacher, one arrives too quickly at the name of Timothy Mason, who mounted the campaign against the shapes. William L. Chappell, a local compiler/publisher, even solicited singing teachers in his advertising, hoping they would adopt his book. So we must conclude with the evidence that the singing school may have been promoted in Cincinnati, but it was not an institution of great influence.

Shape Note Music and the Churches

In the manner of *The Easy Instructor,* most shape note tunebooks were pan-denominational in intent and use. Sometimes churches would sponsor a book, but even then the song selection would often draw as much from the common repertory as from composers who sought to advance the denomination's particular theology. In Ohio, denominational compilers included the Warren family of Noble County, who produced *Warren's Minstrel* (1857) for the Universalist Church (Brasher 1984), and singing teacher A. S. Hayden of Portage County, who compiled *Introduction to Sacred Music* (1838) for the Disciples of Christ (Fletcher 1988). Both were oblong tunebooks that drew heavily from the common style and repertory and added compositions and other features unique to their denomination.

Even without the institutional support a church could provide, tunebooks that were not church-sponsored had a better likelihood of survival. Both the Warren and Hayden tunebooks were soon replaced in their churches by modern denominational hymnals. Outside the churches, compilers could and did go to lengths to insist that they were intended for use in *any* church, seemingly oblivious to the impossibility of a church ever adopting a book not its own. Most included song texts by authors of various faiths, representing various theological positions—all in the interest of catering to the "singing public." Mary O. Eddy, surveying old Ohio families around 1950, came upon copies of patent note tunebooks, including *The Missouri Harmony* and *The Ohio Harmonist,* among Presbyterians, Methodists, Lutherans, and Baptists (Eddy 1951, 20).

The rise of denominational hymnals, of course, reflected the rise of the *denomination* itself—a term, contrasted to the more exclusive *sect,* implying a shared spiritual authority with different outward modes of expression (Hudson 1961, 34). The denominational theory of the church linked the freedom and tolerance of the revolution and the First Amendment to the vast evangelical possibilities of the West, serving to consolidate the efforts of churches. Tunebooks occupied a different sort of public space—not a "consolidation" but a convergence of various doctrines.

But this point is partly moot: in Cincinnati and the Ohio River valley, any supposition of widespread use of shape note tunebooks in the churches appears to be overstated. What may well have been the prevalent experience was that of Chapin's Chillicothe student—that a successful singing school did not lead to acceptance by the congregations from which its students came. Indeed, one searches in vain in accounts written during the period—e.g., Baptist church minutes, Presbytery histories, or diaries of Methodist itinerant preachers—for a description of a commissioned singing school, an account of singing from a shape note tunebook, or the adoption of a tunebook by a congregation. Whereas tunebook sales were apparently strong in bookstores, religious organizations had their own means of distribution—the "book concerns"—where tunebook sales were not at all evident (Sutton 1961, 150). In Sweet's profile of book transactions of frontier Methodist preachers—covering roughly 1812 to 1817 when tunebooks sales in Cincinnati bookstores were strong—cumulative inventories include over 1,500 hymnbooks and not a single tunebook (Sweet 1946, 698–706).

Occasionally, in written accounts by preachers or other travelers, singing is mentioned, but nowhere does one find a suggestion of the enthusiasm of camp meeting music or the complexity of the singing school. For example, Jacob Bower left this account of a Baptist prayer meeting in Kentucky in 1812: "I started verry [sic] early and got to the meeting just as the people were singing. I thought that I had never heard such heavenly music; all their singing—praying—exhortation, shakeing [sic] of hands accompanied with singing, was certainly the sweetest exercise I had ever witnessed" (quoted in Sweet 1936, 194).

Or Peter Cartwright, in his account of frontier Methodism during the first half of the nineteenth century, concluded only that the Methodists "could, nearly every soul of them, sing our hymns and spiritual songs" (Cartwright 1856, 74; quoted in Sweet 1946, 55). On 12 October 1825, the Ohio Conference of the Methodist Church did authorize the Book Agent to publish a new edition of their music book in patent notes, but did not endorse its use (Sweet 1923, 271). A decade later, in his record of the meeting of an Ohio Methodist conference in 1834, James Gilruth reported that the "Resolution appended was That all preachers of this coif [sic] be instructed to line their Hymns in all our publick congregations" (Sweet 1946, 393). Preachers who "lined their hymns" would have had no use for tunebooks.

It should be said that this admittedly scant evidence led music historian Richard Stanislaw to the opposite conclusion, that there is "no doubt" that four-shape tunebooks were used in churches (1976, 139). Stanislaw looked to the tunebooks themselves—to the convincing ratio of sacred to secular tunes, with most employing scriptural paraphrase (138), and to the prominently stated ambitions of compilers that their books be "used in divine worship" (138). The theology of revivalism, moreover, demanded congregational participation in religious exercise, with singing as a centerpiece of worship (140). Tunebooks, he said, "do not specify exactly how churches were to use them" (141), relying instead, we might conclude, on the popular demand for congregational singing as engaged worship. Stanislaw cited a crucial account of the efforts of Charles Finney to introduce a tunebook to a congregation in western New York: they resisted, and only "by degrees" could he win them over (141). Perhaps we need not resolve the matter of whether or to what extent tunebooks were used in churches: if they made such inroads, it was more often by popular support won "by degrees" than by appeals to denominational bureaucracies. As such, tunebooks stood outside the scope of organized evangelical reform.

Shape Note Music and Camp Meetings

The same absence of tunebook involvement appears to be the case for camp meetings, whose period of popularity ran almost identically with the shape note movement. Originating in 1801 just south of Cincinnati in Kentucky, camp meetings were the most visible manifestation of missionary zeal—the Second Great Awakening on the frontier (Bruce 1974; Johnson 1955). Along with circuit riding practices championed by Methodist preachers, camp meetings were an effective means of extending Christianity to sparsely settled areas.

Like public singings, the first camp meetings were pan-denominational affairs (Hudson 1981, 138). In fact, no denomination ever officially endorsed camp meetings, although the Christian Church and the Disciples of Christ were formed independently from camp meeting roots (Bruce 1974, 7). And, of course, their appeal among the Methodists was considerable. Ordinarily they were multiday gatherings, featuring deep emotional involvement in religious conversion (Bruce 1974, 53f.). Camp meeting followers valued verbal skills in their preachers, with education sometimes being viewed as a handicap (Hudson 1981, 148f.). Contemporary accounts of camp meetings, in fact, have viewed them as harbingers of populist democracy in an otherwise repressive atmosphere (e.g., Hatch 1989).

Music was a fundamental part of the camp meeting experience. "Everyone sung what they pleased," one account had it, "and to the tunes with which he was best acquainted" (Rankin 1802, 16; quoted in Lorenz 1980, 29). In fact, camp meeting hymns were necessarily simple so as not to intrude on the conversion process: Revival hymns "were important, for their simple words and images offered a key to the longings of the crowds which sang them, and their simple tunes and meters required no skill and therefore invited everyone to participate in the service. Yet precisely for this reason, they furnished a backbone to a revival meeting, and sometimes they were almost the meat of an entire revival in themselves" (Weisberger 1958, 148).

It is true, of course, that camp meeting tunes entered the tunebooks later, when compilers arranged them in premeditated harmonic parts. Ellen Lorenz, in fact, has noted that "earnest editors" had great difficulty recording camp meeting melodies, and when they did, the results were clearly improvised (Lorenz 1980, 59). But camp meeting music itself was so completely wedded to the principle of instant emotional appeal that tunebooks would have been at best unhelpful, if not an outright hindrance.

As Richard Hulan argued so compellingly, the primary currency of camp meeting music was not the tunebook at all but the camp meeting songster. This genre of religious song collection, which contained printed texts without music, was the exclusive province of the camp followers, even fostering its own genre of poetry composed around camp meeting aims and experiences. Perhaps because they contained no music, scholars of American musicology and religious folksong have grossly neglected the songsters. That these texts and tunes entered the tunebooks is unmistakable. But Hulan examined geographic areas regarded as important in camp meeting and singing school tunebook interaction, particular the area where Wyeth's *Repository, Part Second* (Harrisburg, Penn., 1813) was used, and concluded that the musico-religious repertoire had already been established in oral tradition and songster use (1978, chap. 4). He suggested, moreover, a broader conclusion: that in the West, the tunebook was far more an artifact of education and printing technology than it was of musico-religious experience. The reason, Hulan concluded, that the tune-book has been credited with so much influence is that it has been too convenient a primary source for musicologists. In the West, in fact, it was more often a secondary source—a collection gleaned from musical and religious practice engaged through hymnbooks and songsters (1978, 93–94).

As a barometer of all these influences, we might well use as an example the life of the Reverend James B. Finley, who reported in his diary on a variety of religious experiences in the region in and around southwest Ohio. Finley was born in 1781 and moved to Kentucky, the "new Canaan," in 1784 with his Presbyterian parents (Finley 1857, 2). In his youth, somewhat before the shape note era, Finley recalled the "great excitement in the Presbyterian Church about Psalmody," particularly the introduction of Watts (22). Finley marveled at the "power of *holy* song in rousing the dormant soul," such as Wesley's hymns (20). As an adult, Finley moved north to Ohio where he was successful as a backwoodsman and pelt trader. In 1801, he heard of a great meeting to be held at Cane Ridge, Kentucky, where his father once had preached. Curious, he attended the meeting, where he heard singing, preaching, and noise "like the roar of Niagara" from the crowd "supposed by some to have amounted to twenty-five thousand" (166).[6] Though determined to resist the effects of the camp meeting, Finley succumbed and was converted.

Committed to a life of religious devotion, Finley began a genuine deliberation over which denomination to follow. Eventually he became an itinerant Methodist preacher. But not once did he report a singing school or shape note singing. In 1808, leading a prayer meeting at his house, Finley arose and "gave out a hymn" (Finley 1857, 182). In 1810, at a camp meeting on the Little Miami River in southwest Ohio, he reported that brother John Collins stood up to preach: "Instead of giving out a hymn, as is customary on such occasions, before preaching, he commenced, in a full clear, and musical voice, singing that exceedingly-impressive, spiritual song, 'Awaked by Sinai's awful sound'" (228). In 1818, at the eight-day Steubenville, Ohio, conference, he observed that "when the holy song rises from a thousand voices, and floats out upon the stillness of the night air, the listener must feel that surely such a place is holy ground" (345). In sum, Finley's extensive narrative covering so many religious experiences is noteworthy for its lack of any mention of shape notes, tunebooks, or note reading of any sort.[7]

Sacred and Secular Hymns

If the tunebooks were not part of religious observance, what was their religious significance in frontier areas such as Cincinnati? Let us return to the urban phenomena of newspapers and advertisements, where the most activity seems to have been evident. Mostly because it reflects the reform influences of Timothy Mason and Lyman Beecher, I will examine the musical world described in the *Cincinnati Journal*, a Presbyterian weekly newspaper. The *Journal* was "one of the most popular religious journals . . . which at one time had a circulation of four thousand" (Lesick 1980, 22). So extensively did the Beechers influence the *Journal* after their arrival that it was called their own "family newspaper" (Johnston 1963, 142; Wilson 1941, 116). Consequently, its theological stance tended to be New School Presbyterian. Between 1832 and 1835 when Mason came to direct musical activity at the Second Presbyterian Church, the paper frequently acknowledged the popularity of shape notes.

In 1832, the *Journal* began featuring a hymn and hymn tune in each issue. The tunes "will be composed in *patent notes,*" the paper explained, "so that those who have never studied music as a science, may have an opportunity of joining in this pleasing part of divine worship" (3 February 1832). The first series, lasting through most of the year, consisted of compositions in two parts, many named for Cincinnati neighborhoods or nearby towns, printed in treble and bass clefs on separate staves. Beginning in November 1832, the printed selections were excerpted from *Christian Lyre*—a patent note tunebook sold in Cincinnati bookstores, one of which regularly advertised in the newspaper. The compiler, Joshua Leavitt, wrote that the plan was to issue, along with hymns, "some of the most popular tunes used in family worship, revivals, four-day and camp meetings" (quoted in Buechner 1979, 29). These musical selections most often were printed in four parts on separate staves.[8] In 1834, after Timothy Mason's arrival, however, the paper began using songs from *Mason's Sacred Harp,* which was extensively advertised in and promoted by the paper.[9]

Furthermore, where the *Journal* advertised or endorsed books printed in shape notes, this fact was noted prominently. Even the advertisement for *Mason's Sacred Harp* (which was published in shape notes over Mason's stated objection), proclaimed, "The publishers would further remark that 'The Sacred Harp' is printed in patent notes, under the belief that it will prove much more acceptable to a majority of singers in the West and South" (29 August 1834). Were they correct? A notice on May 8 of the following year boasted, "It has been printed but a *few months,* and has already reached a *seventh edition!*"

The most important taxonomic feature was the distinction between those books which included printed music and those which were text-only metrical hymnbooks or psalters. An advertisement for Cincinnati's Corey and Fairbanks's Bookstore, for example, was organized in this way (27 June 1834):

HYMN BOOKS	MUSIC BOOKS
Watts' psalms & hymns	Handel & Haydn collection
Dwight's do, do	Bridgewater collection
Assembly's do, do	The psalmist
Village hymns	Missouri harmony
Alexander's do	Western lyre
Christian lyre hymns	Juvenile lyre
Clelland's hymns	Juvenile harmony
Church psalmody	Christian lyre
Vedder's hymns	Musica sacra
Miller's do	spiritual songs
Methodist do	Am-Sunday-School psalmody
Episcopal do	Blank music paper
Dover selection	
Brown's psalms	
Psalms of David	

Because their hymns and other texts were set to music, the shape note tunebooks (*Missouri Harmony, Christian Lyre,* and *Western Lyre,* for example) were considered "music books," not "hymnbooks." With them in the category were the Handel and Haydn Collection and even blank music paper. "Music books" thus included both sacred and secular titles. On the basis of their musical notation, they were sold separately from hymnbooks.

At the top of the list of "hymnbooks" was *Watts's Psalms and Hymns*, at the time a Presbyterian favorite. No hymnbook was so enthusiastically endorsed by the *Journal* during the Mason period. For example, in a review of two other hymnbooks, the *Journal* felt it necessary to insist:

> We have been solicited for an opinion on the question of whether any one of these books is a proper substitute for *Watts,* for the public worship of the Sabbath; and we do not hesitate to give a decided, negative reply. We think we do not mistake the views of the editor, nor of three-fourths of the [Presbyterian] churches in the United States, when we say, that the book of Watts, as it was, or as it now is, by approval of the general assembly, should retain its standing; and we believe it will. (13 June 1834)

Later, the *Journal* considered the culmination of plans to publish a collection of all of Watts's hymns, along with popular works by other hymn writers, in one book:

> we then gave [the plan] our most cordial approbation, believing it to be the only plan upon which a book could contain general circulation in the Presbyterian church. (13 March 1835)

And in an advertisement for this book, which included endorsements by churches across the region, the *Journal* had this to say:

> Great pains were taken both by the compiler and the publisher, in getting up the above work, to produce a hymn book that should be *acceptable* to the *whole Presbyterian church,* and free from *all party suspicion.* (13 March 1835)

Even before an official church hymnal had been compiled, even in the very ecclesiastical setting in which Timothy Mason would be called upon to "improve" the quality of music, it seems that shape note tunebooks were never being considered for adoption or use in the church.

All of this may be overstating the case, as I am sure critics of this depiction will want to insist. But the fact is that frontier settlement was sparse and transient in the early nineteenth century, with every reason not to produce the highly charged musical atmosphere that had prevailed in New England over the previous century. As we turn to the rhetoric of reform, with patent notes and singing schools elevated to leviathan proportions, we will know better what truly lay in the path of music reform. By manufacturing a moral enemy, reformers gained control of the publishing industry and perhaps also the public will.

Locating the books outside the church during the time of their publication is important. It means that the reform effort targeted popular musical tastes, and the effects intended by the reformers, albeit emanating from religious institutions, were meant to embrace secular musical society. In rural areas, where reformers would have had to confront individual taste and community tradition, this would not have been so easy. But in the emerging nineteenth-century frontier cities, a transcendent municipal culture was developing that concentrated cultural influence through newspapers, urban mainstream churches, and public education.

"NERVES RENT ASUNDER":
THE MUSICAL CRISIS IN THE WEST

And when I see the cause of temperance, and missions, and revivals all moving the right way, and such dark clouds dispelled as just now threatened earthquake, fire, and storm over a large portion of the Church, and see the tears flow, and hear the song, "Blest be the tie that binds," sung at the close of the most stormy session of a great ecclesiastical body ever experienced, I can not believe that God intends to give the ministers of New England up to the infatuated madness and folly of rushing into an angry controversy; and if they should do it, I could not perceive it to be my duty to remain and wear out my strength and spirit in contending with good men after the Holy Spirit had left us, and the voice from the West still rose above the din of battle crying Come over and help us.

LYMAN BEECHER, farewell sermon,
Bowdoin Street Church, Boston, July 5, 1832

> [Lyman Beecher] could not endure that [the musical] part of
> worship should be thus neglected and marred. He soon sent to
> his friends in Boston, saying, "Come over the mountains and
> help us," or (to use the language of Billings) our "nerves will be
> rent asunder" with discordant, unmeaning singing in church.
>
> NATHANIEL D. GOULD,
> *Church Music in America* (1853),
> on the Second Presbyterian Church, Cincinnati

By the time Lyman Beecher arrived in Cincinnati in 1832, the call for relief from "discordant, unmeaning singing" had become common. We cannot be certain whether this particular lament referred to singing schools or to congregational singing. But reformers seemed to conflate the two, and launched the most deliberate attack at the singing schools as if that would lead to better singing in congregations. This may suggest that singing schools were meant to train singers in shape notes for congregational singing, and that singers, some of whom learned from any of a variety of tunebooks, would then sing memorized melodies from text-only hymnbooks in the churches. One can imagine a number of situations of competing protocol that might indeed have been thought chaotic.

In the Ohio River valley, early voices of discontent included that of Harvard graduate Timothy Flint who, in 1816, only months after he arrived in Ohio, published the *Columbian Harmonist*. Flint had come west from Lunenburg, Massachusetts, "where he had left a pastorate in the face of increasing opposition to certain of his opinions" (Hamm 1958, 301). No less opinionated in Ohio, Flint was disturbed at the poor literary and musical taste in the region. Apparently in response, he hastily assembled the *Columbian Harmonist,* with an expository preface, "Dissertation on the True Taste in Church Music," which attacked American fugue-style composition as "Babel-confusion." Only reluctantly did Flint employ patent notes in his arrangements:

> The compiler, wishing to satisfy all, as far as he could in consistence
> with duty, found it difficult to decide between the conflicting claims
> of the patrons of this work. A part, to whose judgement he thought
> much deference was due, preferred that the impression should be in
> the form of notes. Another, and a much larger proportion, were de-

sirous of having the patent notes. The compiler fears, with the former class, that the patent notes tend to form superficial singers. (Flint 1816, iii)

Perhaps Flint was pleased, then, at the formation of New Jerusalem Singing Society (1820–1830) and a Haydn Society (1819–1824) in Cincinnati and, soon after, a Handel Society in Columbus—all of which sought the advancement of European music (Osburn 1942, 9; Stevens 1943).

Timothy Flint was influential, articulate, and outspoken. We can be sure by his report that the discourse of reform was available in the West during the nearly two decades that preceded the arrival of Lyman Beecher and Timothy Mason. Moreover, any local discontent was surely bolstered by critical writing from outside the region that targeted the West as a bastion of bad taste. For example, Thomas Hastings, influential author of the reformist *Dissertation on Musical Taste* (1822) and editor of the *Western Recorder* (Utica, N.Y., 1824–33), made this connection between Little and Smith's shape note system and the culture of the West:

> Little and Smith, we regret to say, are names which must stand in musical history closely connected with wholesale quantities of "dunce notes." Probably no other book in the country had ever such an amount of purchasers as theirs; or did so much in the day of it to hinder the progress of taste. . . . Even at the present time [1835] there are some excellent men who are filling the Valley of the Mississippi with patent notes which are destined, we fear, to hold back the progress of musical improvement in that region for a half a century to come. (quoted in Metcalf 1937, 96)

With a wealth of resources, influence, and articulate spokespersons, we can rightly wonder why all of this had so little effect in the region during this period. But the fact remains that it had nowhere near the impact of the array of institutional resources that the Beecher-Mason minister-musician team assembled in Cincinnati in the 1830s.[10] Before observing the dramatic changes that they brought about in Cincinnati, let us first look back "over the mountains" to the East where their careers began.

Much credit for advancing musical reform is often given to composer and educator Lowell Mason. This is surely true of Cincinnati: Lyman Beecher sought out Timothy Mason precisely because Lowell had been so effective in Boston. Born in 1792 in Medfield, Massachusetts, Lowell Mason was trained in singing schools as were most of his contemporaries. In addition to singing masters, however, early influences included a local organ builder and a nearby violinist. At age sixteen, around the time Samuel Gilman's narrative was set, he conducted the local parish choir (Rich 1946, 6–7). At twenty, he relocated to Savannah, Georgia, where he became choirmaster and organist for the Independent Presbyterian Church and superintendent of Savannah's only Sunday School. He studied harmony and composition with Frederick L. Abel, a German and a student of Swiss educator Johann Pestalozzi. Biographer Carol Pemberton dates the influence of Thomas Hastings on Mason to his Savannah period, including regular correspondence and ultimately a thorough study of Hastings's 1822 *Dissertation on Musical Tastes* (Pemberton 1985, 29). In any case, Mason emerged from Savannah as a professional musician who could return to Boston and "look on the task of sweeping away the last crudities of the old New England music as in itself a divine mission" (Stevenson 1966, 58). Called by Lyman Beecher to Boston's Hanover Church, Mason found a staunch ally in Beecher, who, like Mason himself, brought daring ideas to a city set in its ways (Henry 1973, 125, 138, 158).

The substance of these ideas was a considerable departure from the previous generation of reformers' appeal to "ancient harmony." Instead, Mason looked to the German Enlightenment for "scientific" principles of composition (Stevenson 1966, 76–78). Whatever else this implied, its status as science provided an alliance with academic training and with the emerging unassailable truths of the natural world. In the name of science, popular tunes from this canon, when they were reprinted, were reharmonized by Mason and others to bring them into line with these "scientific" principles of composition.

Ironically, there was an opposite cultural force at work. Mason was also an educator, and he had become a follower of the educational theories of Johann Heinrich Pestalozzi (1746–1827). A disciple of Rousseau, Pestalozzi sought in music what could be expressed or experienced naturally. In pedagogy, this meant teaching children material they could naturally understand, rather than the "chattering of mere words" (Rich 1946, 80).

Consequently, Pestalozzian pedagogy consisted of various educational and developmental stages, with particular lessons and skills identified for each stage so that pupils could fully grasp the moral and intellectual properties of the lesson (Heafford 1967). In truth, Pestalozzi knew little about music and considered it important primarily as a device for moral teaching (Jedan 1981, 60–61). Moreover, as it would for Mason in America, "morality" meant to Pestalozzi and his followers not religious doctrine so much as conventional public culture (Heafford 1967, 64).

As interpreted by Lowell Mason, Pestalozzianism shifted in its focus somewhat from the student to the teacher.[11] For example, the concept of nature was applied not simply to the natural abilities of the student but to the natural instincts of the teacher (Rich 1946, 80–81). Where Pestalozzi rejected the influence of prevailing pedagogical theory, for example, Mason rejected "explanation, description, assertion, or declaration"—devices central to shape note pedagogy. In keeping with the practice of learning by stages, Pestalozzians disassociated rhythm, pitch, and dynamics from one another and taught them in separate stages. In shape note tunebooks, introductory sections of "rudiments of music" normally divided music this way, too. In practice, Mason integrated rhythm, pitch, and dynamics; again, this was likely the practice in singing schools. All three systems (Pestalozzian, Mason's, and singing schools), of course, used the movable "do" and "sol-fa" syllables. In theory, differences in musical pedagogy were not that great. Mason did develop special programs for children, whereas the singing school was a social institution that appealed to men, women, and children indiscriminately and taught them in unsegregated classes.

Pestalozzi's theory drew also from Kantian "faculty" psychology, attributing to the mind (an immaterial reality) a priori intellectual faculties—memory, reasoning, imagination (Ellis 1955, 8–9). "The mind is exercised and disciplined by it," Mason wrote of his system of musical instruction, "as by the study of arithmetic; and the voice by reading and speaking" (Mason 1834, 21). Consequently, this also meant constituting a musical culture of childhood and the professional adult institutions to manage it. Singing schools appealed to the young, but they were holistic events, not based on a separate naturalized culture of childhood. On this basis, reformers could argue, Pestalozzian pedagogy was better suited to the public schools and to music academies. Support for the culture of singing schools and shape note tunebooks fell to segments of American culture that did not advocate the institutional separation of childhood.

Pestalozzianism introduced an effective weapon in the reform arsenal. Whereas calls for "musical improvement" in the West had been largely ineffective in shaping public taste, this apparatus could link music reform with a host of other moral and cultural devices. Formulated as public morality based on scientific principles imported from Europe, it could direct its appeal at a diverse public, presuming to rise above native theological squabbles. In Cincinnati, which proved to be a fortuitous site, it found the security of a variety of emerging urban institutions. Surely it was all of this, and not mere sound, that provided the balm for Lyman Beecher's "nerves rent asunder."

"THE REFORM HAS BEGUN": THE CAMPAIGN AGAINST SINGING SCHOOLS

The publishers would further remark that 'The Sacred Harp' is printed in patent notes, under the belief that it will prove much more acceptable to a majority of singers in the West and South.

Advertisement for *Mason's Sacred Harp*
Cincinnati Journal and Western Luminary, 29 August 1834

[The publishers announce a new edition of *Mason's Sacred Harp*] printed in round notes; the *patent note* system being a miserable device, a mere shift to clothe ignorance and laziness with the look of science.

Advertisement for *Mason's Sacred Harp*,
Cincinnati Journal and Western Luminary, 21 July 1836

According to Gould, Timothy Mason came to Cincinnati from Boston in 1834 and "found everybody singing and enjoying the Billings and Company 'fuguing songs' and all the rest of the old-time, native New England singing-school stock-in-trade, and using books printed in the popular shape-notes" (Gould 1853, chap. 10). We must assume that he meant that the books were popular with the public, but not that they were used in churches. Finding them objectionable, Mason undertook what Gould would call "the work of reformation in the West" (Gould 1853, 143). But what did this reformation consist of? If Mason actually accomplished this, what institutional powers did he marshall? And what was the effect on singing?

Timothy Mason initially wore two hats in Cincinnati. He was sought by Lyman Beecher to direct music at the Second Presbyterian Church, where Beecher served as minister. At the same time, a group of influential men led by Judge Jacob Burnet founded the Eclectic Academy of Music— on the model of Lowell Mason's Boston Academy of Music (1833)—and sought Mason as its director (Gary 1951, 12). Upon Mason's arrival in June 1834, Academy classes were held in the Second Presbyterian Church. Under the stated auspices of Pestalozzian principles, a special series of classes was held for children; another special series was held for women. Advertisements for the Academy reflected the influence of both Lyman Beecher's moral ideology and Lowell Mason's educational philosophy:

> *Every child and youth in our country should be taught vocal music,* not only as a source of rational amusement, but as a most excellent *moral safeguard.*
>
> The course will be strictly elementary, and conducted upon the PESTALOZZIAN system, which has been so justly celebrated and so eminently successful in Europe and some of the Atlantic cities . . . *fully to the comprehension of children Six years old.* (*Cincinnati Journal and Western Luminary,* 13 June 1834)

As influential as Mason's presence in Cincinnati must have been, his work was largely indebted to the ideas of his contemporaries. But throughout 1834/35, Mason's work was apparently limited to his Eclectic Academy subscribers. The *Journal* had enthusiastically supported the activities of the Eclectic Academy, but it continued to uphold popular tastes—printing hymns in shape notes, endorsing Watts's hymn collections for church use, and printing advertisements for a variety of shape note books and activities. If there was to be reform, more was needed. The break came late in 1835, when the *Journal* made a substantial commitment to the musical reform effort, reflected in a series of polemical articles on the subject of music. The series was a rhetorical masterpiece, sustaining a comprehensive argument over the course of a year and a half. Whatever its actual effect on readers, the fundamental meaning of hymnody or even music in general as reflected in the *Journal* underwent an extraordinary transformation over this period in the series. It warrants our attention.

The Discourse on Music

It was not customary for the *Journal* to offer discourses on music, so early installments of the series entitled "Music" attended to technical subjects of lesser consequence.[12] Installment no. 5 (18 February 1836), for example, addressed the relationship between pronunciation in common speech and in poetic and musical meter. In lines such as "Nature, with heavy loads oppressed," the writer objected to the transformation of stress—from "NA-ture" as spoken to "na-TURE" as sung—which was called "a real destruction of *sense*." The writer gave some correct examples, calling them "illustrious specimens of the good taste of compilers of books of Psalmody."

Installment no. 7 (March 10) attacked the fugue on a similar basis. Imagine, the writer asked, the pretty line, "Life is a shadow—how it flies," transformed by the fugue into the following: "Life is a shad—life is a shad—life is a shad—ow [Oh!] how it flies." Of this, the writer concluded: "Not that all fugues deserve indiscriminate censure. In the hands of a skillful composer, *occasionally* they heighten the effect powerfully. We censure their *indiscriminate* use, and use them to illustrate the necessity of avoiding any arrangement of harmony destructive of sense." These were serious attacks, but they were directed at specific habits of style and not at the shape note or singing school institution as a whole.

With calculated restraint, installment no. 9 (March 31) began the assault on fundamental structures. Under the rubric of "Good Performance," the writer attacked congregational singing, in which "every body must sing 'on *his own hook*'—and the 'hooks' will be as different as the different notions of the individuals." In its place, the writer advanced the institution of the choir with its single leader, its opportunity for sustained training, and its devotion to musical skills as "effective as a vocal body." As if too much had been taken for granted, however, the next four issues were devoted to raising and countering objections to choirs and may have reflected real or imagined objections raised by readers.

Some of the stated objections and their replies illustrate salient moral dimensions of the discussion as well as the contorted yet urgent logic of the writer. To the objection that choirs would consist of "gay and thoughtless" young people, the writer countered that this was not the way choirs should be (April 7). Besides, the argument continued, the same was already true of congregational singing. (Indeed, singing schools were popular social events for young people.) To the objection that choirs would remove an important part of worship from the hands of the congregation, the writer replied that members of the congregation would be inspired to learn to sing and join the choir (April 7). To the objection that choral singing was scientific, hindered feeling, and was unnatural, the writer replied that the trained singer could "continue to keep perfect time and tune, as if it were by INSTINCT, for habit is a second nature" (April 14).

Singing Schools and Musical Rules

Installment no. 14 (June 2) outlined a pivotal argument. It consisted of a Socratic dialogue between two singing school students: P, an ostensibly innocent but manipulative questioner, and Q, an experienced singer accustomed to shape notes. Initially, P proposed that Q solicit students for a singing school. But Q had never before considered teaching and was reluctant yet intrigued by P's encouragement. So Q asked how he might conduct the school, and the writer, through P's enthusiasm, pursued the plan to the point of absurdity. For instance, when Q reported that he couldn't read music, P replied: "'Read notes? time?' fudge! don't be troubled, you needn't teach them any thing about that."

They turned then to a discussion of the value of shape notes, and Q, although a seasoned singer, confessed that he didn't really understand the rules but merely followed them. P replied facetiously: "but this learning the rules after all is a great plague; and I never got any good by it myself, nor my classes either; so it's best to get through it as *spry* as possible." Q objected, asking that without understanding, what were the rules for? P replied, again facetiously: "it's the way they always do to keep a singing school; and we must take things as we find them; however it's only a little troublesome along at first, you get through it all in three or four evenings at most, and then the rules may go to Jericho."

Q was relieved to hear this: "Well, I wish they would go, and never come back; what else must I do?" Then P described the singing school procedure of going over the scales, learning tunes, and then "putting the words on." By this time Q was overjoyed: "Is this all? I never dreamed of keeping a singing school before; but now, if I don't have one in less than no time, my name is not Q. But suppose I did not take the patent notes, what then?"

The argument took a crucial turn at this point. Having established the simplicity of singing schools, P could now allude to the more advanced activities of scientific musical "rules." He answered that without shape notes, "Why 'twould be much harder to get along. I believe you'd have to know something about the rules, have 'em so you could say 'em, or something another." He described the difficult process of detecting the scale by observing the key signature, and then concluded: "For my part, I expect this round note system will go out of fashion soon, it can't stand much longer."

By this time Q's curiosity was aroused beyond hope. Who, he must know, does know the rules? Now P had him trapped: "Why, yes, some great musicians I 'spose, who make tunes, and write note-books; but there ain't many, I can tell you; it's so dry, I don't see how anybody can bear to study it; however, they can't keep schools any better; if they go making the schools learn them by heart, why, they get tired of it directly; some don't half learn them, and none understand them, it only makes a plaguy fuss about nothing."

Driven to absurdity, Q was nonetheless blissfully undaunted and vowed to "commence an expedition next week." With consummate irony, P concluded the dialogue with an exhortation of encouragement: "Well, good luck to you; but remember—look bold—sing loud, and flourish your hand stoutly, and if anybody asks you questions about what you don't understand, just turn up your nose at them, and turn away contemptuously from them saying, 'Hooh! don't you know *that!*' "

The Moral Climate of Singing Schools

Having made the point on musical terms, the writer raised the stakes in installment no. 15 by taking on the moral implications of the debate. We can now marvel at the delicate progression of the argument, each stage fully dependent on ground won in the last. In no. 15, time had passed—Q was now routinely operating singing schools. The author began by lamenting that he or she had represented things too favorably in the last installment. Determined to set things right, the author turned to another dialogue, this time between two of Q's students: X, a "typical" singing school pupil, and Y, a "serious" student of music.

As the dialogue began, X was surprised that Y did not enjoy the school held on the previous night. Y explained: "I might have been foolish in going for any other purpose [than flirting], I grant, considering the bright eyes, blooming cheeks, and ruby lips I saw there, and the obvious effect they were producing upon many a chanting swain: but to tell you the truth, I went there with the expectation of learning how to sing."

Seduced into agreement, X replied this was not the purpose of the school. No one at all, he said, was really there to learn, even the teacher: "And do you suppose Master Q. would ever line his purse if it wa'nt for the *gals?* Why that's all the fun!" With this interchange, writer gave X the unlikely task of *defending* the moral disrepute of singing schools! Clearly no person would do such a thing, and by manipulating a fictional dialogue designed to represent reality, the writer could, in a setting where objections should otherwise have been forthcoming, stigmatize singing schools without a chance of real disagreement.

Y persisted, outlining his intention to understand music, including its rules. Thus they parted, having moved from the illusion of agreement to hopeless, unresolvable dispute. Y: "I shall not waste any more time in a flirting school for the sake of any thing, or any body. Good morning X." X: "Good morning Deacon Y. Ahem!" But this impasse was only an illusion. The writer had given Y the moral high ground and had aligned the readers' feelings with that position.

In several concluding editorial paragraphs, the writer could then link the presumed immorality of the singing school to the patent note system itself. Earlier the writer had printed some musical examples in round notes (March 24), but up to this point it would have been premature to assail patent notes directly. The writer finished the installment, concluding that the patent note system "has accomplished its mission of wide spread evil in the deterioration of sacred music: and as sure as the progress of truth against error, IT MUST CEASE."

The Plan for Reform

The next series of installments resumed the expository style, presumably having completed the task of aligning the emotions of readers. Having already identified and countered objections to choirs, installment no. 16 (June 16) could now outline the faults of singing schools: (1) singing schools were not taught by religious persons; (2) the teachers did not generally teach with understanding; (3) the teachers did not have musical training; and (4) the schools were restricted almost entirely to adults, from the erroneous notion that children could not learn to sing. The writer concluded, "Such singing schools, it is to be hoped, wide-spread as they are, will ultimately cease; and be succeeded by others, which, in a future number we will endeavor to describe. The reform has begun. Boston has led the way, the City of the Pilgrims. Cincinnati is following rapidly in a similar career, and promises to take a stand worthy of the Queen of the West." Having inflamed the readers' sense of musical accomplishment, moral propriety, and regional loyalty, the writer prepared the readers to receive the plan that at this point was yet to be described.

Transitional installments addressed various peripheral matters. In installment no. 16 (July 7) the writer introduced the notion of the "musical faculty" to advance the idea of comprehensive musical education, with music elevated to the status then granted to arithmetic and natural history. Installment no. 17 (July 14) returned to style and assailed the nasal twang, guttural style, and bellowing of congregational singing. It concluded, again manipulating the Romanticist sense of nature, that "nothing is more unnatural than this same *natural* singing." Equally distasteful were the "marches, rondos, and jigs" that populated shape note tunebooks.

A continuation of installment no. 17 (July 21) drove the argument home, outlining the plan that Gould would later call "the work of reformation in the West." Surely echoing Beecher, the writer spoke of "God's plan of conducting the church . . . by a combination of means," any of which could undermine the plan if neglected. This was especially important in matters of national influence, for "what will mould the character of a nation quicker than its music?" Any other means employed (singing schools, we presume are meant by this) were a part of another great combination—"Its author the devil, its aim the subversion of the church. *What must be done?*"

1. Abolishment of the singing schools.
2. Raise the standard of lyrical poetry and musical composition such that no piece be tolerated in a collection that is not fit to sing and that does not unite science with nature.
3. Establish the institution of *choirs* in churches and, temporarily, give up the system of congregational singing.
4. "Every church should make vigorous efforts *to procure, and to support continually by a regular compensation,* a teacher of music qualified by his talents, and his thorough education, to lead the services of the sanctuary, and to commence among the *children of the congregation,* and carry on, that regular progressive system of musical education, of which we shall hereafter speak—thus establishing this part of church service upon an immovable basis."

Three columns to the right, in the same issue, the *Journal* announced the new publication of *Mason's Sacred Harp* "printed in round notes; the *patent note* system being a miserable device, a mere shift to clothe ignorance and laziness with the look of science."

Music and Public Education

We cannot know the effect this had on readers' opinions, nor do we presume that this Presbyterian periodical actually changed the course of musical and religious practice. Nonetheless, it served as a kind of discursive momentum that provided leverage into public institutions. In 1836, Professor Calvin Stowe of Cincinnati's Lane Theological Seminary toured Europe, studying its schools with his wife, Harriet Beecher Stowe (Lyman's daughter, and author in 1852 of *Uncle Tom's Cabin*).[13] His report, delivered to the Ohio legislature, concluded that "whoever visits the schools of Messrs. Mason or Solomon, in Cincinnati, will have a much better idea of what [the European method] is than any description can give" (Gary 1951, 13; Stowe 1838, 217). The following year, as Mason was offering the first volunteer classes in the common schools, Mason and Charles Beecher, Lyman's son, presented a report to the Western Literary Institute and College of Professional Teachers, "Vocal Music as a Branch of Common School Education" (Mason and Beecher 1837).

In this report, they undertook to convince teachers of literature that vocal music could be learned by all. So, comparing musical notation to the alphabet, they concluded that "the power of learning the shape, name, and uses of one set of characters, is the power of learning the same of any, or of all characters" (160). (Since shape notes more closely follow the principle of the alphabet, this is an ironic conclusion; indeed, we will see that the same argument was used by shape note proponents. But for this audience, the writers did not need to acknowledge the dispute over various musical notations.) They addressed faculty psychology, suggesting a danger in neglecting any particular faculty in educating children. Music, they said, uniquely exercises the faculties of force, time, and tune. Finally, they presented the compelling case for the moral properties of music education, in which "religion shall bear sway over an enlightened intellect," and America will, "with the voice of millions, solemnly swell the harmony of our national song to Him" (178).

Eventually, this report played a significant role in establishing music programs in Cincinnati's public schools (Osburn 1942, 11). After 1841, only one tunebook in shape notes would be introduced by Cincinnati publishers active at the time.[14] Even the *Missouri Harmony*, owned by a Cincinnati publisher but sold far outside Cincinnati, issued a "revised and improved" edition in 1835, including a supplement that "would have appealed to those who preferred the emerging 'genteel' style" (Bean 1994, xi). In 1844, music was made an official part of the school curriculum

(Hamm 1958, 305; Osburn 1942, 11 gives the date as 1845). A few years later, after several music teachers had been employed in the city, Nathaniel Gould made surprise visits to the schools and, having caught them "when there was no chance for display," observed that "there was no greater evidence of thorough training in the first principles of music, of attention, and ambition on the part of the scholars, than in Cincinnati" (Gould 1853, 142). In 1848, Elisha Locke and Solon Nourse's *School Vocalist* was adopted as the official music textbook. In 1853, a third Mason brother, Luther (1818–1896), traveled to Louisville, Kentucky, and pioneered music education in the primary school grades there. In 1870, Charles Beecher was appointed state superintendent of public instruction in Florida.

If reformers achieved their aim of injecting an atmosphere of secular piety into music instruction, the overall result contained perplexing contradictions. It was ironic, for example, that the movement directed its moral attack at music that was largely sacred, neglecting a host of other secular forms prevalent in the city. In 1841, after Mason had left the Eclectic Academy for public teaching, the Academy named as its orchestra leader none other than Joseph Tosso, a violinist who achieved fame in Cincinnati theaters with his humorous "Arkansaw Traveler" skit (Cist 1841, 137; Smith 1947). But unlike singing schools, Tosso made no pretense of moral authority and thereby posed no threat to reformers' aim of shaping public moral consensus.

It is worth wondering if reader response had any bearing at all on the effect of the series—if, rather, it was meant only to shape the reasoning of those who were building public institutions. After installment no. 7, the *Journal* editor had printed an objection to a section that attacked the use in song texts of explicit religious doctrine, didactic passages, or descriptions of prayers (March 17). Apparently in response, the writer had dropped the matter completely until much later (November 17), when the argument was recast in terms that did not restrict the promotion of religious doctrine in song. On the whole, a discourse of this nature would surely have provoked the readers to object—the paper was, after all, taking on as adversaries some of its foremost advertisers.

Nothing could signal the *Journal*'s perception that the war had been won more than its wholehearted endorsement of the round note edition of *Mason's Sacred Harp,* which only two years earlier it had promoted in patent notes. The book's instructional "rudiments" section was thoroughly infused with explicit Pestalozzian pedagogy. It contained a modest sampling of Revolution-era American tunes, but it also conspicuously appropriated the titles of some popular pieces—"Northfield," "Chester," "Sherburne," and "Swanton"—to entirely different tunes composed by Mason and Hastings. Meanwhile, the *Journal* continued its dramatic reversal, turning on one of the paper's own writers, James Gallaher, who had edited the series of shape note hymns a few years earlier. Comparing him unfavorably to Lowell Mason, the writer said of Gallaher that he was "not a professional musician, and cannot fairly be supposed to be so well acquainted with the principles necessary to be observed, in preparing a collection expressly for singing" (December 22).[15] Surely the *Journal* risked a loyal readership in taking such a stand. But what really was at stake? To answer this question, we must turn to the theological context in which the debate took place.

A PLEA FOR THE WEST

The thing required for the civil and religious prosperity of the West, is universal education, and moral culture, by institutions commensurate to that result—the all pervading influence of schools, and colleges, and seminaries, and pastors, and churches. When the West is well supplied in this respect, though there may be great relative defects, there will be, as we believe, the stamina and vitality of a perpetual civil and religious prosperity.

LYMAN BEECHER, *A Plea for the West* (1835)

If we gain the West, all is safe; if we lose it, all is lost.

LYMAN BEECHER, 1830

The urgency of the assault on shapes is remarkable, particularly since the matter of the method of printing music would seem on the surface inconsequential. It is understandable that tunebook compilers and singing teachers disagreed over pedagogy and notation. But why should this practice, which had so little to do with the conduct of worship, have been of such great concern to the churches?

THE UNITED EVANGELICAL FRONT

According to the plan described in the *Journal*, the improvement of music was part of a systematic and united effort to articulate "God's plan" and extend the domain of moral influence far outside the churches and into American civilization as a whole. The movement originated in eastern churches whose leaders feared that in the religious outcome of the West much was at stake. As the Second Great Awakening took shape in the early nineteenth century, the greatest initial successes in the West were achieved by lay-clergy denominations—Baptists and Methodists. Among those inclined to more centralized authority, however, a fear arose in the East over the moral chaos that was imagined on the frontier. It was in this environment that a "united evangelical front" arose as a deliberate plan to link conservative Christians of a variety of denominations (Foster 1960). Working through an impressive array of tract, Bible, Sunday School, temperance, and other societies, proponents circumvented divisive ecclesiastical authority to form a powerful evangelical movement.

As an urban center predisposed to religious discourse, Cincinnati was an ideal setting for the movement. In 1816, Timothy Flint had found in the city "many societies for diffusion of religious knowledge, instruction, and clarity." The presses "teemed" with polemical religious pamphlets, and those he distributed were "devoured eagerly." He called Ohio the "Yankee state," noting its "disposition to dogmatize, to settle, not only their own faith, but that of their neighbor, and to stand resolutely, and dispute fiercely, for the slightest shade of difference of religious opinion" (Kirkpatrick [1911] 1968, 66–68, 78).

It was not until the 1830s, with Lyman Beecher's arrival in the city, that a unified vision began to emerge out of this discord. Beecher and others in the evangelical milieu sought to forge a comprehensive millennial society— to infuse fundamental social institutions with religious principle. Stymied by the recalcitrant authority of both Congregational and Presbyterian polity, he found an outlet for his ambitions in the institutions of the evangelical movement (Foster 1960, 129). Beecher's move to Cincinnati in November 1832 was partly motivated by a "Valley Project," devised in 1828. In this, the American Tract Society (founded in 1825), the American Bible Society (founded by Beecher, 1816), the American Home Missionary Society (1826), the American Sunday-School Union (1824), and the American Education Society (1816) almost simultaneously laid plans to flood the Mississippi River valley with evangelical materials (Foster 1960, 192).

Surely this would not be universally supported in the West: "Missionaries who come out from New England," the secretary of the board of Lane Theological Seminary wrote Beecher in 1832, "are held up as heretics, and every obstacle is thrown in the way of their efficiency and success" (Beecher [1864] 1961, 2:188). Beecher might also have heard of Cincinnati's "infidel paper," the *Western Tiller,* which ridiculed the excesses of the western priestly class (Aaron 1992, 197). Or he might have received reports of Congregationalist ministers sent out by the American Home Missionary Society after 1827 who "professed amazement at the ignorance they found in southern Illinois when they first encountered frontiersmen from Kentucky and Tennessee who had known no Puritan tradition in education" (Smith 1967, 690).

Yet the main source of resistance was not the "infidel" press at all but an entrenched elite establishment of old Calvinists, rooted in Cincinnati's Old School Presbyterian churches. Echoing the division in New England Congregationalism a century earlier, "Old School" Presbyterians held fast to the doctrine of election—the theology of the people of God within the family of God—and opposed the Arminian-tending methods of "New School" evangelicals, whose theology revolved around the mission to the unbeliever. The success of Methodism in the West, for example, followed a wholesale adoption of evangelical theology, providing for the widespread employment of missionaries and itinerant preachers. But Presbyterians at that time and continuing until the merger of 1870 were divided along strict Calvinist ("Old School") and Arminian ("New School") lines. This division, and not the imagined depravity of the West, ultimately defined the scope of evangelical work in Cincinnati in the mid-1830s.

In Cincinnati, the "able and contentious leader" of Old School proponents was the Reverend Joshua L. Wilson (1774–1846) of the First Presbyterian Church. One writer called him "an uncompromising Calvinist and heresy-hunter, vigorously opposing the so-called New England theology" (Presbyterian Church 1968, 127). Whether by necessity or choice, it was Wilson's Old School establishment that arose as Beecher's chief obstacle in the West. Ultimately, little else stood in the way of reform other than a decisive and visible victory over Wilson.

Cincinnati's Second Presbyterian Church, where Beecher came to preach and Mason to sing, had occupied a new building in 1830—a "fine edifice" downtown on Fourth Street, with a muscular Greek revival facade. As Cincinnati's wealthiest congregation, it was apparently less entrenched in Old School sentiment (Aaron 1992, 192). Although one authority called it "ultra-Calvinist" (Pitzer 1966, 102), its establishment in 1817 was clearly linked to a dispute several members had with Wilson (Hightower 1934, 11; Nutt 1991, 33). Consequently, Beecher, the outspoken New Schooler, inserted himself into a volatile atmosphere that included opposition to his own employment (Caskey 1978, 58–59). As it turned out, winning over his own congregation was far less difficult than might have been thought. During Beecher's ministry, the Second Presbyterian Church became the largest congregation in the Synod. More difficult were votes over ordination of candidates to the Presbyterian clergy whose theological views divided the Presbytery along New School/Old School lines. When George Beecher, Lyman's son, was approved for ordination without a single crossover vote, the stage was set for a major controversy.[16]

Just two months after the vote, on 11 November 1834, Wilson filed formal charges of heresy against Lyman Beecher, accusing Beecher of teaching false doctrines. Beecher's defense at the trial, held the following June, could not have been more inflammatory: "I do not say that I have not taught the doctrines: but I deny their being false doctrines. The course I shall take will be to justify" (Nutt 1991, 36; Stansbury 1835). Charged with opposing Reformed theology in saying that the human will was left untouched by the sin of Adam, Beecher drew from the work of Jonathan Edwards for his response. Edwards had distinguished moral ability, which is corrupted from birth, from natural ability, which provides for human freedom and thus human responsibility for sin. Beecher found evidence for natural liberty in the Westminster Confession and held that Wilson's rigid view negated any exercise of the will in sin.

Beecher was convincing: the Presbytery acquitted him on all but one charge and failed to assess any discipline at all. As for Wilson, the Presbytery voted to censure him for bringing before them inferential and unfounded charges. The trial was covered extensively by the press, even outside Cincinnati. Beecher's highly publicized victory over his staunchest adversary regarding the issue of free will and sin earned acceptance of his ideas in the Presbytery and cleared the way for unimpeded reform in Cincinnati and the West. He had secured, as one of his contemporaries had described it, "the union of these two doctrines of *activity* and *dependence,* which are so commonly felt to be subversive of each other; [and] the bringing of both to bear with undiminished force on the minds of the impenitent" (quoted in Caskey 1978, 35).

As this theological dispute raged, another controversy found Beecher at its center. Beecher's original appointment in Cincinnati had been as director and professor of didactic and polemic theology at Lane Theological Seminary. In 1834, Beecher allowed students to hold a debate on the question of abolition of slavery. As the debate and subsequent antislavery activism of the students spilled out into the community, Beecher and the trustees, under pressure from the citizens, took a hard stance against the debate and abolished the students' Antislavery Society. As a result, most of the students and some of the faculty—the so-called Lane Rebels—left the seminary, many for the theology program at the Oberlin Institute (now Oberlin College) in northern Ohio (Fraser 1985, 115–27; Lesick 1980).

Beecher had sacrificed academic freedom and perhaps a personal sympathy for the antislavery cause for the stability of Lane Theological Seminary—at a tremendous cost. The seminary had been preserved, although it never again attracted a student body to match this class. Nonetheless, his theological principles had been defended. When the new students arrived in the fall of 1835, the burden of these acrimonious struggles had been lifted from Beecher's shoulders. He could turn his attention elsewhere, to "the work of reform in the West"; the series of articles on "Music" began appearing at this time in the *Journal.*

EVANGELICAL THEOLOGY AND MUSIC REFORM

Order is heaven's first law.

LYMAN BEECHER, Address to Union Literary Society,
Miami University, 1835

The chief importance of the Second Great Awakening to music reform was to vastly amplify its moral dimensions. As the case of Cincinnati demonstrates, earlier attempts at reforming musical taste were largely inconsequential. But once music reform was linked to moral pedagogy, the results were apparently swift and compelling. And at the critical moment of transition, Beecher's most formidable obstacles to moral reform were unruly and idealistic seminary students and the Cincinnati's Old School faithful. Consequently, the symbolic containment of youth and the discursive appropriation of the autonomous church were priorities of the highest order. Singing schools, where both of these properties lay unmolested and fundamental, stood as an auspicious target.

Both of these principles, so active in the confrontations with the Old School faithful and with the idealistic students at Lane, were central themes in the preoccupations that soon followed. As the new class assembled at Lane, Beecher turned his attention to the character of public education—surely mindful of the upheaval he had endured. Invited to address the Union Literary Society of Miami University in nearby Oxford on the occasion of its tenth anniversary, Beecher seized an opportunity to articulate a plan for comprehensive public education, printed the following year as *A Plea for Colleges*. In the address, Beecher fabricated a plan with mental discipline—achieved by rigorous mastery of a uniform curriculum—as its governing mandate. "Order is heaven's first law," he said, describing an educational machinery, and by extension a public discourse, whose moral dimensions could be rigidly controlled (quoted in Fraser 1985, 144).

The heresy hearings were even more important. Beecher had made human responsibility for sin a public concern, and he now had the institutional machinery of Western Presbyterianism at hand to control it. Presbyterians, who had been outpaced in the West by lay-ministry Baptists and Methodists, could now use their unique strengths—centralized authority and doctrinal constraint—to better advantage. Called to execute "God's plan of conducting the church . . . by a combination of means," they aptly turned their attention to schools, civic morality, and music.

Yet Beecher's vision did not come in Cincinnati, nor did he formulate his defense against Wilson's heresy charges in the West. His theology of revivalism was inherited, as a student at Yale, from his mentor, Timothy Dwight, a Congregationalist minister and grandson of Jonathan Edwards. At the time of the Revolution, Dwight began composing poetry, most notably scriptural allegories celebrating the founding of the American nation. But after the Revolution, he grew increasingly alarmed as the reality of republican ideals began chipping away at the status and influence of New England Congregationalism—and "infidel philosophy" swarmed to fill the vacuum. Inaugurated as president of Yale in 1797, Dwight found a student body organized around deeply entrenched Enlightenment thought. Beecher, by his own account, had reluctantly endured this atmosphere since entering Yale in 1794; he immediately came under Dwight's influence and was converted "quick as a flash of lightning" (Henry 1973, 38–40; Fraser 1985, 14). With Dwight's arrival, the prevailing winds of skepticism at Yale were halted and reversed—soon to gather the momentum that became the Second Great Awakening.

Dwight's theology stood squarely on the shoulders of Edwardean revivalism, which had lain dormant during the Revolution. Whereas for Edwards, conversion came supernaturally, as God "inscrutably chooses to impart spiritual motives," Dwight expanded the domain of revealed religion to include secondary "means of grace"—regularly operating quasi-religious ordinances (Berk 1974, 53). Whereas strict Calvinists had focused on an inner state of grace to mold moral character, Dwight preached a theology of paternal guidance—a matrix of religious and secular institutions designed to channel the will in a virtuous direction (Berk 1974, 76, 106). Dwight's stated intent was to supplant the functioning of the Standing Order and thus to restore the theocratic state that the Bill of Rights had brought under legal assault (Berk 1974, 75–76; Silverman 1969, 94–95). Consequently, Dwight considered democracy a plain violation of God's government because it set subjects over rulers and fostered "infidel philosophies," such as Deism and Unitarianism. Ultimately, Dwight believed, democratic government would lead America into the hands of a widespread anti-Christian conspiracy (Berk 1974, 107, 128–30).[17]

Despite his proximity to tunebook and singing school activity, there is little evidence that Dwight had any systematic interest in music. He was adopted by the Federalist movement as an advocate for loyalty to the Standing Order (Berk 1974, 40; Silverman 1969, 101), which may or may not have led the Federalist supporters also to embrace "ancient harmony" and the rhetoric of strict public morality with which it was advanced. Dwight was also well known for his widely popular edition of Watts, identified as a replacement for Barlow's "infidel" edition. But the direct link of music reform to the Second Great Awakening seems to have been made first by Beecher and only after his contact with Lowell Mason at the Hanover Street Church. Accounts of Beecher's early revival preaching, however, depict him as singularly uninterested in music. He often worked on his sermons until the last minute and then "dashed up the aisle as the hymn was closing—or occasionally as it was being repeated to give the tardy pastor time to arrive" (Fraser 1985, 52). Once the connection was made between Mason's Pestalozzian moral pedagogy and Beecher's revival theology, there was apparently an effortless discovery of shared purpose that nourished them both. The nature of Beecher's intellectual inheritance from Dwight and the combative theological atmosphere surrounding Beecher's tenure at Hanover Street both suggest a crucial link of nineteenth-century music reform with this lingering eighteenth-century New England theological schism.

This link has less to do with music reform per se, of which much has been written, than with the moral and pedagogical umbrella that nourished the reform movement. Indeed, at the time the *Journal* series appeared, the advancement of public education as an extension of Protestant morality was widespread and included both allies and enemies of Beecher (Fraser 1985, 182; Smith 1967; Tyack 1966). Yet it was not the infrastructure of common schooling that articulated evangelical secular morality, but the array of pedagogical materials, developed around Pestalozzian principles, that translated the explicit Federalist agenda into a generalized culture of childhood. Because of their extraordinary success and because of their formative connections to the Beechers and the Stowes, we can justifiably assess this process by way of the series of readers compiled by William Holmes McGuffey. Ultimately, these readers were broadly influential in infusing common school pedagogy with the comprehensive morality of revivalism, explicit to the extent that they illuminate the workings of the discourse.

The first of McGuffey's *Eclectic Readers* were published by Truman and Smith, who had made the pivotal decision to print the revised round note edition of *Mason's Sacred Harp*. Winthrop B. Smith had envisioned his company's future in schoolbook publishing and approached Catherine Beecher about a series of readers. She declined, but by one account she recommended William Holmes McGuffey. McGuffey was already an outspoken advocate for common schools and, with Calvin Stowe and others, had lobbied the Ohio legislature for that cause. An agreement with McGuffey was made in 1833 to publish the readers, and in 1836 Truman and Smith published the *Eclectic First Reader*, the first in the series that would be revised and reprinted many times over the course of the next century (Westerhoff 1978, 49–54).

The *Eclectic Readers* were essentially collections of pithy narratives, drawn from a variety of sources and each redesigned around a pedagogical and moral lesson (Lindberg 1976). In the design of the narratives, perhaps no moral trait was more fundamental than the rhetoric of paternal benevolence that emanated from God through sanctified institutional "means" (Mosier 1947). The readers obscured the popular image of God as deliverer of the oppressed and advanced in its place a doctrine of moral stewardship. This doctrine extended sanctity to wealth as the vehicle of benevolence and as the reward for thrift, industry, and hard labor. The readers formulated a moral world beyond the world of nature—where wealth, the priestcraft, and government, as described by the conservative synthesis of Hamiltonian Federalism, all prevailed over natural law, equality, and democracy.

Yet it was not so much their substance that made them exemplary as their propensity to work through narratives, describing an American cultural mainstream of narrow moral dimensions and obscuring the heterodox atmosphere from which the readers arose. Indeed, confrontation was systematically supplanted by paternal benevolence as the means to gain the rhetorical upper hand. For example, where conservative polemics raged elsewhere against Catholic immigrants (with Beecher's *A Plea for the West* prominently among them), McGuffey's *Rhetorical Guide* quietly noted the unreasonableness of attacking "speculative doctrines of faith" (quoted in Mosier 1947, 84). Even the designation "eclectic" was incorporated into the series title as an Americanized codeword for Pestalozzianism, described only as originating in European countries where "the subject of education has been deemed of paramount importance" (*Third Reader* [1837]; quoted in Lindberg 1976, xx–xxi). This was the process of an evolving "civil religion," in which secularized religious doctrine was grafted onto American public culture. Its impetus was the formation of universal religious symbolism; as a consequence, those forms of religious practice which resisted this process drifted toward the margins of American culture (see Williams 1980).

For the most part, the readers did not participate in music reform. They merely contributed to the cultural atmosphere that sustained it. Poetry appeared in all the readers in substantial quantity, but music was suggested only occasionally by the indication of a well-known tune. Truman and Smith, in fact, published separate juvenile music instructors, including Timothy Mason's *Young Minstrel* (1838). This work contained not a single common psalm or hymn—only bland versified homilies set, according to the explicitly stated method, exclusively to European airs. In advertisements for these publications, however, the *Eclectic Readers* served as a platform for advocating Pestalozzian musical instruction. The *Fourth Reader* (1837) even contained a full page on *Mason's Sacred Harp* inside the front cover, stating the hope that the round note edition "will take the place of the numerous worthless music books now so widely circulated." The patent note edition, still in stock, was mentioned less enthusiastically, with this warning: "Persons who order the above work must be very particular, and specify whether the *round* or *patent* note edition is wanted."

One particularly vivid example will illustrate the dramatic change that reformers exacted in the moral compass of American musical culture. Since the time of Billings, the tunebook idiom abounded in patriotic poetry, most dramatizing the revolution and the founding of the new nation.

In the tunebook context, however, these songs—arguably more genuinely patriotic because they emerged directly from the cause of the Revolution—stood as prototypes of patriotic sentiment but not as national hymns. Many of these songs were retained in the shape note tunebooks as the idiom moved west and south. For example, Oscar Sonneck cataloged several dozen nondescript printings of the tune "To Anaceron in Heaven" under various titles and with various texts, some patriotic and some not, between 1795 and 1813—all before Francis Scott Key used the tune for his poem "The Star-Spangled Banner" and long before the song was adopted by Act of Congress as the national anthem in 1931 (Sonneck [1909] 1972, 24–27). Similarly, one of the innumerable tunes and texts to use the title "America" appeared in a likewise unexceptional presentation in *Mason's Sacred Harp*. But on the final page of *McGuffey's Fourth Reader* was the complete text of the song, the Reverend Samuel Smith's 1832 poem ("My country, 'tis of thee"), which had first been performed by Lowell Mason's choir at a Sunday School celebration on July 4 (Sonneck [1909] 1972, 73–78). McGuffey boldly proclaimed the song "'America'—National Hymn—Mason's Sacred Harp." [18] It was this type of transformation that so contended against the tunebook idiom. Where tunebooks had faithfully celebrated the cause of the Revolution in music and poetry, reformers enlisted these same materials in the service of a new cause, one which called for the wholesale transformation of the musical idiom.

In other respects, the Second Great Awakening has long been considered an ally to the shape note movement, stirring camp meeting enthusiasm in the West and the South and contributing a new style and repertoire to the tunebook idiom. In this regard, Lyman Beecher was influential precisely because he shunned enthusiastic revivals, interpreting the theology of means as a call for reform and decorum. He was disturbed by the excesses of emotion and noise characteristic of such fiery preachers as Charles G. Finney in part, and ironically, because the disrepute brought on by them would weaken him in his battle with the Unitarians (Fraser 1985, 64). Perhaps most important, Beecher was confronted by Finney—forcing him to refine his position on the manner of conducting revivals—

during his tenure at Hanover Street, just as his bond with Lowell Mason and Pestalozzianism was taking shape. In Cincinnati, the dangers of un-controlled revivals were again called to mind by Theodore Weld, a Finney disciple, who led the student revolt at Lane Theological Seminary. And precisely at the point Beecher arrived in Cincinnati in 1832, the *Journal* began printing, in shape notes, music from *The Christian Lyre,* compiled by another Finney disciple, Joshua Leavitt (Buechner 1979; Downey 1986) So much, it seems, led Beecher toward confrontations over the con-duct of quasi-religious observance that comprised such institutions as singing schools, public singings, and revivals.

Few places would have been better suited for the work of the Masons and the Beechers than Cincinnati. As a frontier city, Cincinnati provided an institutional base in music publishing, public education, and frontier Presbyterianism. Even the presence of bookstores and music schools, such as Mason's "Eclectic Academy," provided a sales outlet unavailable in ru-ral areas where itinerant singing school teachers operated. Yet in Cincin-nati there was little evidence of any grassroots resistance to reform. In topical magazines, especially those devoted to music, reformers encoun-tered a lively debate; the *Journal,* a local newspaper under denominational control, did not print responses or letters. Joshua Leavitt, who had else-where mounted an energetic defense against Thomas Hastings, would have been one to protest the cancellation of his tune series in the *Journal,* but no such protest appeared. Leavitt, of course, was not a local resident, and there were no other resident tunebook compilers invested in their own books or notation system.[19] The absence of genuine dialogue only en-hanced the effects of the invented "dialogues," co-opting voices of dissent to advance the reformers' own brand of orthodoxy. It is not that this sort of thing was uncommon but, rather, that the local influence of the *Journal* was decisive.

There were other circumstances that also amplified the effects of music reform in Cincinnati. The development of music pedagogy was closely allied with the development of public schools, providing a powerful in-stitutional base against which the efforts of independent tunebook com-pilers could only have paled. Moreover, the Second Presbyterian Church in nineteenth-century Cincinnati was a visible concentration of urban wealth. This provided lasting associations of music reform with genteel "high" urban culture and contributed to the disbursement of musical style by social class—a commonly recognized feature of nineteenth-century American music (Chase 1987, chap. 8; Seeger 1957; Levine 1988). Yet the most important circumstance may well have been accidental: at the time of the reform efforts, there was a massive influx of German immigrants in Cincinnati. In 1840 the city's population was one-third German born. This continued throughout the nineteenth century, producing a following with far more liking for the prevailing European musical canon than for the idiom sustained by American shape notes. Both by accident and by design, Cincinnati proved to be an auspicious site for reform. It seems extraordinary how meager was the resistance and how rapidly the essential changes were exacted.

These circumstances, of course, had an important effect on the character of the discourse. Beecher set out for the "New Jerusalem" of the West steeled for battle against Romanism, barbarism, and skepticism, his plan not formulated around the needs of the West but carved out of the polemics of post-Revolutionary New England. His view of westerners as "prey to Satan's wiles" unless rescued by eastern evangelical aid was "constantly corrected by Westerners" themselves (Fraser 1985, 185). It was no accident that he encountered his fiercest enemy in frontier Presbyterianism. Echoing the vision of Paul in Acts 16:9, Beecher and Mason answered a call of their own making to "come over the mountains and help us"—the West, and its urgent need for reform, an image affixed each in his mind's eye (see Keller [1942] 1968, chap. 4).

RESISTANCE, NOSTALGIA, AND REVIVAL

Now, if a man were to offer me the choice of two fields to farm in corn: one rough, stony, stumpy and steep; the other smooth, level and free from stones and stumps, which would I as a man of common sense take to farm? I suppose the round-head, or swell-head, would take the rough field for fear he could raise no corn, unless he could first clear the land of stumps, stones and other rubbish. Foolish bigots, they know they are wrong, but they have not honor enough to own up to the facts. I have seen round-note teachers teach a whole winter, whose classes could not sing in the spring what they learned in the winter. Some round-note fellows say that they can't sing by position or letter, as you claim, for patent notes just stand where round shapes do, therefore you ought not be bothered by shapes if you sing by letter. Too thin, gentlemen; too thin!

ALEXANDER AULD, letter to the *Musical Million*, 1880

And well I feel the magic power,
When skilled and cultured art
Its cunning webs of sweetness weaves
Around the captured heart.

But yet, dear friend, though rudely sung,
That old psalm tune hath still
A pulse of power beyond them all
My inmost soul to thrill.

HARRIET BEECHER STOWE,
"The Old Psalm Tune" (1858)

In the wake of reform, American music history became, by its own account, a largely uncontested record of the moral progress of music reform. Carried through the technologies of burgeoning public institutions, there emerged from this discourse a "mainstream" that marginalized and obscured competing discourses. Against this backdrop, the nineteenth-century tunebooks of the West and South took their place as an American musical idiom. Yet reform also set in motion a powerful dialectic. The Golden Age of the singing school movement very soon became a historical expedient, a style and period of an idealized past that absorbed what was no longer viable in the authorized present. This past also became a kind of contested territory, with form and function, and past and present, foregrounded or obscured in various measures to create a usable history. Some histories were designed explicitly around the genteel tastes of public culture, and others around the historical, theological, and experiential aspects of the singing school idiom. Eventually, these functions would accumulate around the folksong idea, built against the widening gulf of cultural isolation in America.

Resistance

This process did not go entirely unchallenged, and it behooves us to briefly examine instances of genuine resistance. In 1831, Thomas Hastings, then editor of the *Western Recorder,* and Joshua Leavitt, then editor of the *Evangelist,* carried on a vituperative debate through their publications over the function and conduct of worship and revival music, with neither yielding the upper hand (Buechner 1979). In a similar vein, one of the most articulate and outspoken defenses of shape notes was mounted by Alexander Auld. Auld was a singing school teacher and tunebook compiler, based on a farm near Deersville (Harrison County), Ohio, to the east, at considerable cultural and geographic distance from Cincinnati. He published several tunebooks relatively late in the shape note era, some, as account sheets of book sales reveal, reaching audiences far outside Ohio (Miller 1975, 256). Beginning in 1835 and continuing for over fifty years, Auld taught in the public schools during winter months when farming did not demand his attention, and in summer he taught singing schools. The first of his shape note tunebooks, the *Ohio Harmonist,* was introduced in 1847, so Auld and his books would have borne the full brunt of the campaign against the shapes.

In response, his defense was tireless. In the preface to the *Ohio Harmonist* (1852 edition), he took up the alphabet analogy, reporting that he had found some "who affirm that there is no difference about the name of the note." He continued, "I would ask that head of wit who undertook to drown an eel, if he can give the sound of the vowel A by naming X, or the sound of O and name W?" (quoted in Miller 1975, 252). In *The Key of the West,* he assailed the necessity in round note notation of using double sharps and flats.

Campaigns in support of singing school pedagogy and style by book compilers such as Leavitt and Auld were articulate and on the surface effective. But they reveal the overall limited influence on public culture of published debate in the absence of sustained musical institutions.

Nostalgia

At cultural sites where reform had had its greatest impact, there arose a different response—a longing for a simpler past. In a process of cultural loss and nostalgic restoration that is now recognized as common, there arose immediate yearnings for the singing school tradition at the very locales in which it had been driven out. As early as the 1830s, Boston saw the founding of a Billings and Holden Society, modeled after the Boston Handel and Haydn Society. In a cultural atmosphere where music compilations only reluctantly included singing school tunes—and then "reharmonized in accordance with 'scientific' criteria"—the society aimed instead to republish singing school tunes "as originally written" (Chase 1987, 135; McKay and Crawford 1975, 200).

Later, at midcentury, public performances of old New England psalmody flourished. The most influential of these was a professional venture, the Old Folks Concerts. Not quite vaudeville, not quite costumed recital, the Old Folks presented the music theatrically, dressed in eighteenth-century attire (Crawford 1984; Steinberg 1973). Through extensive touring—six thousand performances, it was said—the group reached millions of people across the nation. Organized by "Father" Robert Kemp (1820–1897) of Wellfleet, Massachusetts, the troupe featured "sacred, ancient, classic, and national melodies," but they specialized in New England psalmody. Sometimes they adopted roles as specific colonial luminaries such as George and Martha Washington, John Hancock, Daniel Boone, and Thomas Jefferson.

In their presentations, the Old Folks devoted scant attention to the religious sentiment of the texts and caricatured the social disposition of the schools by exaggerating their recreational atmosphere. In the absence of such social and religious integrity, the troupe isolated discrete minutiae to assert the authenticity of their performances. Promotional material, for example, boasted of using the pitch pipe that had belonged to Daniel

Read, or claimed to feature the "old fashioned *fa, sol, la* of the choir, in 'taking the pitch'" (Steinberg 1973, 604–5).

The "Old Folks" played in Cincinnati, 17–29 January 1859, as part of a seven-month western tour, and mustered sufficient attendance for ten performances. On January 8, advertising began a daily run in the *Cincinnati Enquirer,* calling the group the "largest concert troupe in the world . . . consisting of thirty-seven Ladies and Gentlemen Vocalists, together with their GRAND ORCHESTRA, all from Massachusetts, clad in COSTUMES OF ONE HUNDRED YEARS AGO." The *Enquirer*'s "amusements" writer gave generous endorsements before ever attending a performance:

> Their music is of that kind which touches the heart and appeals to the sympathies of every one. It calls to mind early associations long since buried in the "dead past," and revives the pleasantest recollections of the spring-time of existence, when "life was full of sunny years," and our hearts free from the "mountains of care" which weigh them down in after years. (19 January 1859)

Upon seeing the show, however, the writer was quick to recant this testimony:

> We frankly confess the indiscretion of having written during the early part of their engagement, and before we had heard them, a few lines in their favor; but having since stood the infliction of this New England psalm-singing for an hour or so, we hasten to recall any thing we have said that might induce any one else to be similarly bored. What there is about this un-kempt troupe—unless it be the ridiculous costumes in which they appear—to attract such crowds of easily-satisfied people, we are at a loss to determine. They would make an excellent choir in some village church, but to attempt giving concerts throughout the country is drawing rather extensively on the credulity of the public. Again we say, "*J'adoube.*" *Vive la Humbug!* (23 January 1859)

This turnabout set "the entire pack of the press barking at our heels ever since," the critic wrote a week later (30 January 1859), and then offered a surprising defense of the remarks. Some from this "pack" would have been expected to complain, the writer said, since they were "capacitated by nature and art for preferring the flippant, shallow music of Lowell Mason to the ennobling strains of Meyerbeer, Mozart and Rossini." "To those who regret the departure of the Old Folks," the writer concluded, "we recommend a visit to the Ninth-street Baptist Church every Sunday, where they will hear better singing in every respect."

In his own *History of the Old Folks' Concerts,* Father Kemp skirted this controversy entirely, writing only of the extraordinary following that assembled to bid them farewell:

> We left Cincinnati on a beautiful morning. Thousands of people covered the banks of the river, while the windows of the houses in the vicinity were crowded with ladies, waving handkerchiefs, and making other demonstrations of sorrow or gladness (I never was fully convinced which) at our departure. As the steamer moved away from the wharf, we sang "Sweet Home," and several patriotic airs, which were loudly cheered. (Kemp [1868] 1984, 54)

The tour proceeded down the Ohio River by steamboat, with Cincinnati remembered as one of the more enthusiastic receptions.

In 1862 the Continental Old Folks performed in Cincinnati, led by Mr. J. T. Gulick and modeled after Father Kemp's group.[20] Promotional material, which ran in the *Cincinnati Enquirer* during the week before their arrival on April 7, described them as dressed in "Ancient Costumes." "Granny Slocum, Aunt Rachel, and Cousin Reuben will also be present in all their antiquities," the advertisement continued, "and jine in the singen." The *Enquirer*'s reviewer called them a "perfect picture of the choirs that sang when the Pilgrims tabernacled at Plymouth" (April 7). After the second performance, the writer added, "These good old people sang the Psalms of David, the Songs of Solomon, the Hymns of Doddridge, Wesley and Watts last night at Smith & Ditson's Hall. Father Gulick 'deaconed' the hymns and gave the pitch from a veritable pipe of 'ye olden time'" (April 8).

Notwithstanding the considerable efforts to identify the music as antique, the writer was equally moved by the polished performances of this "drilled chorus." Particularly impressive was the group's "nightingale" mezzo-soprano, Mrs. Emma J. Nichols, "a lady who would ornament the highest walks of musical science" (April 9). Whereas the writer initially acknowledged "misapprehension . . . regarding this quaint old troupe" (April 7), by the end of the run the group could be said to have been "greeted last night by a large, fashionable and highly-intelligent audience, who relished their unique entertainment throughout" (April 11).

The Old Folks phenomenon was an important step in the management of public historical consciousness regarding the singing school idiom. Having been marginalized only a generation ago, this music could now be rediscovered and performed as "good old songs" with the conspicuously deliberate artifice of costume, dialect, and pitch pipe. By this time, it was tied to "associations long since buried in the 'dead past.'" The Mason family—Lowell's sons, at least—were repulsed by the whole affair and attacked Father Kemp through their *New York Musical Review and Gazette* (Steinberg 1973, 609). Their complaint was based only in part on the caricatures Kemp employed; they also disapproved of glorification of singing schools, which Lowell Mason had long ago deemed unprofessional. In Cincinnati, Timothy Mason, who died in 1861, must have been pained by all of this: in the interest of "better music," the *Enquirer* critic had associated Kemp's music with "the flippant, shallow music of Lowell Mason."

In 1888, a publication with the presumptuous title of *Presto! From the Singing School to the May Music Festival* recalled Cincinnati's esteemed celebration of German music, the annual May Festival. The report gave an ostensibly generous account of the singing schools that once populated the city:

> The Singing School is an American institution, which may account in a measure for its unpopularity with a class whose exclusive idiocy for things foreign needs no extended advertisement. It was a source of knowledge, and a place where study was most pleasantly combined with innocent, healthful, social intercourse and a medium for the spread of musical knowledge—shall it be condemned because that knowledge was limited? . . . Numbers of the men who presided over its early destinies were earnest and able and quick to encourage and

foster natural ability. Everywhere they were welcome guests and the honor of the family circle was safe in their hands. They accomplished great good. . . . They labored to inculcate a knowledge of the simpler rules of theory and reading at sight was a favorite practice. . . . Sometimes on foot, with instruction books strapped in a snug bundle and thrown over the shoulder, he may be seen making his way along a country road to the next objective point, humming, perchance, a favorite melody that was last in rehearsal and which still engrosses his mind. It is only a few years ago, that one of this traduced class was moving sturdily along one of the common highways in old Auglaize county. He was well advanced in years, but the light of the contented spirit was reflected in his face that was rich in nature's bronze. A substantial farmer driving by with a friend remarked, as he drew up his team:

"Hold on. I must speak to this man. He taught me the little I know of music," and he sprang from his wagon to meet, on a common level, the humble minister of song. (Tunison 1888, 8–9)

By this date, the entire institution of the singing school could be personified in the character of the old man. Of this figure, all symbolic value had vanished except the fleeting memories of a farmer. Only after leaving his wagon, the writer took care to note, did the farmer engage the man "on a common level." The reader, of course, was well insulated from this scene and would very soon be distracted by the glories of the May Festival. Presto!

In 1922, the *Cincinnati Enquirer* ran an article on music publishing in the city (Fetta 1922). According to the story, a substantial portion of music typesetters in the United States worked in Cincinnati. Of these, typesetters who worked for the Armstrong Printing Company were specialists in "Buckwheat" notes, the kind used in books "sold in Southern States and rural districts where 'sings' are very popular among people lacking in musical training." The writer concluded, "The books are never sold in the North and would be "practically unintelligible" to the average northern singer, yet this company alone sends hundreds of thousands of books each year to the South."

Gone, by this date, were fond memories of the singing school. The shape note culture was now relegated to the South, its notation practically unintelligible to the northern singer. Most important was the complete transformation the pedagogical system had undergone. No longer was it called unscientific or immoral; no longer was it even linked to pastoral life. Rather, the system was now associated with those lacking in musical training. The singing school had no pedagogical or spiritual value at all.

Revival

Within the realm of public culture, there would seem to have been few alternatives to nostalgic display. But one response arose that, like the Old Folks movement, addressed the old forms of singing across the historical chasm of reform, yet retained, on principle, elements of the subjective experience of singing. This response was the quasi-historical world of old New England described in the writing of Harriet Beecher Stowe, in which, beginning around midcentury, the singing of hymns in the old style was an important element in her reconstructed and romanticized Calvinism.

There was a generational element to this: the Beecher siblings were said to have experienced, in response to their overbearing father, "a marked alienation from the Presbyterian way of doing things" and decided "to strike out boldly for even more unorthodox ideas" (Caskey 1978, 66). At the time of the Old Folks movement, for example, Henry Ward Beecher compiled the Plymouth Collection (1855), which advocated the use of revival tunes. "There is such a thing as Pharisaism in music," he wrote. "Because [revival tunes] are homebred and popular, rather than foreign and stately, we like them none the less. And we cannot doubt that many of them will carry up to heaven the devout fervor of God's people until the millennial day!" (quoted in Lorenz 1980, 46).

At about the same time, with the nation poised at the brink of war over a cause she helped define, Harriet Beecher Stowe turned away from the contentious theological and political world that had accumulated in her father's milieu. In its place, primarily in a series of novels, she reconstructed the New England of her childhood, deriving the better sentiments of her characters from the most nurturing elements of the Puritan ethical world that surrounded them. This was the central theme of her New England novels: to restore the consoling spiritual community of Puritanism, without its harsh doctrine.

One element of this transformation was to extract hymn singing from the world of liturgy and doctrine and release it to the community, to the home, and to the unfettered hearts of its singers. For example, in Harriet's writing, hymns no longer were invested with liturgical authority as they were for Lyman; rather, they spoke directly to the heart and often derived their spiritual power from the people who loved them and sang them. Where Lyman, for example, had boasted of Lowell Mason's knack for choosing the perfect hymn to complement his sermon, Harriet wrote that when the minister rose to give his sermon, the music (Billings's fuging tune "Majesty," composed in 1778) had already "done its work on the audience, in exalting their mood to listen with sympathetic ears to *whatever he might have to say*" (*Poganuc People*, 1896, 11:50, emphasis mine).[21]

The singing community, moreover, could provide a far deeper spiritual experience than the choir. The polished choir—the "grand orchestral strains" from "foreign lands"—could weave "webs of sweetness" around Stowe's "captured heart." But it was the "old Psalm tune," she recalled in a poem in 1858, that had the "pulse of power" to thrill her "inmost soul" ("The Old Psalm Tune," 15:309–11). Only in the "rudely sung" psalms and hymns of her youth did she hear the "voices of the loved and lost" singing "far above those earthly notes." These old tunes may have sounded discordant, but for their heavenly singers they achieved a deeper harmony:

> Their life is music and accord;
> Their souls and hearts keep time
> In one sweet concert with the Lord,—
> One concert vast, sublime.

In Stowe's vision, the professional choir lacked the articulated personal connection—with family members, beloved friends, and the spiritual community—that the old congregational singing fundamentally provided.

But music reform was not her deepest concern, nor was it central to most of her writing. Rather, music was one element in a crisis of national scope resulting from the "loss of the old dignity and purpose of the colonial Calvinist society" (Crozier 1969, 91). Significantly, this was not an appeal to restore Calvinist doctrine—which she had privately come to reject—but rather the spiritual sustenance of the Puritan community. Such a charter, she rightly perceived, called not for theological debate, which could only by its nature contend against the very qualities she sought to celebrate. Rather, with narrative fiction, she could develop characters who possessed innate spiritual gifts and she could describe the qualities of the Puritan spiritual community—including the various psalm and hymn singing venues—that nurtured these characters. As a writer, this approach situated Stowe, unlike her mostly Unitarian counterparts of the American Renaissance, in a unique literary tradition of Calvinist Romanticism (Buell 1980, 1983).

Often this strategy involved setting the rational and theological Calvinism of male characters against the more effective emotional and spiritual Calvinism of female characters. In this way, the most positive traits of her own religious upbringing were personalized and feminized, resulting in a transformation of Calvinism derived directly from Puritan orthodoxy. In *The Minister's Wooing* (1859), a young Mary Scudder was urged into marital engagement with a discernibly more analytical Dr. Hopkins, her pastor and her family's middle-aged boarder—whose character was based on Calvinist theologian Samuel Hopkins (Buell 1980). All the while, she was being enthusiastically wooed by the young, unconverted James Marvyn. On the advice and manipulation of female attendants and the cooperation of Dr. Hopkins, she married James, securing a more authentic happiness. *The Pearl of Orr's Island* (1862), set in a remote section of Maine, chronicled the life of the orphaned Mara, a kind of "angelic heroine" whose innate spiritual gifts enriched and reassured those around her (Crozier 1969, 136). *Oldtown Folks* (1869) followed the lives of the orphans Henry and Tina Percival, the theological climate of colonial New England, and the life of the not-too-visible narrator, Horace Holyoke. Much was invested in the relative emotional sustenance that Henry and Tina received from various adults—and thereby also in the adults' spiritual grounding—throughout their chaotic childhood. *Poganuc People* (1878), the most autobiographical of the four, recounted Harriet's youth through the eyes of Dolly Cushing, whose keen and innocent sensitivity to benevolence measured the spirit of various theological squabbles of the community of Poganuc Centre, most involving her father, a Congregationalist minister. One night at family prayers, for example, after the Democrats won in elections sufficiently to foresee the end of Establishment, young Dolly had to console her despondent father, who felt "for the Church of God." Privately, however, Dolly thought of kind acquaintances and wondered, "How could it be that such good people were Democrats?" (11:71–73).

On numerous occasions, hymns and psalms were set distinctively in the world of emotions and against the world of rational and analytical thought. In *Oldtown Folks,* Harry and Tina, after a sequence of harsh experiences as orphaned children, came under the care of Miss Mehitable, who earned Tina's elusive trust through the deep empathy they shared about a hymn the children had sung at their mother's deathbed. Tina's hymn, in fact, had led to Miss Mehitable's conversion. As Stowe described it, "The child had entered so earnestly, so passionately even, into the spirit of the words she had been repeating, that she seemed to Miss Mehitable to be transfigured into an angel messenger, sent to inspire faith in God's love in a darkened, despairing soul" (9:240; Crozier 1969, 142). In another passage, Sam Lawson, a character marginalized for his concern for others' mishaps and neglect of his own personal industry, found Horace Holyoke alone, sobbing over the death of his father. He consoled Horace with the image of his father, in death, looking "as peaceful as a psalm-tune" (9:41). He sang a fragment from a psalm, but his consolation was interrupted "like the crack of a rifle" by a call to duty from his wife.

More than once, as in that scene, an abrupt interruption marked off the singing of a hymn or psalm as a ritual circumstance, invaded by some less spiritually enriched activity or person. In *The Minister's Wooing,* Mary was singing a contemplative psalm ("Life is the time to serve the Lord") in her room—a kind of inner sanctum in the temple of domesticity—when she was surprised by James at her window (5:24). Later, the day after James went to sea, Mary Scudder was preparing breakfast and singing from the kitchen ("Truly my waiting soul relies") as the studious Dr. Hopkins listened, busy with his exercises of devotion. When he heard her singing cease, he "looked up from his Bible wistfully, as missing something, he knew not what" (5:93).

More often, as when Miss Mehitable gained Tina's trust, hymns and psalms were the pivotal figure in a swell of transcendent empathy. In *The Pearl of Orr's Island,* the castaway Moses was grief-stricken at the imminent death of Mara, the woman into whose family he was long ago adopted—and with whom he only then realized mutual feelings of true love. After Moses saw her hopelessly ill with tuberculosis, the Reverend Sewell made an awkward and discernibly orthodox attempt to console him ("My son, despise not thou the chastening of the Lord"). Moses, seeking solitude, retreated to a favorite grotto alone. As evening approached, he was found by Captain Kittridge, who with "child-like ignorance" had "ventured upon a ministry of consolation from which a more cultivated person would have shrunk away" (6:385). What he brought to Moses was Mara's hymnbook and some hymns that Mara had chosen and sung for him. He pointed to "There is a land of pure delight, where saints immortal reign" and added: "We must kind o' think of it for her, 'cause she's goin' to see all that." Moses still resisted consolation, but Captain Kittridge persisted, recalling the heavenly promises made in Revelation and the many occasions Mara had prayed for Moses. He concluded, "This 'ere old Bible—why it's jest like yer mother,—ye rove and ramble, and cut up round the world without her a spell, and mebbe think the old woman ain't so fashionable as some; but when sickness and sorrow comes, why, there ain't nothin' else to go back to. Is there, now?"

Presumably, we feel his agonizing grief and the ineptitude of religious doctrine to comfort him. It was only through the strength and example of Mara's lived spiritual faith and the persistence of a family friend that there was any comfort. This comfort came to him through Watts's reassuring hymn, a text deeply invested with personal meaning by the community of singers who loved it.

On the whole, Stowe's historical fiction was an important alternative to the prevailing depictions of a period that had come to be saturated with historical meaning. It was a nostalgic depiction—in some respects engaging history to serve an ideal much as did the Old Folks. Stowe, in fact, articulated her own brand of nostalgia—historicizing the singing traditions, advancing no institutional support, and replacing it with contemporary fiction. But Stowe's New England writings differed from Old Folks nostalgia in two important respects. First, they constituted an implicit and occasionally explicit critique of reform, demonstrating that the visible yet superficial effects of reform were achieved only by sacrificing the precious spiritual qualities that were fundamental to the old forms. It was essential in her writing that the transcendent spiritual community never achieved its ideal but remained in constant tension with the surrounding world. Second, her characters, precisely because they were fictional, were not entirely historicized but were infused with transcendent sentiments and values accessible to readers. Indeed, the impetus of her work was to restore to American culture the experiential world that she believed had been eroded in her lifetime, in part, undermined by theological and musical reform.

Moreover, Stowe was not merely writing historical fiction: she believed that her contemporary Americans stood to gain by drawing from the well of spiritual community by which Puritan hymn singing derived its fundamental meaning. In her own way, she actively pursued a "revival" of the way of life that surrounded the singing community, one uniquely invested in the values nourished by that community. Father Kemp, who foregrounded the historical features of the music against a backdrop of suppressed fiction, could manipulate and even ignore the spiritual underpinnings of the music to cater to the nationalist mythology that his audiences craved. Stowe, by constructing a fictionalized narrative whose characters were animated by complex and historically rooted principles, could explore and advance values—associated with the music—that had long ago lost their popular significance. By investing these values in marginalized characters, Stowe constructed a transcendent spiritual world inaccessible to the discourses of progress and reform that raged around her.

In her four New England novels, Stowe had sought "to aid and admonish her contemporaries in the severe problems of their own time by interpreting to them the significance of their past" (Crozier 1969, 93). In that past, hymns and psalms were personal sacraments and consequently were of the most fundamental type of religious expression—part of a "ladder to heaven, whose base God has placed in human affections, tender instincts, symbolic feelings, sacraments of love, through which the soul rises higher and higher, refining as she goes, till she outgrows the human, and changes, as she rises, into the image of the divine" (*Minister's Wooing*, 5:66).

These sacraments emanated not merely from the spiritual paradise that beckoned but also from the human soul itself in its earthly strivings. Even the most mundane events had extreme spiritual significance. In one scene, readers encountered Mary Scudder with Miss Prissy, the seamstress and female confidante in *The Minister's Wooing*, a minor character who ultimately had a great deal to do with the outcome of the narrative (see Schultz 1992). Miss Prissy was sewing and discussing with Mary Scudder her appreciation for Dr. Hopkins's impressive theological and rhetorical talents. But the scene unfolded with swelling irony, since for each expression of praise she extended to Dr. Hopkins, she revealed her own profound insights into the everyday world that Stowe believed was, of all earthly things, preeminently sacred. First it was her description of a ruffled shirt she wanted to make for him, then her singing of a psalm from Watts ("From the third heaven, where God resides") that she said reminded her of Dr. Hopkins. Miss Prissy ceased her singing abruptly, distracted by the stitching at hand, and then Stowe took over the narrative to explore what had transpired:

> So we go, dear reader, so long as we have a body and a soul. Two worlds must mingle, the great and the little, the solemn and the trivial, wreathing in and out, like the grotesque carvings on a Gothic shrine; only, did we know it rightly, nothing is trivial; since the human soul, with its awful shadow, makes all things sacred. Have not ribbons, cast-off flowers, soiled bits of gauze, trivial, trashy fragments of millinery, sometimes had an awful meaning, a deadly power, when they belonged to one who should wear them no more, and whose beautiful form, frail and crushed as they, is a hidden and a vanished thing for all time? For so sacred and individual is a human being, that, of all the million-peopled earth, no one form ever restores another. The mould of each mortal type is broken at the grave; and never, never, though you look through all the faces on earth, shall the exact form you mourn ever meet your eyes again! You are living your

daily life among trifles that one death stroke may make relics. One false step, one luckless accident, an obstacle on the track of a train, the tangling of the cord in shifting a sail, and the penknife, the pen, the papers, the trivial articles of dress and clothing, which to-day you toss idly and jestingly from hand to hand, may become dread memories of that awful tragedy whose deep abyss ever underlies our common life. (5 : 149–50)

Here was a solemn meditation on the divided consciousness, described not as an affliction of the dispossessed but as a necessity for a fulfilling spiritual life. Almost as a unifying theme, the narrative progress of Stowe's protagonists was woven around misfortune—far more so than evil—and around the coterie of supporting characters who drew strength from their mystic proximity to the "awful shadow." It was in this transcendent world—where the personal was sacred—that her characters encountered the subtle power of hymns and psalms, proffered to God.

But Stowe did not invent the mystic power of marginality, nor, once conceived, did she project it onto some cultural other. Rather, she described, as historical self-discovery, the spiritual and cultural space that had been forsaken by neo-Edwardean theology. And just as the genteel world erected in Stowe's lifetime endured—even a century and more later—so also did the powerful spiritual world that it obscured. It should hardly surprise us that others, like Stowe, have sought to experience it.

Chapter 2

SACRED HARP AS CULTURAL OBJECT

> A strange, uncanny feeling comes over one when one stumbles
> upon survivals of the supposedly dead past. Rip Van Winkle
> must have felt this way when he met the little old man toting
> the keg. I had the same feeling when I first came in touch last
> summer with a sort of lost tonal tribe which was plying its mu-
> sical art in pure pre-revolutionary form.
>
> GEORGE PULLEN JACKSON, "The Fa-Sol-La Folk" (1926)

> Great crowds gather for [a Sacred Harp convention], and natu-
> rally the music must be judged as one judges the work of a large
> chorus. The singers form in a hollow square facing the center,
> in which stands the leader. . . . The singers are then asked to
> sound the first chord. This being done, the leader remarks,
> "We'll sing the music first." Singing "the music" consists of
> singing the shaped notes by name. The result is astonishing and
> most ludicrous to the uninitiated ear.
>
> CARL CARMER, "The Sacred Harp Singers" (1928)

"Great crowds gather," wrote Carl Carmer, providing urbane readers of
the *Yale Review* with the rhetorical means to comprehend Sacred Harp
singing from a considerable distance. Carmer's article and one by George
Pullen Jackson two years earlier might be taken as the beginning of the
"culture writing era" in the history of documentary accounts of the shape
note singing tradition. Never before had a style of writing been used to
describe singing that was designed so completely for readers unfamiliar
with the singing tradition. Carmer, Jackson, and others, in the decades to

come, would formulate singing as folk music, introducing the forgotten music in discourses of discovery, often to the very Americans who had become institutionally separated from it.

The folksong idea is not a simple one. Even applied to the shape note movement it can carry a variety of motivating implications. Yet depictions of singing as folksong have long held as a fundamental feature that the music emerges from the common experience of an indigenous group of people. By implication or explicit reference, this depiction can be thought to *represent* the totality of indigenous experience: a song performance can easily stand as a symbolically overdetermined object for the homogeneous culture or tradition as a whole. Sometimes it may also be extended to represent some larger idea—American heritage, social class culture, regional culture, the culture of religious dissent, a nostalgic remnant of the past, or a "pre-revolutionary form," for example—that seems to be emulated by that indigenous expression.

Folksong revival relies heavily on this process. By linking otherwise unrelated traditions under the folksong rubric, proponents appeal through these larger ideas to a potentially vast audience, some of whom may have no other interest than to reclaim the "survivals of the supposedly dead past." Ordinarily this is innocent enough: a flyer for a contemporary Sacred Harp singing convention in a folksong revival area might quote from a newspaper account: "wild sounds of the frontier," or "distinctly American music," or "one of the oldest, purest musical traditions in this country." In practice, the impact of these exhortations is negligible, for anyone who attends a singing must immediately confront far greater complexities than any of these expressions convey. Nonetheless, they are purposeful remarks that occupy a certain symbolic space, and for those who are or were exposed to Sacred Harp only through recordings or public performances, they may be the preeminent initial motivating condition.

How did this happen? How is it that this music, once a movement championed by progressive Harvard-trained clergy, has come to so reliably evoke from the public the stock sentiments associated with American folksong, particularly when they are deemed by traditional singers as alien to the experience of Sacred Harp singing? Some may call this a trivial question, but I hope to show it has nothing like a trivial answer. Beginning with this chapter, I mean to reconstruct the various writing practices that have come to define this cultural space. This chapter observes the origins of the so-called culture writers, the next will explore the Sacred Harp's own writing traditions, and the last will look to the convergence of these in what some have recently called the Sacred Harp revival.

The classic instances of culture writing treat singing tradition as a cultural object, employing a style of writing similar to the style of "ethnographic realism" in that it seeks to represent or allude to a whole world, culture, or form of life (Clifford and Marcus 1986; see also Marcus and Cushman 1982; Rabinow 1985; Webster 1982). That is, the written account of singing as culture is meant to represent to outsiders singing as a whole; in turn, singing is meant to represent the comprehensive way of life of the singers. In most instances, culture writing arose on the assumption of a vast cultural difference between the world of the writer and readers on the one hand and the written subjects on the other. In recent years, the illusion of cultural autonomy and the writing devices that accompany it have come under scrutiny. "Cultural criticism" has exposed the occluded cultural, social, and political links between the worlds of the writer/ readers and the subjects. It is now observed that writing does not merely represent but actually constructs the worlds of writer, readers, and subjects, and it manufactures the distances between them.

So it was with Sacred Harp. It was through ethnographic realism that the "discovery" of singing was announced and its participants named "fasola folk." Under the spell of cultural discourse, Sacred Harp reentered public culture as folksong, participating in American musical culture only ironically, as existing in spite of itself.[1] *Yale Review* readers could marvel at the fact that "great crowds gather," for example, because across the vast gulf of cultural isolation they would not otherwise have expected it. It was ironic because it was measured against a backdrop of self-evident public culture. Of course, to establish this irony, the rhetoric of culture writing has neglected competing forms of documentary writing. In short, whereas cultural description is presumed to have been "objectively" guided by an observed event, its underlying irony motivates a form of employment built solely around the writer's experience.

In this chapter and the next, I will examine these competing documentary forms: one that constructs Sacred Harp as a cultural object, and the other, the self-evident "custodial" mechanism that manifests the subjectivity of the singing itself. Certainly not all accounts by outsiders since the 1920s have taken this approach. But because the devices of culture writing have been widely duplicated in the mass media, because they have been used by and for outsiders to singing, they have been influential not merely in shaping public perception of Sacred Harp. They have also, by default, defined public culture and the role of the "outsider" to singing. This has been a key component of Sacred Harp revival.

The strategy of this chapter will be to look at preeminent strains of cultural description of Sacred Harp at their earliest stages to examine how they have evolved and what avenues of integration they have provided for Sacred Harp revival. I will examine several of the important cultural sites from which cultural realism has arisen, beginning with one of the most significant: Birmingham, Alabama, at the turn of the century.

THE "MAGIC CITY" AND THE "LOST TONAL TRIBE": MODERNISM AND ITS DISCONTENTS IN THE SOUTH

> Then I grew up and put away childish things, or tried to. I became a student and a rider of musical hobbies. Through a chain of circumstances my interest centered eventually on the poetry and art-music, and then the folk-song, of some European nations; and I learned of the European recognition of the importance of folk-song both for its own sake and as the proper basis of poetic and musical art-developments in their lands. Such observations led me subsequently to cast about in my own land, to see if perhaps similar folk-song conditions and intelligent recognition of them obtained here; for I was culturally quite patriotic, with a touch of the missionary. But I soon found the American scene rather dark. No one seemed to know or care whether we had any folk music or not. This, in the first decade of the present century.
>
> GEORGE PULLEN JACKSON,
> "Some Enemies of Folk-Music in America" (1939)

In 1895, Birmingham was a youthful industrial boomtown. Earliest censuses recorded 3,086 residents in 1880, 26,178 in 1890, and 38,415 in 1900. Although bitter labor disputes, cholera, and a nationwide depression had recently quelled municipal zeal, speculators still dreamed of a "Magic City," founded at nothing more than a proposed railroad intersection, where rich coal and iron ore deposits lay in wait. Even in 1887, an enterprising visitor concluded that the railroads, "reaching every part of the country by their connections and tributaries, furnish rare facilities for the development of the wealth that abounds here" (Riley 1888, 65). The most radical proponents of development even dreamed of the day when the South would no longer depend on labor for the return of prosperity:

> The dismal cloud of the 'Reconstruction' era in Alabama had this silver lining, and only this: it urged individuals of hope and courage to seek in the mining and manufacturing resources, lying in such untold prodigality at their hands, a diversity of industry which would secure commercial connections, and thus operate to work a reform in the public spirit, to the ultimate liberation of the energies of the whole people. Labor was no longer capital and the release of labor from the *status* of capital had swept out of existence $350,000,000 ... of assets in Alabama, only on that single item of account of losses of the revolution. The statesmanship of the day was to create capital afresh from the ground, as the basis of reorganized society. (DuBose [1888] 1976, 747)

Turn-of-the-century Birmingham was still a gleam in the eye of "New South" optimists in Alabama, vying for prominence with Atlanta and Nashville. Industry would supplant agriculture, and hope would replace the despair of war and reconstruction.

Much as in Cincinnati earlier, civic promoters in Birmingham yearned as much for cultural advancement as they did for economic growth. In shaping the musical tastes that would reflect municipal culture, they looked to other prestigious cities for their models. In 1895, the *Birmingham News* reported that Prof. Benjamin Guchenberger (later Guckenberger), with credentials from Cincinnati's College of Music, had accepted an invitation to come to the city and direct the new conservatory of music.

That same year, Miss Emile Von Navarra, formerly of Vienna, London, and New York, opened a college of music. In her promotional material in the *News,* she took care to remind readers that she was "a most celebrated artist, teacher and vocalist, who bears recommendations from such authorities as achieved the greatest success in the *most musical cities in the world"* (17 May 1895, emphasis mine). Four years later, the city began planning its first May Festival, based on the model provided by Cincinnati, intending to promote the image of Birmingham as a music-loving and cultivated city (Anderson 1978, chap. 1). If vernacular culture followed the migration patterns of a region's inhabitants, civic culture imitated the accomplishments of other cosmopolitan cities.

It was in this setting that George Pullen Jackson encountered the most urbane sensibilities of turn-of-the-century American music. Born in 1874 in Maine, his family came to Birmingham when he was a youth; there his father established himself as a manufacturer, eventually rising to the presidency of the Houston Biscuit Company. In 1890, the Jacksons were among the 2,000 northern-born citizens of the city.[2] Perhaps this led Jackson to his early endorsement of "better music": in 1895, he delivered a graduation address at Birmingham High School entitled "Imaginary Address to the Board of Education upon the Value of Vocal Music in the Public Schools." Only five years before this, in 1890, Birmingham's board of education had approved the "National System of Vocal Music" for use in the public school curriculum.

A precocious musician, Jackson began earning money performing in bands. As a member of Grambs's Military Band, he performed occasional cornet solos. Fred Grambs, a New York native, had come to Birmingham in 1883 as its first professional director, organizing an orchestra for the new O'Brien's Opera House. On July 6, 1895, the Military Band performed at Capitol Park to a crowd of two thousand people. The following year, Guchenberger directed St. Mary's Choir in twelve choruses of Handel's *Messiah.* "A young musician," Birmingham's *Age Herald* reported, "George P. Jackson, was featured playing the cornet at the performance which was called the 'grandest musical triumph in the history of this music-loving people'" (31 December 1897, p. 6; quoted in Anderson 1978, 22). When in 1902 Guchenberger took a job in Massachusetts,

Jackson was chosen to present to him a bronze statue from the choir and deliver farewell remarks on the second of a two-evening farewell program. "We do not want to say good-bye to you," Jackson said in closing, "but 'auf wiedersehen'" (9 April 1902, p. 2; Anderson 1978, 54–56).

Jackson was well positioned, then, to view shape note singing as folk culture. Surely he had a voracious appetite for music; equally certainly his musical career was launched on the optimism of the "Better Music boosters," whom he would come to abhor. Jackson reflected on his upbringing in 1933, in the opening pages of *White Spirituals in the Southern Uplands:* "I lived in cities of that section for many years and was in touch with its musical life and thought as they exist in urban environments, long before I heard of these country singers." From this perspective, he would refer to his encounter with vernacular singing as a "discovery" and would call the discovered people, "as contrasted to music and musicians as they are known in occidental urban culture, a sort of 'lost tonal tribe'" (Jackson 1933, 3–4).

Moreover, raised by Yankee merchants in the post-Reconstruction South, Jackson would have been both an insider and an outsider to the highly charged class sensibilities that afflicted working people in Alabama (Flynt 1989). He may have looked to music to resolve conflicting feelings about the South, finding equal refuge in the reformist logic of "New South" boosterism and the authentic moral purity of the "fa-sol-la folk." But Jackson soon left the South to study in Germany and did not return for any substantial period until his 1918 appointment at Vanderbilt University in Nashville. Thus we must pause momentarily to examine the emerging antimodernism that was developing even in his absence.

"WEIRD AIRS" COME TO BIRMINGHAM

For many years music was taught in the schools after this [shape note] method. In the old days, pupils in the backwoods school had never heard of a piano, or even a spinet, but the air rang with sound.

"Weird Airs Handed Down by Sacred Harp Singers,"
Birmingham News, 15 July 1910

Two years ago, F. L. Blaugh of Indiana was elected supervisor
of music for Jefferson's rural schools; and under his management there has been remarkable progress made in this phase of
the county school work. . . . Mr. Blaugh visits the schools
throughout the county, advises with the teachers in regard to
the music, takes charge of the instruction for the day, or hears
the teacher give the lesson, and plans the work of succeeding
lessons.

"Music in Rural Schools of Jefferson County,"
Birmingham News, 25 May 1913

During the latter half of the nineteenth century, Sacred Harp singing had
spread westward from Georgia into Alabama, where singings and conventions had become common in some northern and eastern counties (Cobb
1978, 139–41; Jackson 1933, 104–9). In Winston County and surrounding areas, Seaborn Denson devoted fifty-one years to teaching some ten
thousand students from *The Sacred Harp,* beginning in 1874! Surely Denson stands among the most effective Alabama musical educators of that
era. We might wonder how George Pullen Jackson, who wrote an essay
on music in the schools in 1895, would not have heard of Denson's prolific
work, based only fifty miles to the north, until the 1920s.

We might also wonder why someone of Denson's stature and enthusiasm allowed musical reform in Birmingham to occur without a struggle,
and why Birmingham reformers saw no need to campaign against the
shapes as they did elsewhere. In fact, in the period of Jackson's youth,
Sacred Harp singing had probably not come to the municipal culture of
Birmingham. Whereas Cincinnati arose a hundred years earlier as a frontier cultural center, Birmingham was built as an economic enterprise designed to extract wealth from natural resources. The "New South" that
Jackson's family entered was economically and culturally isolated from its
surroundings.

Several factors contributed to this isolation. Alabama's elite planter
class did not support the founding of the industrial site at Birmingham
and would have had a diminished impact on its culture.[3] Nor was there
an institutional basis for working-class influence: in the surrounding area,
mining camps nourished the city's economy, where discontented laborers,

some of them prison convicts, worked under the most austere conditions (Ward and Rogers 1965, esp. 12). Those who were lured to the mines from small farms might only stay a few months before returning to the land (Flynt 1989, 161). Thus, they also would not have had cause to establish municipal cultural institutions. And in the hills where Alabama's "plain folk" operated small farms, resentment was building among those who saw promised prosperity sapped by industrialists (eventually dominated by northern companies), professionals, merchants, and large planters (Owsley 1949; Rogers 1970).

It was in these rural areas where small farms prevailed that Sacred Harp singing had achieved its most substantial vigor. After 1900, however, both Sacred Harp singers and music reformers sought to expand their influence. In 1911, Jefferson County (Birmingham) installed a supervisor of music for its rural schools to visit teachers and provide curriculum materials. Sacred Harp singers, likewise, sought to expand into urban areas and urban institutions. The movement began in Georgia, where in 1904 Joe S. James had organized the United Convention in Atlanta, hoping to establish there a permanent headquarters for a central Sacred Harp organization (Jackson 1933, 102–3).[4] By similar reckoning, in 1910, organizers located the first Alabama State Sacred Harp Singing Convention in Birmingham.[5] For the Alabama convention, the initial site was Birmingham's Southside Skating Rink, although the following year the convention began its lengthy run in the symbolic seat of municipal affiliation, the Jefferson County Courthouse. That first year, planners predicted that five thousand singers would converge on the Magic City! The *Birmingham News* covered the meeting, granting it front-page status. This was a significant cultural event.

Yet the presentation of the convention in the *News* had an odd tone to it: "Weird Airs Handed Down by Sacred Harp Singers," it proclaimed in its Friday (July 15) headline, followed by "Without Use of Pitch Pipe or Reed with Which to Sound Key, They Acquired the Art." Already, long before it was to be identified as folk music, Sacred Harp singers were being described by and to their Birmingham neighbors as exotic relics of bygone days! On Saturday (July 16) the headline read, "Some Singers of Ye Olden Days," and the article described Brother R. J. Langston leading "Canaan's

Land": "White-haired fathers sang, harkening back to the days when first their fathers had taught them the air." On July 17, the *Birmingham Age-Herald* described the music as "unique in that no music is had for accompaniment, the singers relying entirely on the melody of their voices."

The effect of this was to formulate Sacred Harp so that it did not compete with reform efforts. With Sacred Harp safely projected into the past, music teachers could be sent into rural areas as if no music existed there at all. A 1925 assessment of music in Alabama by the Alabama Federation of Music Clubs included only a few paragraphs contributed by Mrs. W. S. Wilson of Dothan (Wilson 1925, 27). She wrote of practices long out of vogue, though still surviving in shortened form in the Dothan County courthouse singings. In other rural singing strongholds, however, where the New South movement had not penetrated, newspapers did not take this approach. Even as late as 1932, the local newspaper describing the rural singings at Mt. Zion, Georgia, gave an account in the sparse style of Sacred Harp recorded minutes, providing the names of all leaders and officers and mirroring the sequence of events in its form.[6] Titles of the articles employed the language of the tradition: "Report of Thirty-eighth Annual Session of Mt. Zion Sacred Harp Singing" (1930) and "Report of Mt. Zion Memorial Singing" (1931). Even at this date, after nostalgic depictions of singing were common elsewhere, this rural newspaper found no advantage in such devices.

Generally, journalists outside the sway of New South modernism were inclined to replicate the descriptive mechanisms of the tradition until the discourse of "culture writing" became fashionable. As chapter 3 will discuss in more detail, newspapers initially printed convention minutes verbatim, but over the course of the first half of the twentieth century rhetoric was increasingly employed that "translated" Sacred Harp events for a public not presumed to be a part of singing culture. Unlike culture writers and other observers, however, native southern modernist journalism had a unique characteristic. That is, old-time singing was associated with the past, yet it was still "owned" by native journalists as native music. Only later, after the onset of systematic observation, was the tradition visited by outsiders—"strangers"—who constructed accounts that presumed to reach out to readers across great distances.

THE "STRANGE COUNTRY": REGIONALISM
AND SACRED HARP

Like a character in imaginative fiction, I feel that I stepped into
a past that lives and is concurrent with today.

CARL CARMER, *Stars Fell on Alabama* (1934)

Although his account is not universally accepted as reliable, the most influential "stranger" to observe Sacred Harp was Carl Carmer (1893–
1976). His exposure to singing probably predated the appearance of published observations by others—thus the extravagant style of his accounts
was at least in part his own. A New York native, Carmer earned a master's
degree in literature from Harvard, taught briefly at the University of Syr-
acuse and the University of Rochester, and served in World War I. In 1921,
he accepted an appointment in creative writing at the University of Alabama at Tuscaloosa, situated in an area where Sacred Harp singing was
well established. Carmer was widely popular and notoriously gregarious
both on campus and among Tuscaloosa's elite (Raines 1990).

Although Carmer was by profession a creative writer, his initial interest
in folk music was not as literary source material. In 1924, the University
of Alabama campus newspaper announced that, assisted by his "English
Eleven" American literature students, Carmer was embarking on a collection of Alabama folklore, intended for publication in the *Journal of
American Folklore*.[7] He identified other southern state folklore projects as
models for his study: C. Alonso Smith's work in Virginia, Frederic Koch's
in North Carolina, and an unidentified book from Kentucky. Oddly
enough, his first exposure to Sacred Harp singing may have been as sponsor of the campus glee club, of which he reported in 1926, "It is not an
unusual occurrence at the University of Alabama for an aspirant to membership in the Glee Club to announce that he can sing only by shaped
notes."[8] By 1926, Carmer's ideas on singing had begun to include issues
that would occupy scholarship on spirituals throughout the 1930s, including the role of spirituals as America's "national music," the role of
reclusive Calvinists in the endurance of the tradition, and the potential for
traditional singing on the concert stage.

Carmer left this position in 1927, but returned to resume contact with folklorist Ruby Pickens Tartt (1880–1974) of Livingston, Alabama, the mother of one of his students. In this seat of sedate planter culture, Mrs. Tartt had drawn strength from a family tradition that included unusually ambitious women. She benefited from progressive schooling at Julia Tutwiler's Livingston Female Academy and a cosmopolitan college education at Sophie Newcomb College and New York's Chase School of Art (Brown and Owens 1981, 3–15). Returning to Livingston, Tartt married into a banking family and, defying the conventions of southern matronage, turned her considerable talents to community projects and to collecting and preserving the folk culture of Sumter County. She would later achieve significance as a WPA Writers' Project agent, and she so extensively influenced folklorists and ethnomusicologists working in Alabama that Carl Carmer remarked, "Miss Ruby had made little Livingston a Mecca for folklorists of the nation" (Carmer 1993, 187).

But Carmer was the first outsider to take systematic interest in her knowledge of west Alabama folk culture. Indeed, he later identified her as a major influence in the outcome of his work in Alabama, even though there were others who helped his collecting efforts and certainly other publication models. Nonetheless, upon hearing that he planned to send his materials to a scholarly journal, he credits her with having insisted, "Notes! You must write a book" (Carmer 1993, 184). The book so urgently anticipated was *Stars Fell on Alabama* (1934), written after Carmer returned to New York. In it, Carmer took cultural distance to its absurd extreme, depicting Alabama as a "strange country in which I once lived and from which I have now returned" (Carmer 1934, xiv). Confirming his outsider status, the book was partly organized as a tour Carmer took through Alabama, guided by only partly fictional natives. Tartt was disguised as Mary Louise (Brown and Owens 1981, 11).

Initially, a reader might presume, Carmer shunned scholarly style because he was fundamentally a fiction writer or because he could reach a larger audience with a popular book. Yet his characters have the effect of absorbing responsibility for the book's authoring: Carmer wanders haplessly into scenes or is whisked here and there by his hosts. His considerable editorial manipulation appears less forced, his exaggerated emotional responses less contrived, because Carmer reveals himself as not having manufactured the scenes in which his characters appeared. The entire Alabama chapter of his life, he said in the book's afterword, was "an unreality stumbled upon long ago" (Carmer 1934, 270). Yet the characters *were* real; their identities even had to be disguised, he said, "to avoid causing them serious embarrassment" (xii). Thus later, when Carmer did attribute to Tartt a presumably comprehensive role in the matter, he effectively appropriated her as a voice that guided the work as a whole.[9]

The book is relevant here because it included a vivid and influential account of a Sacred Harp singing. The chapter "All-day Singing" (49–57) originally appeared as an article in *Theatre Arts Monthly* (1930), but surely it had no significant influence on public perception until it appeared in *Stars*. In the book, the account served with other observations as evidence that ever since an 1833 meteor shower—the day the "stars fell"— Alabama and its people had been enchanted, the powerless apprentices of sorcery. What was truly a matter of cultural discourse, of course, was the depiction of various traditions linked within the web of a cultural whole; the unifying "spell" is Carmer's own contrivance. But at every opportunity a reader might have to question the reality of a scene, Carmer would "stumble" in some way and pass along the descriptive authority to a native voice.

This spell seems to have affected the singing—or Carmer's account of it—in several ways. Foremost was the sound of the singing, which to him consisted largely of screeches and rumbles and stood far beyond conventional notions of musical beauty. At a second level, this enchantment sprang from an undercurrent of urgency and intrigue. Carmer gained access to this world, with the help of his escort, in several engaging subtexts: for example, the escort's solicitation of votes for an upcoming election and a controversy about singing the alto part.[10] For his description, these subtexts had the dual effect of verisimilitude. They served to authenticate the descriptive account by animating the singers and giving the account emotional presence; in turn, the characters' emotional development was lent credibility by the status of the singing as a real event.

All of this was amplified in what was the most disarming subtext, a courtship episode that seemed to persist throughout the singing. In it, Carmer's narrative eye followed, somewhat voyeuristically, a "slim brown-eyed girl in an orange dress" from the front row during the singing to a spring outside during dinner. Inside again, he noticed her missing, and then observed as he left the singing: "We left late—Tom was still vote-gettin' for Knox—but there were still cars and horses in the grove when we rolled away. I glanced back toward the spring. An orange dress burned through the gathering dusk. Beside it towered a dark figure. Behind them stretched a long line of couples, girls no longer shrill and boys no longer shy."

These narrative subtexts operated in tandem with the description of the singing. They helped authenticate the description by providing motives for the singers and presence for the author. In turn, the singing provided quasi-documentary status to an otherwise fictional account.

This typically unplain account of the "plain folk" was precisely the kind of representation that, in its vivid excesses and broad appeal, was designed to bring widespread public recognition to a deserving tradition. It also helped dispel the myth of wholesome planter gentility that was sometimes attributed to southerners in general. But in some ways this was a setup. The more obscure Carmer made Sacred Harp appear, the more ironic was its absence from public discourse and the more readily did the overarching glaze of the "spell" settle over the singing. Carmer provided his characters with a limited set of emotions, not distinguishing in them the forces that might have worked against the burden of southern culture by which he was so completely enchanted. Only Carmer, through his indignation, seemed capable of perceiving social injustice. Romance, jealousy, ambition, and detachment animated the main characters, of which his hosts were the most prominent. Nowhere in his account could one find the sense of spiritual fulfillment, the pleasure of sharing in community, and the satisfaction of musical accomplishment most often found at singings.

Published one year after Jackson's *White Spirituals in the Southern Uplands*, Carmer's book had far greater appeal than Jackson's. In the first month or so after its release, *Stars* was selling a thousand copies a day and required a third printing (Raines 1990, 294). Composer Hoagy Carmichael even took its title as the theme for a popular song, thereby boosting its exposure. We can be certain that Jackson's work was taken more seriously by scholars. But if Jackson provided the more reliable document of the tradition, Carmer did more to define the boundaries that separated public culture from the traditions he described. *Stars* and its imitators provided an emotional roadmap by which Americans for decades afterward, if only in their imaginations, navigated native Alabama culture and Sacred Harp tradition.

Carmer's characters so overwhelm us, in fact, that we notice less what aspects of the book he did presume to have authored. Against the emotional authenticity of his characters, Carmer assessed on his own terms the music he heard: melodies were "haunting," minor keys were "plangent," singing the note shapes produced "outlandish gibberish," and the overall effect was a "fearsome hodgepodge of sound." Orthographic distortion conveyed a far-from-standard dialect ("git down below with that bear's growl o' yourn") in which texture prevailed at the expense of substance. This effect was amplified by Carmer's own relatively texture-neutral, formal written English, which took all of this caricature as evidence that, from his perspective, something indeed mysterious had occurred the night the stars fell.

The account of the singing was woven together with other vignettes—including a square dance and a footwashing—and framed by the geographical span of Carmer's journey, with his arrival in and departure from Tuscaloosa at its boundaries. In this, we are to understand, Carmer conveyed an essential structure of the traditional culture of Alabama. But Alabamians and southerners did not entirely think so. The book was controversial for decades, eventually settling into "a kind of borderland between journalism and imaginative literature" (Raines 1990, 295).

"FEEDING DEEP ON ARCHAIC SPLENDORS": SACRED HARP AND THE AGRARIANS

[The southerner] finds that there is a vast propaganda teaching him, but particularly his children, to despise the life he has led and would like to lead again. It has in its organization public schools, high schools, the normals, and even the most reputable universities, the press, salesmen, and all the agents of industrialism. It has set out to uplift him. It tells him that his ancestors were not cultured because they did not appreciate the fine arts; that they were illiterate because their speech was Old English; and that the South will now come to glory, to "cultural" glory, by a denial of its ancestry.

This is the biggest hoax that has ever been foisted upon a people.

ANDREW NELSON LYTLE, "The Hind Tit" (1930)

Many were the invitations to stay for dinner. Surely we weren't going right now, when the fried chicken and sausage and pie were being set out, from baskets that the women had cooked all Saturday to fill. But we were strangers, the unaccountable folk who must say farewell too soon. We left the Sacred Harp folk under their pines, where in a moment the preacher would ask the blessing of the Lord upon the bounty that His hand and His earth, despite man-made hard times, had given His people; and went our way with the strings of the Sacred Harp still vibrant in our minds.

DONALD DAVIDSON, "Songs of the Sacred Harp,"
Reader's Digest (1934)

Carmer's approach in *Stars Fell on Alabama* put it broadly in the camp of literary realism and folklore regionalism, a movement which ultimately gained ascendancy among American writers and folklorists during the Great Depression. Among folklorists, the most comprehensive statements of this approach came from Benjamin Botkin, who coined the term *folksay* to include literary works based on folklore (see Hirsch 1987), and Constance Rourke, who promoted the view that outsiders could produce traditional works of art by transcending the boundaries of regional culture and articulating the culture's essential structures (see Hyman 1955). If Carmer was successful at this, however, it was not by the mystical procedure Rourke advocated but by the clever use of appropriated voices.

Whereas Carmer's description of Sacred Harp was designed around tensions between folklore and literature, another popular observation of singing was rooted specifically in a movement concerned with southern cultural identity. In 1934, *Reader's Digest* published a condensation of an account of a visit to a singing by Southern Agrarian writer Donald Davidson (Davidson 1934b). Davidson's portrait of Sacred Harp was based on observations made during a year he spent in Marshallville, Georgia, recuperating from fatigue at the family home of his colleague John Wade (Conkin 1988, 97). Unlike Carmer, Davidson was a southerner—a Vanderbilt "Fugitive" from New South modernism who took intellectual refuge in the South's agrarian heritage. In what some call their manifesto, *I'll Take My Stand: The South and the Agrarian Tradition by Twelve Southerners* (1930), the twelve writers who formed the core of this movement outlined a charter for restored southern agrarian culture. For Davidson, the ground on which this "stand" was taken would consist increasingly of folk music: his later publications included a "folk opera," *Singin' Billy* (1952), and an antimodernist novel, *The Big Ballad Jamboree* (Conkin 1988, 162).

The Agrarian argument was a complex one, not restricted to literature or even cultural identity, but one that recognized and sought to combat the threat of a comprehensive modernist hegemony that would feed itself on an indulgent South. According to Andrew Nelson Lytle, Sacred Harp gatherings figured into the Agrarian charter as preindustrial social forms that protected the South's cultural integrity. In contrast, the panacea urged by urban prophets—the fashion industry, modern farm equipment, extractive industries, and packaged entertainment—conspired to extort the southern farmer's precious resources and disturb the system of self-reliance. Sacred Harp traditions, standing as a part of that delicate autonomy, "bind the folk-ways which will everywhere else go down before canned music and canned pleasure" (Lytle 1930, 232).

Carl Carmer, of course, was not a part of this movement. One fundamental difference was that Carmer positioned himself rather completely as an outsider. Consequently, he demanded less of his readers—at times no more than a vicarious indulgence in southern anachronisms—whereas the Agrarians sought to expose the devastating cultural costs of modern conveniences. For this same reason, Carmer's approach was more easily imitated and popularized. It also drew fire from the Agrarians, such as Donald Davidson, who was repelled by Carmer's account of Sacred Harp. Having attended a singing himself, Davidson wrote of Carmer's chapter:

[Sacred Harp] is, in short, an ancient music, Americanized or "Southernized" into a new and astonishing vitality that saves it from being merely a curious relic to be catalogued and forgotten. This is not the view taken, of course, by curiosity-seekers like Carl Carmer, who gives a grotesque and entirely misleading account of a Sacred Harp singing in his rather misleading book, *Stars Fell on Alabama*. It is possible that Mr. Carmer chanced to visit an unusually inept band of singers. I think it more likely that he had no conception of what he was witnessing and hearing. He was as culturally unprepared for a Sacred Harp singing as an Eskimo for a Bach festival. (Davidson 1935, 467)

This was published a year *after* Davidson's own account of singing; nonetheless, we may look to that account to see how, having thrown down the gauntlet in retrospect, he thought it should have been.

Except for a more admiring choice of adjectives, Davidson's account did not differ that much from Carmer's. In the abridged *Reader's Digest* narrative, Davidson breezed in and breezed out—and so would his readers have, too.[11] "In the plantation country of Middle Georgia," he began, addressing them directly, "you can find 'church houses' which keep alive the all-day singings which once were a feature of life in the South" (Davidson 1934b, 83). Surely this opening passage was uncharacteristic of one who had spoken unfavorably of "curiosity-seekers" looking for "a relic to be catalogued and forgotten." Davidson and his mysteriously unidentified companions were greeted, "I see you all are strangers here," as if to suggest that the readers, too, were present. And to liken his own state of unfamiliarity to theirs, he confessed: "We were told that the Cedar Valley people sang in the old-fashioned way, out of 'The Sacred Harp' only" (83). This was scarcely the strategy of the Agrarians, and it seems, to get by, Davidson had to construct himself and his readers completely as outsiders, not even as potential converts to his philosophy. "But we were strangers," he would say in the end, "the unaccountable folk who must say farewell too soon" (86).

Admittedly, there were no distracting subtexts—Davidson focused closely on the singing. Not that Agrarian philosophy would have motivated this decision—politics and romance, which Carmer so vividly noticed, might easily have been included as functional elements of the Agrarian whole. Courting youngsters were mentioned briefly, in fact, as were the cotton fields that surrounded the church, the mule buggies and old automobiles, the wooden benches, the self-reliant confidence of the singers, quaint expressions rendered in dialect, and the antiquity of the music. Davidson's account followed the structure of the singing, darting more briefly than Carmer's in and out of parenthetical observations. At one point, his authorial gaze having drifted to the outskirts of the singing, he took care to remind readers that the Sacred Harp "was Lord in that place" (85).

Agrarian principles emerged most strongly from the music. The first song "went beckoning into the woods and fetched the people in" (84). "The device of rotating leaders," he observed, "was a revelation of the sturdiness and good sense of these musical democrats" (84). Explaining why the music would not have pleased a "trained chorus leader," Davidson wrote that the singers "were singing to please themselves, to feel their own emotions in song" (85). And for the singers, whose souls were "feeding deep on [the Sacred Harp's] archaic splendors," Davidson observed, carefully quoting: "it was 'the most beautiful music in the world'" (85). We may suspect that in this, in endorsing the powerful spiritual effect the music has on singers, Davidson thought he had conveyed an essential element that Carmer missed.

But, like Carmer, Davidson navigated these emotions without ever claiming any of them for himself or his readers. Davidson and company left the singing at the end of his narrative, just as dinner was beginning. They encountered "young folk" engaged in courtship but, unlike Carmer, not from a distance. In fact, two couples actually occupied their car and "laughingly made way for us" as the group approached (85). Then came protests over Davidson's leaving before dinner. In these gestures, readers could sense the all-encompassing sensibility of Agrarian tradition, with nothing functionally out of place, urgently appropriating the vain devices of modernity as they lay idle. As the group of "unaccountable folk" drove away, the narrative lingered briefly without them, anticipating the dinner-time blessing of gratitude for the prosperity—in spite of "man-made hard times"—that was spread bountifully before them.

There were other accounts from the 1930s that reiterated this imagery in the media and popular culture. Quoting Carl Carmer as an authority on the subject, *National Geographic* discussed Sacred Harp in a lengthy feature on Alabama culture (Simpich 1931). The article set the old against the new—Agrarian traditions against the "Smoke over Alabama" that rose from industrial development—although the prevailing device was irony and not exploitation. *Time* ran a short column on William Walker and the *Southern Harmony* singing in Benton, Kentucky (Singin' Billy's Book 1939). There were fuller developments in music magazines. *Etude* visited a Texas singing and reported on the "Singers of the Soil" (Fulling 1939). In these, it was not so much that Americans learned of Sacred Harp directly through these accounts. But they provided an authoritative literary model that made its way into local newspapers, travel literature, musical taxonomy, and public programming. Through these media, progress-minded public culture drew further and further away from the world of the "lost tonal tribe," so that the preeminent way for the public to encounter Sacred Harp was, in the manner of Jackson, Carmer, and Davidson, to discover it.

Whatever their approach, these accounts of singing were designed primarily to be consumed as literary products. Even the Agrarians had as a central goal to produce a Southern Agrarian literature. And when *Stars Fell on Alabama* appeared in 1934, Carl Carmer had left Alabama and had turned his attention to other writing projects. But at the time these two works appeared, George Pullen Jackson had produced *White Spirituals in the Southern Uplands,* and a wide chasm in style and purpose separated his work from theirs. Carmer's study gave Sacred Harp a compelling sense of emotional urgency, but it provided no usable ties to contemporary culture other than as a literary object. In contrast, Jackson's view was motivated by an upbringing in New South musical culture and training in German Romanticism. His solution, which he pursued relentlessly to the end of his life, was a revitalization of the music, based on historical and emerging American musical culture. Let us return to his career.

"FROM YOUNG LESSING TO PERCY'S 'RELIQUES'": GEORGE PULLEN JACKSON DISCOVERS FOLKSONG

> [American neglect of folksong] is no less than national disaster.
> It stands in cultural history as perhaps unique. Other nations
> have tempered such disaster or have avoided it completely. The
> ancient Greeks avoided it by building up their culture, includ-
> ing music, on national foundations. Britain made a start in that
> direction before and during Elizabeth's reign and then ne-
> glected the healthful trend as Albion neglected nationality for
> empire. The Welsh refused to be diverted from themselves. An
> authoritative Welsh observer wrote me recently that his nation
> "became a musical people by the simple and natural method
> (of wide participation in their own national music) with the
> result that they have produced but few individual stars but have
> become one of the leading nations . . . in choral, congregational
> and mass singing. As the people became real singers more for-
> mality entered into the picture. The formality, however, did not
> in any manner impair the democracy of it; with the result that
> today little Wales is a land of song, [and *that song*] *belongs to
> the lowliest and mightiest on strictly common ground.*"
>
> GEORGE PULLEN JACKSON,
> "Wanted: An American Hans Sachs" (1947)

We need scarcely look farther than Birmingham's "Better Music" influences to account for Jackson's decision to study at the Royal Conservatory of Music in Dresden in 1897. Yet, ironically, it was this experience,
introducing him to German appreciation of folk culture, that led him
eventually to folksong. The following year, he returned to study briefly at
Vanderbilt, and then finished his degree at the University of Chicago in
1904. Jackson's next period was nomadic, with instructorships in German departments at Kansas State College (Manhattan) and Case School of
Applied Science (Cleveland), the University of Chicago, Oberlin College
(Ohio), and Northwestern University (Evanston, Illinois)—interspersed
with studies at Munich and Bonn. He returned to earn his Ph.D. from the
University of Chicago in 1911, and then in 1913 he took a position at the

University of North Dakota, which he held until his 1918 move to Vanderbilt. Arriving in Nashville that year, Jackson could look back on eleven moves to eight different universities.

At some point, the burden of Jackson's interests shifted from music to German Romanticism. His earliest publication was on "German Student Dueling" in fraternal clubs, a description, sensitive to differences between spontaneous and prearranged duels, that would qualify today as ethnographic (Jackson 1908). He acknowledged the role of the clubs in German national character—in this case, by citing their tacit endorsement by Kaiser Wilhelm. Following this were two articles in *Modern Language Notes* on eighteenth-century German war songs documented by the poet Johann Gleim (1719–1803) that, Jackson argued, predated the development of the idea of folksong by J. G. Herder (1744–1803) in 1787 (Jackson 1911b, 1913).

Many contemporary folklorists attribute to Herder the development of the idea of folklore, and it is clear that Jackson had by then achieved this understanding. We can well suspect that his University of Chicago doctoral dissertation, which is now lost, addressed the evolution of romantic thought that led from the criticism of G. E. Lessing (1729–81) to the folksong collections of Bishop Percy (1729–1811) (Jackson 1911a). Jackson concluded his work on this subject with a formal analysis of German folksong, covering a hundred pages over four issues of *Modern Philology,* that criticized the unnatural separation of music and text that pervaded both folksong study and the training of folksong scholars (Jackson 1916–17).

Closing the last of these folksong essays was a plea that was thoroughly resonant of the thought and style of Herder. Jackson called for an understanding of the "real nature of the folk-song—that subsoil from which the overworked topsoil of modern lyric poetry and modern song draws, from time to time, new life for the bringing forth of its most beautiful flowers" (Jackson 1916–17, 4:38). These were the last words Jackson would write on the subject of German culture.[12] In a transition he would later describe as a consequence of his "cultural patriotism," Jackson's work took an immediate and wholesale shift toward American traditional music (Jackson 1939, 78). Unmistakably, this turn to native music anticipated Jackson's "discovery" of Sacred Harp singing. Surely this enthusiastic discovery was bolstered by his return to his southern roots, but another factor may have played a part as well: the coming of World War I.

Jackson could not have been pleased that his rise to prominence as a German scholar, launched with studies of the culture of militant nationalism, came at a time of unprecedented anti-German sentiment in America. During the war, German language instruction in the United States was widely targeted as an obstacle to ethnic assimilation, part of "the tentacles of the German octopus in America" (Luebke 1974, 216). German books, many undoubtedly important to Jackson and perhaps also to his students, were hauled away from libraries and burned. Students began boycotting German classes; at the University of Wisconsin, German-language enrollment declined 40 percent. And in South Dakota, the State Council of Defense ordered the immediate elimination of German language instruction in all the schools of the state (Wittke 1936, 179). Jackson never commented on this, but he was profoundly motivated by the political and psychological consequences of differing national cultures in America and Germany—of Romantic nationalism weak and undeveloped in America and gone hopelessly out of control in Germany. Repeatedly, he looked to American folklore not as a source of nationalism but as the foundation of an indigenous cultural identity.

Somewhat by default, Jackson seemed to associate his own New South with that rootless America. For example, as a consequence of his upbringing in this culture, Jackson had to "discover" American folksong—and several accounts of that discovery confirm it as a profound epiphany. One obituary claimed he was introduced to American folksong by a high school teacher in North Dakota; another said that "on a hot summer day in 1920, Dr. Jackson walked into a country church in Winston County, Alabama, and heard Sacred Harp singing for the first time." [13] As for his introduction to American folksong in general, he had written in the *Journal of American Folklore*, "As a lover of folk-lore and as an American, the conviction that [Americans are indifferent to the study of folklore] gives me real pain" (Jackson 1919, 438). Later, he would say that he was inspired by his German training "to cast about in my own land, to see if perhaps similar folksong conditions and intelligent recognition of them obtained here" (Jackson 1939, 78).

"A HARMONIC COMPLEX OF SINGULAR CHARM": JACKSON AND SACRED HARP

> He mumbled a few rather rusty tones—a procedure called "keying" the tune—and without further ceremony he raised his head and hand and "lifted the tune."
>
> GEORGE PULLEN JACKSON, "The Fa-Sol-La Folk" (1926)

As for his discovery of Sacred Harp singing, Jackson reports in the opening pages of *White Spirituals* a "chance conversation" with a teaching colleague, Dr. John W. Barton of Ward-Belmont School, in which he learned of country "fasola" singings from shape note books (Jackson 1933, 3). It would seem that his interest in folksong would have put him in contact with Carl Carmer, whose earliest ambitions for folksong, when he was planning a scholarly book, were similar to Jackson's. But there is no evidence of correspondence or collaboration, and neither cited the other's work.

In any case, Jackson would later write that he had "heard about this antique guild for some time" before he attended his first singing at Helicon, Winston County, Alabama, July 4, 1925 (Jackson 1926, 6). Inquiries led him to "a certain Joe S. James of Atlanta," who replied to his correspondence with a *Sacred Harp* book and the printed "proceedings" (Jackson's quotation marks) of the nineteenth United Sacred Harp Convention held in September 1923 in Atlanta. As countless new singers have done since then, Jackson noted in these minutes the occasion of an upcoming singing—the Fourth of July Helicon singing—and struck out for the event, as he put it, "determined to hunt up these Fa-sol-la folk in their own *revier*." His account of this venture bears repeating in full:

> I made the necessary trip to Cullman, Ala., the nearest rail point. Two hours of driving over sandy roads which wound through forests of pine, between fields of young cotton and through a dozen shallow

"branches," brought me to my destination at about noon on Independence day. Helicon was no town. It was not even what is locally termed a "place." It was simply a little aged, unpainted school-house-church off by itself some distance from a cross roads. And I never have learned whether this gathering place for rustic singers and composers was intentionally named after the ancient Helicon, "the favorite seat of Apollo and the muses."

The pine grove round about was alive with men, women, children and, a little deeper in the woods, mules, scores of them hitched to trees. The singers had come in springless farm wagons, conveyances which were now being converted into picnic tables.

Singing was going on inside, so I went in, found a seat, opened my Original Sacred Harp and pretended to be one of them—this partly to ward off any possible suspicion on the part of the natives that I was an unsympathetic intruder from the city or perhaps even a secret emissary from the camp of "operatic, secular and rag-time strains" which, as I had read in the preface to the song book, were looked upon as the subtle influences which "drive away, in place of promoting, religious feeling" and thus retard "the great work of the Gospel and of the churches."

My clothes themselves were, I felt sure, giving me away. But my fears were groundless. The people were all too intent on their singing to take any notice of my presence. Packed into every one of the stiff-backed, rough wooden benches; sweating but not noticing the sweltering heat, sat young men and women, mothers and fathers with babes in arms, grandfathers and grandmothers. Singing had been going on continuously since early morning. Just as I took my seat the chairman was inviting "Brother" Wall to lead a "lesson" for twenty minutes. The brother—a nearly toothless, nearly hairless, drooping-moustached patriarch of popular polyphony, who was wearing the usual blue overalls and combatting the suffocating heat with an advertising fan—walked out into the little open space in front of the desk-altar and looked around for a moment. He held no book. He didn't need one. He had "led" here in Helicon, as I afterward learned, for the whole thirty-five years that these Fourth of July singings had been going on.

He called a number. A hundred Original Sacred Harps opened. He mumbled a few rather rusty tones—a procedure called "keying" the tune—and without further ceremony he raised his head and hand and "lifted the tune."

No instrument was needed to urge these hundred mouths to open. Like a well trained orchestra the singers hit the very first note, dwelt a moment on it and then dashed off at a clip which was twice as fast as the tempo marked in the book, and as regular as an idling gas engine. And now I saw why they had laid so much stress in the "rudiments" on the syllable-names of the notes, for they proceeded to sing the whole tune once through using these syllables instead of the words of the song—a custom which I found was general.

"Fawwww solamefa sol sol," sang the tenors. "Fawwww melamela la la," squeaked the trebles. And the basses and the altos produced also their particular syllabic sequence with equal assertiveness, each indulging in what seemed to function as an individual and group review of the essentially musical part of the piece, a review which prepared the singers for the next time through, when much of their attention would have to be diverted to the sacred words themselves.

And when they did finish with the syllables and came to these words there was revealed a harmonic complex of singular charm. This Sacred Harp harmony is perhaps the most unique musical phase of their singing. (Jackson 1926, 6)

Compared with this, Carmer's and Davidson's narratives seem inundated with the narrative structure, character development, and authorial presence of imaginative literature. Carmer and Davidson wrote as if they knew all along that they were observing a "strange country" or a "land of Eden." But Jackson's narrative was more purely confessional—as if he genuinely did not know what he would encounter and was not yet under the spell of the conventions of ethnographic literature. His actions, his thought processes, and also the outcome of the narrative were laid out, transparent, as if he were not completely sure of their eventual outcome. At the outset, he took "with salt" the advice of his colleagues and "went to work" on the subject of singing "to test out their truth-content." The documents sent to him by Joe S. James "proved to be curious things." Then came his trip: "Two hours of driving . . . brought me to my destination."

Two weeks later, Jackson attended singings at Birmingham and nearby Ensley, Alabama. Not long after this, he corresponded with Sidney Burdette Denson and learned of the Denson family and their remarkable work in music education.[14] In the account of his initial encounter, Jackson had marveled at the facility of the singers in "dashing off" difficult pieces of music "like a well trained orchestra."

All of this was even more extraordinary, he said, in that it was "accomplished in a section of the country where, by reason of the sparseness of population, the public schools have penetrated only slightly if at all." In closing, he pondered the various modernist institutions against which Sacred Harp singers had had to defend their tradition, and then, ironically, he singled out the public schools as the chief threat:

> One of those in-coming institutions is the public school. When urban "education" comes into the "Sacred Harp" country what will be the result? When a set of modern teachers takes charge of the remote Helicons, will the old "leaders" and their art be laughed out? Will there then be presented just one more picture of an uprooted and withering "folk" culture? And in its place the three R's and other forms of realism, all planted in nice little materialistic rows in the young folks' minds, with ample space in between the rows for the weeds of worldly wont to take root, space where once flourished the old-fashioned flowers of fancy?
>
> Will this "new learning" be the death or merely the transfiguration of the Fa-sol-la singing? (Jackson 1926, 10)

Surely the writer of this passage, who long ago had extolled the "Value of Vocal Music in the Public Schools," who had observed in German Romanticism the profound benefits of looking inward for the source of cultural identity, who had then returned to the place of his youth and observed the Sacred Harp tradition flourishing largely in spite of public music education, and who recognized in it that "it is their very own, a part of them, hence it is sacred"—surely this writer must also have seen in that glorious band of singers, tragically, a neglected part of himself.

From that point hence, Jackson adopted the outsider discourse of culture writing and ethnography expertly yet always reluctantly. He would not have been displeased that his biography might someday illuminate the artifice on which such a stance is so often built. Most discovery narratives steer clear of the conditions of serendipity. Of those accounting for Jackson's discovery of folksong, some omit his southern upbringing and others omit his German folklore training. No account is given that does not characterize his discovery of singing as some kind of "pure accident." By such a process, historical continuity is disrupted by omitting key facts; in its place, an atmosphere of serendipity is constructed, leading to the drama of a "pure accident." Actually some kind of law seems to be at work: the more thoroughly cultural isolation obscures traditions, the more compelling the rhetoric of discovery announces their return. One can scarcely imagine institutions more perfectly designed around forgetting and inventing culture than those associated with the bold New South movement that was coming to prominence just as Jackson emerged from his youth.

AN ORGANIC BODY OF AMERICAN FOLKSONG

It is generally assumed that America has no organic body of folk-music, certainly none that is significant in quantity and representative of the American people as that people appears today.

GEORGE PULLEN JACKSON, "America's Folk-Songs" (1936)

Nor is music processing *our* job, properly speaking. We may not even believe in this phase of propaganda. And we may justify our attitude as an unwillingness to defile our folk goods. But if we southern folklorists persist in this conviction, there can be, as I see it, but two possible alternative results: either our folk music won't spread at all, or others will take over the job of processing and spreading it. If it is not spread at all, then the millions of our school will keep on learning and singing folk songs of the Urals and Uruguay; our church-goers will go on intoning synthetic hymn tunes; and the great non-school and non-church commercial-institutional sources of musical influence on youth will continue perfectly free to pander to the lowest common denominator of public taste in purveying what pays best. And if outsiders take over what we say is not our job, if they take our folk songs away from us and process them as they see fit, then we may be sure that they will *really* defile them.

Truly, the price of complacency is a high one.

GEORGE PULLEN JACKSON,
"Why Does American Folk Music Spread So Slowly?" (1945)

Having anticipated and then discovered American folksong over the course of the 1920s, Jackson could now begin to uncover the cultural wealth of which he previously had only dreamed. As did some other folklorists of that time, Jackson viewed the collection and study of folksong and the public promotion of folksong as a single activity. In his case, this unified approach was surely a consequence both of his training in German Romanticism and of his apparently rootless New South upbringing. Sometimes with considerable urgency, his writing on almost any subject was often penetrated with the desire to rid American musical culture of its modernist veneer and reinstill historically rooted, participatory vernacular culture in its place.

To this end, two ambitions guided him: the construction of a national music based on native folksong, and the reinforcement of the original motivating conditions of American folksong. Jackson often conflated the two, sometimes in perplexing contradiction, yet he seemed to understand that each was linked to different institutions of revitalization. National folk consciousness, for example, was something that had to be manufactured anew; in contrast, the motivating conditions of vernacular culture had rapidly declined as a result of unrestrained modernism.

Jackson's initial assessment of the national music came in 1919, when he noted an American "indifference" to folksong. As his career progressed and he grew more sensitive to the sources of that indifference, he began viewing it as a struggle. In 1939 he could actually name the "enemies" of American folksong. In the nineteenth century, for example, hostile forces were mustered by the deliberate "Better Music" reform campaign that launched outright attacks on native religious song. Folksong's twentieth-century "enemies," however, were somewhat less visible: the tendency for Americans to dismiss the cultural value of their everyday affairs, the aggressive promotion of "art-music" as preeminent in the minds and souls of Americans, and the "cultural disease" of musical extroversion that inspired Americans to look to Europe for affirmation. For example, the editor of the most widely used denominational hymnal in America, Jackson reported, was genuinely interested in American folk material. In the new edition of the hymnal, however, the editor included "but a paltry dozen of our folk hymn tunes while other nations were represented in that same collection by many scores of folk melodies" (Jackson 1945e, 2). In each case, Jackson's solution was to raise awareness of and instill loyalty to native material.

The most egregious modern "enemy," however, was the system of public music education. Turning to this institution, Jackson analyzed four music books widely used in American public schools to determine the distribution of songs according to national origin and type.[15] He discovered that these books contained an average of only 13.25 percent native folksongs, indicating "the school music people's approval of the general and long-standing American musical extroversion and footlessness, and their determination to teach it" (Jackson 1946c, 3). In contrast, Jackson praised the efforts of a Pittsburgh teacher who, alerted to the idea of a folksong canon by Carl Sandburg's *American Songbag* (1927), initiated a "Pittsburgh Revolution" of folksong instruction and amateur folksong collecting. The Pittsburgh teachers only needed "time enough to *un*-train a bit" to adjust to handling the oral tradition properly (Jackson 1946c, 6). The emphasis was on the reinstatement of a native folksong canon and not a sensitivity to local vernacular institutions. By virtue only of its presence, a folksong canon would achieve for Americans a firmer sense of national identity.

On the one hand, this argument motivated the public promotion of folksong performance to raise awareness of authentic native forms and reconnect Americans with genuine historical roots. Jackson organized and trained a performing troupe of Vanderbilt affiliates and promoted them as the "Old Harp Singers."[16] Their performances included the National Folk

Festival (1934), the White Top Folk Festival (1934), a National Broadcasting Company radio broadcast, and numerous concert performances. Recordings deposited at Vanderbilt University indicate that they performed both secular folksongs and religious songs, probably from *The Sacred Harp* or the *New Harp of Columbia* (whose singers were colloquially named "Old Harp Singers" long before the performing group took the name). He also organized performances of vocal groups drawn from the ranks of southern tradition. One notable group appeared at the second National Folk Festival (1935). Although Jackson was not credited with any organization role, it seems inconceivable that he had nothing to do with it. The program identified the "officers" of the ensemble—A. J. Wooten as chairman and George Bobo, Bud Dean, Henry Stallings, and Tom Wooten as vice chairmen—indicating that the group's structure was, like traditional singings, of a fundamentally ad hoc nature (Green 1975, 28). In 1941 Jackson relinquished leadership of the Old Harp Singers to Irving Wolfe of Peabody College, but apparently he continued to organize performances of traditional singers. In 1948 he took a group of traditional singers to Detroit for the National Music Educators Conference.[17]

Yet, in his quest for a grounded cultural identity, Jackson drew not only on authentic folksong but also on artistic productions that used folksong or were inspired by native forms. By this reckoning, Jackson championed a variety of southern musical institutions. He was pivotal in the founding of the Nashville Symphony Orchestra (1920), the Nashville Choral Club, and the Tennessee Music Teachers Association.[18] He also contributed a regular column, "Southern Musicians," to the *Nashville Banner,* celebrating the art-music accomplishments of native southerners. For example, of David Guion of Ballinger, Texas, Jackson commented, "With all this bred-in-the-home Americanism there was no evading its influence on his life and work." Of Mary Fabian of Birmingham, he wrote, "To any one who knows how music is fostered in the schools of that city, it will not seem strange that Mary not only discovered during those years that she had a beautiful soprano voice, but also developed an unquenchable desire to become an opera singer."[19] In 1923, the *Vanderbilt Alumnus* wrote of him, with apparently unknowing irony, "'Better literature, drama, and music' are his slogans, for which he has tirelessly been working since boyhood."[20]

Although Jackson's folk music and art music activities occupied separate domains of his life, they were not fundamentally distinct cultural forms to him. He had resolved their apparent distance, according to the model of German Romanticism, with an understanding of the way tradition serves as the foundation of any meaningful national or regional culture. Their separation was artificial, he reasoned, having arisen from the deliberate and unnatural imitation of European culture by nineteenth-century Americans. He wrote of American folksong as "permeating different groups and institutions at a pace measured by the groups' ability and willingness to accept it—their hospitality to change in general" (Jackson 1953, 142).

In this assessment of American folksong, published in the last year of his life, Jackson defined the struggle not as one limited to the empowerment of vernacular institutions themselves. Rather, his emphasis was on the penetration of folksong into the preeminent musical institutions of mainstream society, such as the public schools, churches, recitals, choruses, and symphonies. He took for granted that because all cultural groups had stylistic expectations, folksong would require some "dressing-up" to suit the tastes of the various mainstream musical institutions. Even the large and influential category of "processors and distributors"—such as John Jacob Niles, Jo Stafford, Burl Ives, and Tom Scott—arrayed folk materials in the garb of popular song. If he was unconcerned with their lack of authenticity, it was because this group "may be looked upon as a present-day substitute for the one-time oral tradition" (Jackson 1953, 140). Accepting the coexistence of traditional culture and national musical institutions and forms, Jackson could only hope that Americans would accept the influence of their native forms in whatever way was most accessible.

WHITE AND NEGRO SPIRITUALS

The title of that collection, "Spiritual Songs" [Newbern, N.C., 1806], became the generic name of the then new sort of songs created in the revival atmosphere, and it was used by the rural whites of the South for perhaps a century before the programme leaflets of Negro concert groups brought it to the ken of Northern audiences.

GEORGE PULLEN JACKSON,
"The Genesis of the Negro Spiritual" (1932)

Jackson did not have to venture to Pittsburgh for a model for the revival of American "folk consciousness." Even as he first took stock of American folksong during the 1920s, he could be assured of finding at least one instance of impressive strength: at Fisk University, the renowned Fisk Jubilee Singers had been touring and promoting vernacular spirituals as a "Negro concert group" since around 1871. Like the eighteenth-century Germans, the Jubilee Singers had drawn on the political efficacy of folksong. Almost immediately, they had observed from public reaction that their performances contradicted the debilitating caricatures that were being proliferated in the minstrel shows (Silveri 1988).[21]

Indeed, even as early as the 1860s, the spiritual had been recognized in published accounts as a key source of African American emancipatory thought (Epstein 1977, 241–73). Later, in one of the more articulate statements of this view, *The Souls of Black Folk* (1903), W. E. B. Du Bois had argued that the most auspicious African American theology lay in the liberating vigor of spirituals or, as he called them, "sorrow songs." Du Bois had also learned while studying in Berlin how elitist "culture" had oppressed eighteenth-century European "cultureless" peoples and how this pattern was replicated in America. In response, he identified the spiritual as the foundation of the authentic African American "soul," linking it with other movements that derive national consciousness from folk culture (Bell 1974, 1985; Rampersand 1976; Turner 1974).[22]

Ironically, the cultural qualities of the spiritual that had attracted Du Bois also brought it to the attention of those seeking an authentic national music for America. Even as early as 1867, a reviewer of *Slave Songs of the United States* had identified spirituals as the foundation of a national music, proclaiming, "We utter no new truths when we affirm that whatever of nationality there is in the music of America she owes to her dusky children" (*Nation,* 21 November, 411, quoted in Epstein 1977:

337). But the most celebrated opinion came later from visiting Czech composer Antonín Dvořák, who had called for an American musical identity inspired by authentic folksong—"negro melodies or Indian chants" (Chase 1987, 429; Dvořák 1895, 432). These views were confirmed by turn-of-the-century ethnologists, who began documenting Negro music as folksong. The consequence of this was an odd dovetailing of white and black American notions of the value of the authenticity of the Negro spiritual.[23]

No sooner had this mutual interest in the authentic spiritual been established than it became the basis for conflict. Even though New World slave experiences (and not Old World origin) had first been identified as the primary basis for authenticity, ethnologists began raising questions about the origin of the spiritual. In 1893, ethnologist Richard Wallaschek wrote a treatise on *Primitive Music* that challenged the implicit presumption that they were African in origin. Without having visited America or Africa, he nonetheless claimed decisively that spirituals were "unmistakably 'arranged'—not to say ignorantly borrowed—from the national songs of all nations, from military signals, well-known marches, German student-songs, etc." (Wallaschek 1893, 61, quoted in Epstein 1983, 55). In the ensuing years, studies of American folksong began detailing similarities between white and black religious folk music. Some of these studies retained, by implication or design, the aggressive attack on authenticity that Wallaschek had originated. In these attacks, what might have comprised an obscure scholarly squabble was given widespread significance by the context of the urgent search for an authentic American national folk music.

Jackson apparently was not influenced by this literature until after he had already formulated his initial concerns about Sacred Harp and American folksong. In fact, his 1926 account of Sacred Harp was so innocent of these issues that he did not even use the word *spiritual* to describe the music. Instead, he called it "America's oldest choral art" and its singers "our contemporary musical ancestors."[24] Possibly his innocence was lost in the few years following this discovery: both Newman I. White's *American Negro Folk-Songs* (1928) and Guy B. Johnson's *Folk Culture on St. Helena Island, South Carolina* (1930) attacked the origin question.

White, in fact, documented his contention of European influence with parallel evidence in shape note tunebooks. In any case, it can be said with assurance that Jackson did not invent the origin issue but joined an already heated debate on the subject.

In 1932 he had made the connection and outlined his theory of "The Genesis of the Negro Spiritual" in an article for H. L. Mencken's provocative *American Mercury* (Jackson 1932). At the outset of the article, he noted the influential performing tours of the Jubilee Singers, identifying them, along with the Sacred Harp singing he had observed, as the musical forms whose "geneses" he had come to believe were related. He had been led to this connection, on the one hand, by the established Negro origin debate and, on the other, unlike his contemporaries, by Louis F. Benson's comprehensive history, *The English Hymn* (1915). From Benson, Jackson learned that the term *spiritual song* was of American coinage, though derived originally from Colossians 3:16. It was used in a camp meeting songster in 1806 and was later extended to apply to the form generically. With this connection as a point of departure, he began assembling an array of evidence from printed collections that revealed to him a canon of spirituals among European Americans that preceded the collection and publication of Negro spirituals. A year later, with the publication of *White Spirituals in the Southern Uplands*, Jackson coined the term *white spiritual*, with which he would become inextricably associated.

By this time, it had become common for scholars to test for origin by observing similarities in printed texts or melodies from European American and African American tradition. Then, based on dates of publication or collection, they imposed generational metaphors wholesale on the two supposedly homogeneous canons of song. Jackson's main contribution was his attention, with unprecedented diligence and scope, to tune and text comparison. He indulged heavily in the minutiae of origin theory, gapped scale percentages, and lists of tunes that he had recently found in shape note tunebooks and camp meeting songsters. Contemporary critics, of course, are quick to note that his dependence on printed sources skewed his chronology, overlooking a crucial early period when African American performances had not yet reached print (Epstein 1983; Southern [1972] 1983).

Nonetheless, the burden of the article was the theory, not its consequences for national culture. Based on his observations, he even admitted to the likelihood of a vast African contribution and did not deny the existence of some African songs. But Jackson objected strongly to what he called the "inertia of faith" of African-origin proponents, particularly Henry E. Krehbiel. And he was decisive in calling the main body of spiritual songs of European Americans the "parent songs" of the "Negro offspring" (Jackson 1932, 247).

In 1936, Jackson expanded the scope of his stance on the origin question. During that year, he published only two articles, both devoted to the "national culture" implications of the racial origin issue. In "America's Folksongs," he reassured those anxious about the certainty of an organic American national music that "the people of this land have enjoyed, from the start to the present, one dominant culture and language, that of the British Isles" (Jackson 1936a, 34–35). Complementing this was a comparative study of the melodies of Stephen Foster, who had been touted in the "national music" literature as an exemplar for African influence because of the use in his compositions of African American melodies. Jackson struck at the heart of this argument, providing numerous examples of melodies, to which Foster should have been exposed, that were available to him in printed "white spiritual" tunebooks (Jackson 1936b).

Jackson's theories played easily into the hands of racial nativists (see Whisnant 1983, 237–52, esp. 244). Nor did he raise his voice in protest. In fact, Jackson continued to espouse the view that American folksong was of British origin. For instance, when with Charles Faulkner Bryan he compiled a book of *American Folk Music for High School and Other Choral Groups,* the two defended their decision to include only British and Irish sources:

> "But if we are a mixed people and still sing folksongs," I hear, "why do you single out Britain and Eire as their chief sources?" We don't single them out. History of the Fates did it long ago. (Jackson and Bryan 1947, n.p.)

When reviewing Margaret Bradford Boni's *Fireside Book of Folksongs,* Jackson was annoyed that the compiler had meticulously identified the sources of songs without claiming the collection as a body of national song. Particularly irked by her reference to the Negro spiritual as "America's greatest true folksong," Jackson listed the page numbers from her book that corresponded to songs that he believed were incorrectly identified as having preeminent African influence. "But one searches in vain," he complained, "for her recognition of the fact that 77 of her songs are American by birth or by adaptation or by long-range folk-use and by their character and her firesides of this land are conceived as those of our minorities" (Jackson 1948, 102).

The point of this discussion, of course, is to examine the ideas that propelled the promotion or revival of folksong as a part of public culture. The cultural nation-building endeavor, with its dubious representational theories and generational metaphors, could only lead to a distortion of history in service to part of the population. The key issue was the degree and manner in which the spiritual was depicted as emblematic of race/nation. For Du Bois, depending on how you read him, the spiritual (1) emerged naturally from the transcendent "soul" of black Americans, (2) arose from the "soul" not of race but of the transcendent New World experience of slavery, or (3) had formal properties through which some black Americans could achieve some unity of form and experience that became transcendent consciousness or "soul." These readings, in decreasing degree in the order listed, actually reinforce the notion of race that Du Bois struggled throughout his life to eradicate (Appiah 1992, chap. 2). Others, such as Hampton Institute choir leader R. Nathaniel Dett, formulated views of the spiritual that contradicted essentialist notions of race by locating the "soul" exclusively in the formal properties of the spiritual (Spencer 1994).

On the whole, the terms of the origin debate most often linked spirituals, emblematically, to the *fact* of race. These terms were so essentialist in design, so tightly bound together by authenticity, that it was not always clear that spirituals were an emblem of race or vice versa. Depending on the subject he was addressing, Jackson could be wildly inconsistent on the ontology of the spiritual. At worst, in his origin writings, he inferred homogeneous canons of racial music from text and tune evidence and assigned to them broad generative metaphors (e.g., "parent" or "offspring"). But elsewhere, in much of Jackson's writing, historical causality actually drew him away from the quest for national culture where text comparison nourished the tropes of generation and nation. For example, in accounting historically for the rise of the spiritual form, Jackson recognized the importance of the camp meetings of the Upland South, where frontier conditions, the emancipatory theology of independent Baptist and Methodist churches, and the absence of a predominant slave-based economy provided an atmosphere of cultural integration unparalleled elsewhere in nineteenth-century America. Jackson challenged as insignificant the myth of master-to-slave musical influence, locating the most prominent sites of cultural integration in areas where emancipatory opportunities were greatest (Jackson 1943, 286). Nonetheless, he was never able to break the spell of the origin question, and when addressing it, weighed in unequivocally on the side of European origin.

In the post–World War II era, however, this preeminent sociohistorical grounding of Jackson's work has perhaps facilitated "reading around" nationalistic and racial components of the origin question. That is, no matter what the similarity to or influence of Old World musical forms, postwar folksong proponents recognized several canons of American religious folksong that did not contend with one another for exclusive status as authentic national song. In Jackson, we can trace this line of thinking most clearly to Jackson's participation in Sarah Gertrude Knott's thoroughly pluralist National Folk Festival. In 1935, the second year of the festival, the program of "distinctively American expressions" featured Sacred Harp singers alongside the Fisk Jubilee Singers and also a Negro spiritual chorus of one thousand from Chattanooga (Green 1975; Knott 1939, 117). Jackson seems also to have approved fully of the pluralist model of Carl Sandburg's *American Songbag* (Jackson 1933, 40; 1946c).

Perhaps this was possible because the origin question was not central to Jackson's motivations as a champion of religious folksong. He came first to American folksong with a healthy contempt for the overall disregard by Americans, compared to the German model, of any folksong (Jackson 1919). His distaste for "the present art-cravings of our youth" was based on its indifference to history. With this premise at hand, he discovered in Sacred Harp a historically significant music that had suffered class-based indignities of which he himself had played some part. His desire to see the potential of this music fully realized in American culture seems to have arisen from his own cultural roots and seems to have been his most fundamental motive. Perhaps consequently, in the postwar decades, when Jackson's work served as the basis for the revival of singing from shape note tunebooks, one finds in abundance references to Jackson and to the tunebooks as genuine American music but little enthusiasm for origin theory.

"SING, BROTHERS, SING!" FROM RELIGIOUS DISSENT TO FOLKSONG ACTIVISM

> The war against folksong has been and is being waged by artificial song. It is a case of song dictatorship against song democracy. It is the fight of the proponents of planned singing versus those who would preserve what they deem the inalienable right of lyric freedom. It is Fewman against Everyman.
>
> GEORGE PULLEN JACKSON, "Sing, Brothers, Sing!" (1945)

> It is important to remember also that the religious dissenters here, as ever in English life, were the poor, the at first politically powerless, the socially "wrong people," and that they remained so for a long time. This was most strikingly evident in the south where the "right people" of the Established Order owned all the good tobacco land and most of the slaves. This economic-political-social disability kept the dissenters long in the handicrafts and trades and/or drove them to the backwoods and frontiers.
>
> GEORGE PULLEN JACKSON, White and Negro Spirituals (1943)

When Jackson returned to the South and began to focus the lens of German Romanticism onto his own culture, he was employing a model that, in Europe, had drawn from native vernacular forms to revitalize national culture. In part, this model suggested the kind of cultural nation-building that fueled the origin debate. Eighteenth-century German intellectuals, faced with the preeminence of other European cultures on the one hand and the rise of the Enlightenment and progress on the other, had turned to native materials as a resource for a German national literature (Wilson 1973).

But there was a different aspect to this model that focused less on nation and more on vernacular institutions. For example, the Southern Agrarian approach to cultural and artistic identity sought an end to the South's "bartering away [of] its tranquil ways for the gaudy benefits of industrial American life" (Rubin 1962, viii). Jackson subscribed to this cause in that it drew from native materials for identity rather than imitating modern or foreign culture. Those twelve "Fugitives" (or "twelve apostles," as Jackson called them) who had produced *I'll Take My Stand* were "outstanding individuals . . . who are or have been *provincials by their own choice*" (Jackson 1950, 6, emphasis mine).

In that provincialism, they sought not so much to construct a unified southern regional identity as to reattach southerners to historically rooted culture. That is, the ontological or psychological benefits were derived *from the vernacular forms themselves,* not from the manufactured consensus that was a consequence of their promotion. Even in German Romantic theory, this was a crucial distinction. Constance Rourke, who worked with Jackson as vice president of the National Folk Festival Association, had insisted on such a distinction in her call for attention to the roots of American culture. For Rourke, a fatal error in Romantic thought occurred at the beginning of the nineteenth century, when antiquarian style took precedence over the fundamental substance of folklife:

> But a mild nostalgia quickly took the place of Herder's bold creative concept of the folk as a living wellspring of poetry and song. This was brought about mainly through the selective work of Schlegel and the Grimms, whose explorations of folklore and folk-song had great value but who developed to an extreme the romantic concept of primitive or folk-life which had first been touched upon by Montaigne. Antiquarianism began to cast its long insidious spell, and inquiries as to the folk-arts came to be regarded as minor excursions into the pretty or quaint. (Rourke 1942, 24–25)

Rourke thought it ironic that Americans, otherwise so democratic in their thinking, had been largely uninterested in Herder's essentially democratic theory of folk culture. But some Americans, by largely intuitive principles not drawn from European Romanticism, had sought to develop cultural institutions drawn from the democratic spirit of the new nation. As examples, Rourke cited the movement of singing schools and public singings in the late eighteenth century. This movement was "free to all denominations," designed for "diffusing a knowledge of music among all classes, particularly the poor," and was "native in origin, primitive in character, rural in its main sources and mainly religious, though not wholly so, in theme" (Rourke 1942, 171–72). This was, she might have said, folksong revival by instinct, not by ideology. In contrast, she concluded in *American Humor* (1931), American writers were less consistent in their efforts at a national literature. They toyed in myriad ways with a usable national past, but sometimes they had only indulged in superficial boosterism in the name of literature. "Traditions," she warned, "cannot be improvised in the slow minds of whole peoples" (Rourke 1931, 220). Likewise, for Southern Agrarians such as Davidson, provincialism was a call for an inward-looking orientation, a rejection of imitation, a call to explain why the modern South had produced a "great literature" (Davidson 1950).

Although Jackson allied himself with the Agrarian cause, he took a different strategy. For the Fugitives, a central feature was a southern literary movement animated by Agrarian tradition, and Sacred Harp was one such tradition. For Jackson, the struggle was not merely southern and not merely anti-industrial. Folksong and the forms that contended against it had a preeminent psychological and cultural foundation (Jackson 1939). That is, the ontological status of Sacred Harp singing, or folk music in general, was not derived from agrarian social forms. Its decline, as Jackson knew from his observations of nineteenth-century "Better Music Boosters," was primarily cultural and not a by-product of industrialization. The recovery of its vitality would not be ensured by a return to an agricultural economy.

Rather, the presence of folk music in agrarian settings had less to do with its "natural" affinity to agrarian life than with the indifference of rural people toward cultural reform and to some extent also the indifference of reformers toward rural people. Yet this "protective condition" of rural migration patterns was augmented by another important influence: the theology of primitive religion (Jackson 1939, 81–83). The most important example was the case of the Primitive Baptists. "The Primitive Baptist freedom in singing is due to their refusal to allow instruments in their meeting houses and their renunciation of revivals and Sunday Schools both of which tend to replace singing deliberacy with the lyric jog-trotting which has been characteristic of those environments" (Jackson 1943, 247). He frequently noted as an example the persistence of traditional singing in the Primitive Baptist Church in Hopewell, New Jersey, less than a hundred miles from New York City, "where we are celebrating the glittering material advances of the age" (Jackson 1939, 83). In such cases, singing demonstrated its own capacity for producing social forms, thus folklore theory and folksong activism had an inseparable political foundation.

The capacity in America for cultural revitalization through folksong seemed clear, Jackson reasoned, in the manner by which nineteenth-century musical reformers sought its removal in the first place. "While Arnim and Brentano were collecting and praising the songs of the European Common Man," he concluded in 1946, in the wake of the "appalling destruction" of the war, "our Lowell Masons were striving to stamp out the religious folk songs of our humble forebears" (Jackson 1946b, 216–17). Recovering American folksong, then, was a bold historical act, and the folklorist was an "apostle of a broader, deeper humanism."

The pivotal role of history in Jackson's approach to folksong may well have led to his suspicion of Benjamin Botkin's theory of "folklore-in-the-making," of folklore as a process by which traditions might arise anew (Jackson 1944b, 497). Instead, Jackson believed in a re-creative capacity for folksong, insisting that historical theory was not antiquarian theory. "Every old song re-sung becomes a new one," he maintained (Jackson 1945c, 2). Consequently, Jackson's historical approach was not merely the recovery of the past. Rather, he viewed folksong as a historical act in which we screen the past and "apply the screenings to the betterment of the present and the future." It was an abrupt transgression against the tendency of the historical record of the past to be, as Jackson called it, "aristocratically selected." As a cardinal maxim, he borrowed a passage from Ralph Barton Perry: "The chief source of spiritual nourishment of any nation must be in its own past perpetually rediscovered and renewed" (quoted in Jackson 1946b, 211).

In this, Jackson took an approach to folksong revival that was different from but equally as effective as his canon-constructing efforts. In fact, re-constructing cultural history did not even necessitate the positing of a cultural canon. So, in the contentious setting of the racial origin debate, Jackson constructed a parallel argument that would ultimately have far greater impact on Sacred Harp revival than either his origin theories or his advocacy of national musical culture. It was a novel approach. As most clearly explicated in *White and Negro Spirituals* (1943), he sought to discern, regarding American religious folksong, "the dimness if not indeed darkness which has surrounded its beginnings, and the complete uncertainty which has existed as to the relationship of the white-sung to the negro-sung varieties" (1943, 2). By this date, the literature on religious folksong and origin theory was not small. To what "darkness" could he have referred?

"The high light of the revolutionary century in American history," Jackson boldly greeted a public surely harboring some preoccupation with the consensus-minded war effort, "was its anti-institutionalism" (1943, 7). Foremost in the everyday life of colonial European Americans, he said, was the religious dissent derived or transported from European Lutheran, Calvinist, or Old English movements. In prerevolutionary America, dissenting colonists suffered the oppressive burden of new institutional forms: the Congregational Standing Order in New England, the Presbyterian and Lutheran creeds and practices in the middle colonies, and the Established Order in the South. The most severely persecuted of the European sects—the Baptists, Jackson thought—headed first to New Jersey and Pennsylvania, where they were freer (Jackson 1939, 82).

Relentless in spirit, dissenters found new voices for their cause: the Great Awakenings of the eighteenth century (Calvinist theology) and nineteenth century (Arminian theology). In the nineteenth-century Upland South, initially settled by religious people of a "dissentist mind," conditions of "pioneering storm and stress" prevailed (1943, 284–85). "It was," Jackson said, "precisely those who had refused to follow the straight path of denominational tradition who were the real takers-over of a live personal faith, livers of a vigorous personal Christianity, real mass-insisters that the term 'religious freedom' should mean just what it said" (Jackson 1941, 36).

The camp meeting was the "high point in this trend," when "noninstitutional religious excitement was at its highest." It was "essentially a cross section of the whole religious flux, because it was totally free—free from all political, denominational, economic and social control, direct or indirect" (Jackson 1941, 37). Just as European dissenters first established themselves in freer areas, African Americans found the Upland South the most hospitable environment for their Christianity. Consequently, the camp meeting fostered an atmosphere of minimal racial prejudice that led from both African and European roots to the innovative revival spiritual song form (Jackson 1943, 284–85).

Because their compilers appealed to the musical tastes of this diverse population, nineteenth-century southern tunebooks are virtual catalogs of musical and religious dissent, ultimately surviving into the twentieth century among stubborn antimodernists. "Spiritual folk-song," as Jackson put it, "is down but not out." It survives because its singers "are beyond the reach of the enemy." Its preeminent cultural sites of survival, Jackson said, "are the completely satisfied and unambitious Primitive Baptists, the legions who have the time of their lives at the Southern 'old-timey' all-day singings, and those Negro congregations who have not yet allowed these songs to be cultured out of them" (Jackson 1939, 83).

To understand the slender theoretical channel Jackson navigated, consider some efforts to promote folksong that were undertaken by some of his contemporaries. Most significant at that date was the recent blossoming of a movement of grassroots labor activism and leftist political theory, sometimes united with World War II anti-interventionist interests (Denisoff 1971, 61–98). Without allying himself with this movement, without explicitly fostering political dissent, Jackson could instead identify himself with religious dissent, proclaiming "Dissent thrives on institutional oppression" (1943, 9) as a fundamental axiom of American vernacular culture. The struggle of religious dissenters corresponded to the struggle of eighteenth-century German nationalists. European Americans who suffered religious persecution and African Americans subjected to slavery found each other in the liberating atmosphere of the camp meeting.

Identifying this key link between observed folksong and revived folksong meant that he could promote folksong and support the fact of vernacular dissent without actually supporting the particular causes in question. Why else would his theory and practice seem so at odds? Why else would he explain vernacular singing in terms of religious dissent and then, in practice, "bracket" the experience of religious dissent by redefining it as folksong? Using folksong, Jackson had in mind to remanufacture "pioneering storm and stress"—surely replicating the eighteenth-century German Sturm und Drang (storm and stress) movement—a nationalism based on vernacular culture and sentiment. Unlike the folksong of the American Left, Jackson's vision of folksong was not one given in service of an adopted cause. Rather, it was one of historical recovery—the recovery of the "nine-tenths of life" that historians had obscured through aristocratic selection.

POSTLUDE: "ON KNOWING OURSELVES FIRST"

Sing preferably your own songs, brother. Live your own song life and be proud of it. Don't let the I-don't-know-a-thing-about-music inferiority complex trouble you. Don't let the radio flood of vocal contortionists beat you down. If you are mature, re-learn and re-sing the songs of your youth. If your youth was folk-tonally barren, go to the collections. If you are still young, all the better. All the easier to gain these spiritual riches without price.

GEORGE PULLEN JACKSON, "Sing, Brothers, Sing!" (1945)

If the neophyte chooses a *Sacred Harp* singing for his initial attendance, he will take a seat on one side—either the bass, tenor (melody), "tribble," or alto side—of the hollow square of singers. A man may sing any part he chooses. A woman may feel at home vocally anywhere but among the basses. Someone chosen by the chairman rises, stands in the center, calls out a page number, "tones" its song and leads it by hand movements. Then two more songs in sprightly succession, the three constituting the one leader's "lesson" before giving way to another leader. This goes on till noon when the neophyte will be invited to join the throng of hungry singers in the old-traditional dinner-on-the-grounds. The afternoon is spent the same way. The really *big* singings are often three-day affairs, beginning on a Friday and closing at four on Sunday afternoon. The chairman will never be so rude as to fail to invite the neophyte to lead a lesson. Some accept. Some make a fairly good job of reading the strange looking page of music. But whatever his success, the skilled singers will be endlessly considerate of the neophyte's shortcomings.

GEORGE PULLEN JACKSON,
"Wanted: An American Hans Sachs" (1947)

As shape note singing traditions reentered American popular and media culture in the twentieth century, they did so primarily as folksong. Most often they appeared ironically, as a holdover from "olden days"—as an object of modernist fascination and thus also as an affirmation of modernist preeminence. The emergence of written accounts of singing was guided by rhetorical devices and strategies developed or applied by Carl Carmer and George Pullen Jackson and amplified by many others after them. Throughout this period, singing traditions appeared as cultural objects, existing as representations in historical scholarship, regional writing, recordings, and public performances.

The construction of antiquity as the antithesis of progress actually fueled the symbolic engines of modernism, however. Ultimately working against this modernist burden, however, George Pullen Jackson considered the diminishing prominence of singing traditions as unnatural and sought viable historical accounts for their shifting institutional foundation. Almost inevitably, this strategy led him—most prominently in his historical writings—to make connections between his own past and the roots of the traditions he described. In turn, these historical connections disrupted the fundamental axiom of self and other on which modernist writing so crucially depended. For example, in *White Spirituals,* he had cataloged a list of "exhibits" that demonstrated that many of the most illustrious southern musicians were indebted to native shape note traditions, at a crucial time when many were becoming institutionally separated from that history (Jackson 1933, 429–33).

Indeed, as he searched for answers over the course of his career, he would increasingly look inward. In his presidential address to the South Atlantic Modern Language Association in 1950, Jackson admonished those who would take up the fight for broad cultural wisdom that they must "know themselves first" (Jackson 1950, 4). He told how the Ana-baptist roots of his own Baptist church were until recently a heritage hidden from him, even in the region of the Baptists' greatest world-concentration. This, he said, was his "former self," systematically occluded because it was a heritage the forward-thinking modern church considered uncultured. This circumstance stood in contrast, for example, to Ireland, a nation where modernism had not separated the people from their past as it had in America. To be "cultured" for the Irish meant to be deeply knowledgeable about one's own people, one's former self.

Surely Jackson's involvement with singing traditions had initiated and nourished this inward searching. Where others wrote and ran, Jackson maintained a lifelong affiliation with traditional singing. Objective writing could never completely overtake subjective experience. He also struggled to find for native music traditions a meaningful participation in public culture and public history. He was indignant, for example, when a state supervisor of music in the schools overruled conference planners' invitation for him to present religious folksongs at a southern music teachers conference because the supervisor considered the material "crude, commonplace" (Jackson 1945e, 2).[25]

Jackson considered the schools the weakest link in the chain of actively experienced public history. He knew that the schools' "lyric-musical center of gravity" lay far from the culture of the community or region. Instead, students were "fed on a song fare concocted by professional educationists elsewhere and made largely of ingredients they have found in their own standardized and standardizing minds and in the folk traditions of a dozen *other* lands and *their* regions" (Jackson 1950, 5). Yet, precisely because of this, he sometimes harbored doubts that they could adequately teach the complexities of folk tradition. So there were other avenues to public awareness—folk festivals, the Old Harp Singers, for example.

As vigorously as he championed the shape note cause, however, he almost always did so by way of mediating institutions. But in one postwar article, he concluded that words were "notably inadequate" in conveying singing; instead, "One must sit in on singings and *sing!*" (Jackson 1947, 23). In contrast, American concert attendance, Jackson said, had become a "luxury-article of commerce." The orchestral concert, he said, is "a completely non-social [aesthetic experience]; whereas there is a convivial joy unbound in being one of a hundred peers in a country singing" (Jackson 1947, 25).

This was a wholesale endorsement of singing institutions, unprecedented in outsider writing on the subject. An even more extraordinary endorsement was a portion of a pamphlet on the history of *The Sacred Harp,* a section on "Some Hearers Don't Like It: Why?" Jackson sympathized with "casual hearers" of Sacred Harp who were beguiled into disapproving "snap judgements" by the modernist cultural atmosphere. In defending the tradition, however, Jackson turned to a voice not his own—that of veteran singer Tom Denson:

> "If some of you don't like this music," he told [a singing school class] plainly, "all I've got to say to you is you'd better get out. If you stay here it's going to get a-hold of you and you *can't* get away." (Jackson 1944a, xvii)

It was not merely that Sacred Harp was speaking, through Tom Denson, for itself—this was not so unusual. What was notable was that Denson was given the floor to speak directly to "casual hearers" at a point where Jackson usually had a great deal to say.

Unlike Jackson's customary plea, Denson's confident invitation had few of the trappings of folksong revival discourse. There was no call for a national music, no origin theory, no appeal to an agrarian past, no tragic social history, but in their place was a profound sense of native social theory—of the institutional advantages Sacred Harp enjoyed over other musical forms. In fact, this sensitivity to social theory and American musical taxonomy was borne by Sacred Harp's own traditional writers even during the nineteenth century. These writing traditions paralleled the emergence of culture writing, providing rhetorical distance from the modernist enterprise. In time, some of Jackson's ideas and writing would be integrated into traditional discourse. All of this would constitute a distinct cultural theory. This will be the subject of the next chapter.

Chapter 3

WRITING TRADITIONS OF
THE SACRED HARP

It has been predicted that this type of singing will disappear
entirely within the next decade, a victim of its failure to keep
abreast with modern musical tastes.

> KATHRYN WINDHAM, "Alabama's Disappearing Singers,"
> *Birmingham News Monthly Magazine*, 10 January 1954

We disagree with the prediction that Sacred Harp music is fast
disappearing. If you could go with me any Sunday during the
year, I would show you a group of singers, some of whom have
traveled great distances to enjoy an all-day singing.

. . . I have minutes on hand now listing 237 annual singings
and conventions during 1954 in Alabama and Tennessee alone,
and I have no record at present of the singings which will be
held in Georgia, Florida, Mississippi, and other states.

> J. W. BASSETT, "Voice of the People" (letter to the editor),
> *Birmingham News*, 7 February 1954

There is a disconcerting incongruity in the manner by which American
folksong was defined through its tragic struggle against modernity, and
then so serendipitously discovered, again and again, in such vivid spirit
and vitality. We have seen how the institutional foundation on which Sacred Harp tradition was built so completely eluded culture writers. Let us
then take J. W. Bassett's suggestion and look instead to the corpus of what
might be called "native writing"—work that, by some traditional sanction, is singularly designed to accommodate and appeal to the writing

world of the singing tradition. This does not imply an atmosphere of consensus, nor does it indicate "official discourse." But, for reasons that should be obvious in each instance, it does imply a measure of local control and local endorsement—the kind of documents a singer might claim to have "on hand." It implies written forms that emerge within a writing world and a singing world that are largely coterminous. It implies a body of writing where some of the central themes of the singing tradition have been hammered out.

Specifically, I will look at five written forms and works prominent during various periods with an eye to the way they have organized the world around Sacred Harp—culturally, theologically, and socially. The first stop is B. F. White's nineteenth-century Hamilton, Georgia, newspaper, the *Organ,* in which he published songs, minutes of singing conventions, musical debates, letters from singers, and advertisements for books along with other material he considered newsworthy. Second, I will examine two turn-of-the-century works associated with J. S. James (1849–1930): first, his extraordinary *Brief History of the Sacred Harp* (1904), in which he devised a native historical discourse just as Sacred Harp was beginning to be treated as a historical object, and second, his innovations in the *Original Sacred Harp* (1911), which departed in significant ways from the models set by preceding and concurrent editions of this and other tunebooks. Third, I turn to Earl Thurman's *Chattahoochee Musical Convention, 1852–1952,* a midcentury assessment of changes in the singing tradition. Fourth, I will look at the short essays of Ruth Denson Edwards, who in the 1970s assimilated elements of ethnography into traditional documentary style. Last, I will examine the "minutes," the nineteenth-century form of Sacred Harp documentary writing that has maintained its status over the years as the official record of singing events.

In all of these, a theme persists: a tension between written forms and the social and cultural world they inhabit. Sometimes a sense of urgency prevails, deflecting controversy away from important institutions. At other times, as with the mechanical style of the "minutes," the written word seems impervious to any extravagance at all, reducing singing performances to a discrete numerical unit. Then again, in the case of Earl Thurman and Ruth Denson Edwards, there is a deliberate effort to map out an acceptable style that directly engages broader musical taxonomy. All of these forms, all of these voices, have been directly or indirectly attentive to the role that the folksong concept has played in Sacred Harp singing. If we mean to examine the "Sacred Harp revival," it is essential to look to these voices—preeminently and far more attentively than to the folksong revival itself—to understand that movement.

"A CAUSE SO GRAND AND SO NOBLE":
B. F. WHITE AND THE *ORGAN*

> In short, science itself is but a knowledge of that which before existed; language was certainly in existence before a grammar, calculation before arithmetic, and many songs had already been sung to God before the science was invented or the "Sacred Harp" blessed our people.
>
> Address by the Rev. Jeremiah Clarke, Southwestern Musical Convention, 8 December 1854, Cedar Creek Church, Marian County, Georgia, Printed in the *Organ,* 25 April 1855

"Neutral in Politics and Religion," the masthead proclaimed—"devoted to Art, Science, Education, Morality, and the Advancement of Sacred Music." Founded in 1852 in Hamilton, Georgia, the *Organ* was genuinely a newspaper, the first in sparsely populated Harris County and the only county paper during its run.[1] B. F. White, who compiled the first edition of *The Sacred Harp,* was, in fact, not described as the *Organ*'s editor but as its "superintendent," his voice a designated extension of the Southern Musical Convention. Why adopt a form widely understood as designed for polemics—the nineteenth-century Georgia newspaper—and then proclaim it "neutral in politics and religion?"

At one point (justifying his attack of a "defective" music system), White described his obligation to readers in this way:

> We were appointed Superintendent of the *Organ* as a musical sheet, for the purpose of advancing the science of Music and protecting the system as we think it should exist—and detecting all systems and customs which are found in counteraction. (2 February 1856)

Until March 1855, a separate editor, G. W. Wilkinson, was listed inside the paper with the terms of subscription, just below the inscription "published by authority of the Southern Musical Convention." B. F. White was named in the masthead. "Neutrality," it seems, was meant to cover a specific set of issues in which White took no part. It certainly did not apply to music.

Indeed, surviving editions of the paper (1855–57) indicate that its "neutrality" implied a complex strategy of voicing designed in part to provide a context for debate on musical issues, while insulating that debate from the distractions of a divisive and polemical world. It suggests an awareness of the struggles of book compilers elsewhere in the country and—through the Southern Musical Convention—an understanding of the "Sacred Harp family" that later singers would come to love.

So deliberate was the *Organ*'s pledge of neutrality that it seems imperative to examine what in "religion and politics" its editors meant to avoid. This is important, of course, not only because of potential links to musical taxonomy and folksong, but also in the particular way Sacred Harp came to be conceived as apolitical. What, we can initially ask, might readers have expected from Georgia journalism of this period? What possible advantage could B. F. White have seen in invoking and then explicitly denying its polemical character?

We can be certain that Georgia journalism of this period provided an imposing backdrop. During the 1850s the number of newspapers and periodicals in Georgia grew from 51 to 105, echoing a nationwide trend that was a consequence of growing concern over national affairs, the development of the railroads, a period of relative prosperity, and the settlement of the West (Brantley 1929, 8; Coulter 1960, 301). According to one description:

Most Georgia newspapers were county weeklies, but the most influential journals were dailies published in the leading towns and cities. They were saturated with profitable advertisements and commercial announcements, including rewards for the capture of runaway slaves, and almost all were staunchly committed to some political faction. But even the most politicized papers with the heaviest concentration on legislative and congressional activities found space for a wide variety of other material: letters to the editor, poems and other literary efforts, local news and gossip, jabs at rival journalists, select and sometimes erratic coverage of foreign and national events often taken directly from other papers, and just about anything else an individualistic editor might choose to include except abolition writings. (Boney 1977, 180–81)

Like the *Organ*, many were owned, edited, and published by a single individual—so-called personal journalism. Also, many papers routinely covered public meetings because it was there that editors could collect for subscriptions (Brantley 1929, 10). Unlike the *Organ*, however, autonomy ordinarily provided editors the freedom of unrestrained polemicism; indeed, most papers were linked ideologically to a political party or some divisive issue. In some communities, rival papers "kept up a running controversy that in serious times assumed a very bitter tone." Even the best ones indulged in "lurid rhetoric and flowing phrase" (Shryock 1926, 119). In sparsely settled Harris County, without a competitor nearby, the *Organ* was well positioned to rise above the fray, avoiding undesirable polemicism that might spill over into the Southern Musical Convention.

Aside from its "neutrality" and attention to music, the *Organ* was not unusual. Subscribers and advertisers were frequently admonished to pay their bills. Advertising usually filled most of one of four to eight pages, and included a wide variety of items. Magazine subscriptions for *Peterson's Ladies National Magazine* or *T. S. Arthur's Home Magazine* proclaimed their products the cheapest in the world, with the best steel engravings and the most "thrilling" stories. *Scientific American* offered prizes to its most successful distributors. Schools and academies—even Hamilton High School—announced that they were taking students. Estate sales were announced. "Groceries! Groceries!" enticed readers with exotic new products, sometimes listed using clever typesetting. Patent medicines were perhaps the most aggressively pitched products; "Great Southern Remedy—Jacob's Cordial" appeared frequently.

Considerable space was devoted to articles on contemporary topics. Oddly enough, coverage of state and regional events was not always extensive. More space was given to short expositions or reports on moral subjects (e.g., character, hypocrisy, temperance) and to a panoply of world and national events. Many items describing world events were taken from other papers or were "telegraph bulletins" (Brantley 1929, 130). Longer stories ran on the first or second page; shorter pieces were included under "General Intelligence" on following pages. In this latter section, for example, an article from the *New York Times* reported that slave trade was being carried on in Cuba (6 September 1854). From the *London Times* was quoted a description of the Cossacks in battle (28 February 1855). A letter from Philadelphia cited a German newspaper there that reported that a secret society called the "Know Somethings" was attracting numerous followers (6 September 1854). There was even a report from Arvine's *Cyclopedia of Anecdotes* on Sir William Jones's knowledge of twenty-eight different languages (28 February 1855).

Local news most often consisted of announcements. The *Organ* was authorized to run legal advertising, for example, mortgage foreclosures or notices to debtors and creditors. One issue (28 February 1855) included an announcement of a public meeting at the Hamilton Court House on the subject of a proposed railroad, a report of a railroad meeting in Griffin, a brief report on the Washington's Birthday celebration in Columbus, and a report from the *Macon Journal and Messenger* of a suspicious individual passing off counterfeit bills to unwary citizens. The *Organ* gave enthusiastic support to the railroad project, perhaps at the behest of the "Many Citizens" whose collective signature appeared with the announcement of the Hamilton meeting.

The *Organ* gave far less explicit (though perhaps no less enthusiastic) support to the swelling tide of sentiment for secession. Attitudes about slavery varied widely in Georgia in the 1850s, with most support in areas where the soil supported a plantation economy. Printed verbatim on the third page of an 1855 issue of the *Organ* was a secession resolution adopted at a meeting in Columbus, Georgia, and later endorsed by "a very large and respectable portion of the citizens of Harris county" (6 June 1855). Following this was a similar resolution from a Muscogee, Georgia, meeting, including the names of committee members who drafted it, and then a poem from the *Columbus Enquirer*, "The Southern Union," that the *Enquirer* editor called "the honest expressions of a true Southern heart." If the *Organ* took an official stand on an inflammatory issue—as was the case here—it was careful to establish its readers' prior endorsement.

Throughout the run of the *Organ* one could find, interlaced with the events of the world, its trademark feature: a preeminent concern with sacred music. Much of this was the routine business of local and regional singing events and of the Southern Musical Convention. For example, a notice announcing the arrival of a shipment of *Sacred Harp* books might have been placed with this advertising:

> *Sacred Harps.* LATEST EDITION. Just received, a lot of *Sacred Harps,* which will be sold wholesale and retail, for cash or *approved* paper. B. F. White, Organ Office, Hamilton, Ga., Aug. 2d. (15 February 1854)

On the front page, sometimes under the heading "Communications," the complete minutes of a singing or convention were printed (see appendix 1). Or, always just under the masthead, new compositions appeared, arranged in parts for singing and printed in shape notes just as they appeared in *The Sacred Harp.*

But not all was routine. There were ongoing discussions of music theory and pedagogy, suggesting a general populace far better schooled in music than nowadays. So great was the social import of these musical discussions that sometimes writers would submit letters anonymously or under pseudonyms, probably to avoid being associated with a particular stance on some issue. One regular contributor, from Hogansville (thirty miles north of Hamilton), adopted the pseudonym "Georgia Boy." So serious were these discussions that one writer told of some unnamed music teacher who "labored arduously under a false system" and, upon having his errors exposed, "retired and committed suicide by shooting himself through the head" (2 February 1856).

Letters would also come from distant communities, suggesting that the sphere of influence of the *Organ* extended beyond B. F. White's colleagues and the Southern Musical Association. Overall, musical writing in the *Organ* sought to *incorporate* musical controversy in its rhetorical compass, whereas articles on other events were more inclined to report on matters whose import remained outside the scope of the paper's concerns. This relationship between musical and other news was reflected in the contrasting roles of "superintendent" B. F. White and "editor" G. W. Wilkinson. Musical correspondence meant as doctrinal commentary was addressed to "Mr. Superintendent," "Dear Major" (from White's acquaintances), or "Brother White," or was addressed directly to writers of previous letters, for example, "Friend Georgia Boy." Other business was addressed "Dear Editor."

When White sought to present a particular view of an issue as standard, he would sometimes do so in the guise of pedagogical dialogue. He might even assume a kind of paternal role, such as in "Answers to Little Susa's Questions" (17 May 1854), giving the impression that there were simple answers to controversial questions. In the following excerpt White established that sharps and flats were invented by Guido long ago to avoid moving the clefs, and then continued:

Q. Has there ever existed any other keys besides the two present keys, namely the major and the minor?

A. Not primarily; there were the variety of substitutes, and bore the name of Keys, without attaching the names of major or minor to them, and were only subservient to a kind of artificial taste, without any substantial value, and were of but short duration.

Q. What is Sacred Music?

A. Sacred music is of that quality of composition which is calculated to produce a sacred effect, in strict accordance with the true principles of religious devotion.

In a similar lesson, "Answers to Mr. Sikes," White taught that the interval sounded a perfect fifth above the tonic was more basic than other fifths, that likewise the fourth below was more basic than the fourth above the tonic, that the location of the leading tone (mi) was different in the major and minor scales, and thus the seventh in minor music was not a leading tone (25 April 1855).

Apparently Little Susa was not the only intended recipient of this lesson. Preceding her "lesson" was the regular column, "Musical," in which B. F.

White, writing on behalf of the Southern Musical Convention (the articles were signed "Sup."), would address musical issues of general concern. In this installment, White had urged that all music be "systematically composed" on "one fundamental principle"—the tonic note as the foundation, "just as though the notes were to be called by a given name to express their proper position in intonation." White anticipated opposition to this and was concerned enough to call for debate: "Let us hear from the opposer, and we will go into the investigation at length."

Indeed, there were apparently music teachers in his sphere of influence who were advocating alternatives to the diatonic scale. Those who had confused Little Susa were advocating more than two (major and minor) keys. Some taught that no semitones (and thus only one key) existed, with no distinction between major and minor scales ("Musical," 28 February 1855). Likewise, in another letter, the anonymous "Georgia Boy" returned to the subject of Mr. Sikes's lessons because some teachers were insisting that the seventh be raised in the minor scale. As he put it, "Sharping the seventh sound of the minor scale is an artificial composition" (2 February 1856).

The larger import of such challenges, of course, was to disturb the order of the Southern Musical Convention. "A spirit is abroad in the land," as White described it, "to contend against a custom and system of music which has been in use, unmolested, for one hundred years or more; as new musicians spring up, new ideas spring up with them" ("Musical," 28 February 1855). In this instance White took care not to mention the names of the "new musicians," but elsewhere this was not the case. On several occasions he and other writers took on as adversaries Isaac Holcombe, Lowell Mason, Thomas Hastings, and Isaac Baker Woodbury, who advocated European principles in the name of "scientific" music.[2] These men, particularly Holcombe, were cited on several occasions as representing the opponents of the old "custom and system of music."

It is worth considering that in the "spirit abroad in the land" White was referring, by clever indirection, to something much closer. Throughout the early years of the Southern Musical Convention, from 1845 through 1867, B. F. White was the predominant influence. He was "elected" president of the convention for all but two meetings of that period. In 1868, according to Joe S. James, "a very serious split occurred in the convention," in which Professor E. T. Pound was elected president after contending for the use of other books besides *The Sacred Harp,* some of them compiled by Pound and printed in round or seven-shape notes (James 1904, 59).[3] Since he served on the revision committee for the 1859 *Sacred Harp,* Pound himself probably would not have opposed the old system as early as 1855. But others—those who would have comprised the majority who had elected him—may by this time have already been experimenting with gospel music, seven-shape books, and "modernized" musical styles. It would not have been unusual for White to have addressed indirectly those he opposed but did not want to offend.

Whatever the case, the only names White associated with the contending spirit were northern writers. Once, in his regular column in the *Organ,* White had even analyzed a composition by Holcombe, pointing out some "errors."[4] Holcombe defended his composition in a letter printed in the paper, asserting an alliance with Woodbury, Hastings, and Mason. In his reply, on the subject of closing a piece of music at a place not at the end of a measure, White was unimpressed:

> If those distinguished musicians referred to in the article, intended such to be perpetuated as a rule, why have they not given us a *rule* for them? Because Messrs. Woodbury, Hastings, Mason and others, who are distinguished musical writers, introduce a custom without any rule for it, is no logical reason why it is correct. . . . We are still of the same opinion, that he [Holcombe] *must* be young in the cause of Composition. (1 August 1855)

White questioned the principle, allowed Holcombe's alliance with "distinguished musical writers" to go unchallenged, but then, on the principles being advanced, addressed all of them.

Undaunted, Holcombe and Woodbury apparently contributed their opinions again the next year in favor of the raised seventh (minor scale, as leading tone) and fifth (major scale, used as modulation). This time, the anonymous "Georgia Boy" took up the defense, labeling as "artificial" the accidentals in "Greenwich" (*Sacred Harp,* 183, raised seventh in the alto part, seventh measure) and "Phoebus" (173, raised seventh in the alto part, eighth measure). He also took issue with the implications of Holcombe's reference to "Windham" (38), "as it is written," as a model scientific composition:

> Yes, sir, we understand the above connection.—You aimed a blow at the standard works of this country. I mean works written by men of the South, and adopted by the Southern people. I find that those standard works that you have reference to do not seem to suit the taste and wishes of our Southern people. They are somewhat like yourself—rather hard to be understood. (2 February 1856)

I presume that the writer was referring to the practice of overriding musical notation (such as raised sevenths) in traditional performance, and was defending the practice on the basis of a regional consciousness.

Lest this practice be attributed too much to blind adherence to "tradition," it needs to be emphasized that nineteenth-century singers knew well the basic physical properties of musical sound and the function of notation. They believed that the diatonic scale was "natural," that there were two modes (major and minor), and that the use of accidentals was artificial. They knew the location of various intervals: where the semitones appeared, where various fourths and fifths appeared, and which of these were most pleasing to hear. Moreover, they could relate these principles to the physical properties of sound: in September 1855, Columbus Howard read a circular before the Southern Musical Convention that demonstrated the mathematics of musical intervals by string-length experiments.

On the whole, such tonal principles were systematically inclined to favor the old melodies and arrangements that were already in *The Sacred Harp.* They also served to temper modernizing tendencies, facilitated by the system of written music, that contradicted the musical idiom of unwritten folksong. Furthermore, the sometimes contentious spirit with which these principles were debated in the *Organ,* in contrast to their perfunctory treatment in the "Rudiments of Music" section of various editions of *The Sacred Harp,* indicate that they were understood by leaders as having the moral dimensions associated with the "science of praise."

When one compares this dispute with the one reported in the *Cincinnati Journal* two decades previously, it seems the "Better Music Boosters" had little chance of success in Harris County. Yet writings in the *Organ* do not indicate that this was due to any organic link between singing and rural life. What insulated western Georgia from the effects of musical reform was that there were no elite institutions with eastern connections that might exert influence on musical practice, as there were in Cincinnati. Of course, B. F. White edited the only local newspaper and for a time served as mayor of Hamilton. And while he seems to have offered readers a more genuine dialogue than did the *Cincinnati Journal,* any challenges to locally accepted musical practice would not have been entertained without vehement rebuttal. In the *Organ,* dissent ultimately empowered local tradition by providing a meaningful venue for singers to articulate their stance on reform. And so many did: musical argument advanced by singers in the *Organ* had more the character of a popular movement—with letters, short articles, and texts of speeches—than it did the reasoned and single-authored exposition and the contrived dialogue in the *Journal.*

Consequently, *Organ* readers were exposed to a thorough understanding of the social and religious dimensions of their singing institutions. Already in the 1850s, Sacred Harp musical practice was being constructed on a foundation of deeply experienced fellowship and on the quality of praise that singing could invoke. The Reverend Jeremiah Clarke's anniversary address before the Southern Musical Convention explored the religious obligation to learn to praise God by singing, based on the premise that singing is *natural* (25 April 1855). In another discourse, "Georgia Boy" echoed this view—that singing is a gift or faculty that God has bestowed upon mankind with an obligation to improve (3 May 1854). And G. H. Perdue, after recognizing the abundance of song in nature, characterized in this way mankind's solemn obligation to sing:

Surely man will not degrade himself below the insects and birds, in thus letting one of this noblest faculties lie dormant. To improve this faculty is a duty we owe to God and ourselves. It is a duty we owe to our Maker, for it is clearly taught in the Bible that music should be a part of worship. . . . How sad a spectacle, and how discouraging to a Minister, to enter a Church in which the congregation can hardly make music of even the oldest tunes. Verily, one would be ready to exclaim, that such a community has come short of its glorious privileges in this land of freedom, and age of improvement. (31 October 1855)

Because singing derived its status as a fundamental form of worship directly from Scripture, it could be presumed to fall within the concerns of all churches.

But "improvement" was also the ablest weapon of reformers. Had Perdue appropriated the idea as a means to preserve the old "custom and system of music?" Indeed, what truly distinguished southern practice was the specific way that singers understood "improvement." In an address to the Southern Musical Convention in 1854, the Reverend Jeremiah Clarke explained that the *talent* by which one might ordinarily be thought to excel in singing is useless unless accompanied by dignity of character. Furthermore, he said:

> We do not mean by dignity of character, that kind of *democratical aristocracy* which exalts one above his fellow creatures, but that principle which makes one bend, or aspire to every thing [that is] honorable, yet too high-minded to [entertain] vice, or condescend to a mean action. (25 April 1855)

Christ, who "took upon himself the form of a servant" (Phil. 2:7), exemplified this virtue, so Clarke called upon mortals to dwell on Christ's suffering as a means to acquire this spiritual attitude.

One of the surest ways to demonstrate or assume this attitude was to attend singings. "Brethren! Where are you?" several singers wrote urgently at one point (17 May 1854). They were somewhat content with the contingent of Alabama singers at their west Georgia singing, but "desired it to be much larger." They directed a few mild barbs at those music teachers who might think so highly of their talents that they only attend singings if engaged for a fee. Instead, teachers should "have the glory of God before your eyes," the writers urged, "as well as the expectation of remuneration for your services."

In another letter, noted Sacred Harp composer H. S. Rees urged his "brethren and sisters of the musical fraternity" to pay their subscriptions. He went on to warn:

The cause of music is badly behind in this part of our country. We have haters of the cause even in our delightful settlement, and some of the woeful sounds are heard in God's sanctuary. I sometimes think that hog-grunting and ass-bellowing is as good music as some I hear offered up by human beings to their Great Benefactor.

Elsewhere, Rosetta H. reminisced about the days when "we were all together as a social band, singing Psalms and praises to the almighty King," and she identified by initials or name quite a few prominent singers she had not recently seen (14 February 1855). "Boys this is not the way to do business," she proclaimed, "be up and doing all the while, for your stay is but short at best." She characterized the obligation to attend as follows: "There is a few of the boys yet that have not faltered, but are still in the field and with 'Helmet, sword, and shield,' laying most all opposition to Sacred music."

Here, as they fended off unwanted pedagogical innovations, White and other *Organ* writers were forging the idea of a transcendent "custom and system of music," based on a delicate hierarchy of theology, science, and aesthetics, and originating in a remote past too pure and too primitive for the vagaries of innovation. The *Organ* provided Sacred Harp singers a powerful means not merely to construct the tradition's own boundaries, but to devise a rhetoric that could subordinate those issues that threatened their customary way of singing to one preeminent concern—singing together in praise of the Creator.

Without assigning too much credit to the brief run of the *Organ,* it is nonetheless true that some of the notions of the singing tradition that were developed in that venue would have been difficult to convey outside the print medium. Furthermore, because this was done in the context of a public newspaper, the debates had—or at least had the appearance of—widespread public significance. Although it seems almost self-evident, we can better sense the significance of presenting singing in a newspaper by considering some of the alternatives. The *Organ* was not a religious or topical tract, nor was it a musical magazine, even though there were numerous available prototypes for these formats. Thus Sacred Harp singings and other musical issues were given preeminent attention in the context of the events of the world. These musical matters were fundamental dramas of everyday life around which readers organized their values. As was the case with the *Cincinnati Journal,* musical practices were advanced not only on theological principles but also on the basis of secular morality.

Because the *Organ* was a newspaper, it provided singers a means to circulate ideas among a diverse population, establishing sacred music as a form of praise so primitive that it preceded and transcended the formation of religious dogma. Their cause was not outside the church but prior to it. "Show me a church without music," one supporter wrote (5 July 1856), "and I will show you one that is cold and in the back ground, and has but very little religion." Writers in the *Organ* could seek consensus in a divisive world because the ideas around which they rallied were so fundamental and so simple. Sacred music, as G. H. Perdue put it, addressing the Southern Musical Convention in 1855, was so much a "balm for every wound" that it could turn churches into places "where all shall delight to go" (31 October 1855). Its "happy effects" are so numerous, he concluded, "let us no longer 'hang our harps upon the willow,' or cease our co-operation in a cause so grand and noble."

"SEEKING THE OLD PATHS": JOE S. JAMES'S THEOLOGICAL HISTORY

> To first make a few observations on the subject of music, the greatest art and science which has attracted the attention of mankind since the advent of the human family into the world. God Himself, in the beginning, set all things to music, even before man was made and it has continued from that time up to the present, and will continue throughout eternity.
>
> J. S. JAMES, *The History of the Sacred Harp* (1904)

By the end of the nineteenth century, the *Organ* had long since ended its brief ascendancy and, with it, the most salient means of struggle against "systems and customs which are found in counteraction." But White must have envisioned an equally contentious future when, in the preface to the 1869 edition of *The Sacred Harp,* he bequeathed to his followers Sacred Harp's most influential epithet:

The scheme which our prolonged and laborious examination has inclined us to prefer to all others has had the sanction of the musical world for more than four hundred years; and we scarcely think that we can do better than abide by the advice—"Ask for the old paths, and walk therein."

Although White was commenting here specifically on the rise of seven-shape notation (see Cobb 1978, 89), his "old paths" have served a variety of conservative causes.

Of all those at the turn of the century who sought to articulate the sentiments of the "old paths," Joe S. James seems to have best succeeded. The 1911 James Revision, produced by the committee he chaired, was adopted in most of the old singing areas until succeeded in 1933 by the Denson Revision. According to most accounts (e.g., Cobb 1978, 95), the success of the book was most indebted to James's wholesale loyalty to the musical content and style of the nineteenth-century editions. But James introduced several innovations that actually seemed to amplify his stance against modernization. In this section, I want to examine his unique appeals to history and theology both in his 1911 revision and in his 1904 *Brief History of the Sacred Harp*. Surely, these rhetorical innovations would have been ineffective without his allegiance to the popular old songs and to traditional rules of composition and arrangement. But in concert with this musical base, James's rhetorical strategies wedged the Sacred Harp tradition firmly into its own self-described antimodernist niche.

J. S. James's Brief History of the Sacred Harp *(1904)*

When J. S. James undertook to "give some insight to the character, standing and unselfish purpose of the principal author, promoters and composers of the music contained in the Sacred Harp" (James 1904, 3), he had in mind a particular audience and a particular deficiency in historical consciousness.[5] After a period of decline in the late nineteenth century, *The Sacred Harp* was undergoing a "rapidly increasing revival use . . . in many sections of the country" (4). Furthermore, the Cooper Revision of *The Sacred Harp* had been published in 1902: even though it staked its own claim to B. F. White's "old paths," most of its compilers were not White's students. A "brief history" could only enhance the esteem of the White lineage for the new converts, formulating a past to which the present would be seen as indebted.

Of James himself, too little is known, certainly less than his contributions to the Sacred Harp tradition would warrant.[6] He was an attorney—raised in a musical family, self-educated, from Douglasville, Georgia—whose father was a friend of B. F. White. At age twenty-one he was made justice of the peace; by thirty-six, when he was elected mayor of Douglasville, he had already served three terms in the state legislature. Other notable accomplishments include campaign orator and elector at the 1892 Democratic National Convention for Grover Cleveland, founder of the Atlanta Telephone Company in 1895, and founder and editor of the Douglasville, Georgia, newspaper, *New South*. It is ironic, as will become apparent, that nothing in his illustrious biography would have predisposed him to antimodernism.

From his own account, the *Brief History* "entailed a great deal of hard labor" owing to his reliance on oral data (3). For this, moreover, James was apologetic, admitting to defects and imperfections of memory. Oddly enough, James, a lawyer, neglected legal documents. For these imperfections, James's critics have not relented. Jackson wrote that the work is "poorly organized, its language is hard to understand, and in the few instances where I have been able to check up on its data, I have found a quite considerable number of errors" (Jackson 1933, 82).

Anticipating this, James nonetheless felt a great urgency in publishing the book—"an abiding faith," he called it, "that this effort, on our part, will be of service to many people and that it *does justice to the memory* of those who have long since died" (4, emphasis mine). If he was deficient in supplying the facts, James nonetheless defined the historical agenda *in terms of memory,* particularly of that constellation of devoted singers whose contributions to the tradition would otherwise erode with the passing of time. When we observe today the extraordinary role that active memory plays in the continuity of the singing tradition, we can better assess the significance of James's work. And when we observe the esteem that oral history has earned, we can appreciate James's perseverance under hostile conditions.

This said, one notes immediately that James felt obliged to frame the book in terms that extended far beyond the historical scope even of "those who have long since died" (see appendix 2). After all, James wrote, music was "the greatest art and science which has attracted the attention of mankind since the advent of the human family into the world" (5). James continued, echoing the primitive theological grounding that writers had articulated in the *Organ:* "God Himself, in the beginning, set all things to music, even before man was made" (5). And he provided ample evidence: Jubal, "the father of such as handled the harp and organ" (Gen. 4:21), the use of music to deliver the Jews from Egyptian bondage, God's account of the Creation spoken to Job through a whirlwind (Job 38:7), and the "hundreds of places in the Old and New Testament" where "music is mentioned as being one of the crowning events of life" (7). This historical and theological strategy, Buell Cobb has noted, was inherited in the tunebook tradition from Thomas Symmes's 1720 treatise, *The Reasonableness of Regular Singing* (Cobb 1969, 57–58). As further evidence, James enumerated examples of music in nature, and then gave accounts of the psychological benefits of music, such as the effects of the grand choruses at the 1866 Peace Jubilees in Boston (8).

Where the beginning section of the book addressed the historical and theological scope of music, the closing section of the book, which James considered a companion to the history of music, discussed the "History of Four-Shape Notes." By this he meant the history not of shapes as musical notation but of the use of syllables to name the notes. Thus James could locate the origin of the four shapes in the music system of the ancient Greeks, who "had four notes, or syllables which they applied to sound their *tetrachord*" (156). The four-shape system, "by uniting the mind of the practitioner with the ideas of the different syllables with those of intervals, facilitates the recollection of the several sounds which were of very ancient adoption" (155–56). James noted that America, just as Europe, used only four shapes "for a long time," and he cited *The Sacred Harp, Southern Harmony,* and *Missouri Harmony* as examples (156). (James knew of *The Easy Instructor,* but perhaps did not know of its significance.) Thus both in Europe and America, James's "history" consisted of an original, well-established four-note system and subsequent, yet fruitless, attempts at its improvement.

Between these two sections, comprising the bulk of the work, was the history of *The Sacred Harp* and its singers. In these pages, James established or set in print some of the tradition's stock rhetorical and historical devices. In the section "A Brief History of *The Sacred Harp*" (11–14), he introduced the practice of chronologizing the tradition by listing its revisions. In this case he quoted verbatim the prefaces of each edition; significantly, he omitted the Cooper Revision of 1902. In "Revision of *The Sacred Harp*" (17–27), he repeated the chronology, this time listing the names of the revision committee members for each edition. By distributing the historical recognition among the committee members, he broadened the base of support. He also listed the sources from which all but the "original" songs were taken (e.g., *Southern Harmony* or *Baptist Harmony*), partly to illustrate that the songs "in point of tone, word and sentiment . . . are fundamental and constitutional" (21). Later, in "Changes Made in the Sacred Harp" (83–88), James again listed the revisions, this time introducing the extraordinary practice of "tracking" page numbers through the revisions. The implication of page tracking, of course, is a transcendent *Sacred Harp,* of which the actual revisions are but tangible manifestations. Even through the 1991 edition, maintaining page continuity has been the revisers' solemn duty.

Following the chronology of revisions was the first of several biographical sections, "Prof. B. F. White" (27–37). In it the reader encounters a man of impeccable character, with meager beginnings, who triumphed by way of unrelenting religious faith and devotion to the cause of religious song. Following this were shorter accounts of "B. F. White's Children and Grandchildren" (39–53), "The Composers of the Sacred Harp" (89–118), "Additional Composers of Tunes in *The Sacred Harp*" (119–24), "Prominent Leaders of the Sacred Harp" (125–44), and "Leaders of Music in the Sacred Harp" (145–52). In all, hundreds of names were mentioned, if only to say of them that "he had a very strong bass voice and was a fine leader" or "she was one of the best treble singers in the Southern

Musical Convention." Even the controversial Professor E. T. Pound, elsewhere credited with the demise of the Southern Musical Convention, was said to have been "a hard student" who had "done much to advance music in Georgia" (114). These biographical sections formed most of the book and established, if only through reiteration, its basic historical devices. Never, with James, was there an effort to generalize, as in culture writing; rather, his preeminent mode was to personify and enumerate. Consequently, for literally hundreds of singers, "history" is and was a description of personal commitment and not extraordinary achievement.

The remainder of the book was an extension of the enumerative principal, this time focusing on the conventions. James began with the earliest, the "Southern Musical and Chattahoochee Conventions" (55–70), founded, respectively, in 1845 and 1852. He listed chronologically each meeting of the convention, identifying the location and the names of each of the officers. Sometimes an unusual circumstance was noted; for instance, for the 1861 meeting of the Chattahoochee Convention, the following appears:

> 1861, New Hope, Coweta County. J. P. Reese, president, and Mr. Blalock, secretary. Mr. Blalock was sheriff of Merriwether County. When the war came on the convention did not meet any more until 1865.

For the more recent conventions, James gave the date of organization and a general description. In such cases he often added, "Shortness of time has prevented us from getting the names of the leaders, and further data about this convention, but it is growing at each session." As with the biographies, the consequence of this was that James extended the "ownership" of the singing tradition to each convention that adopted *The Sacred Harp*.

In the general plan of the *Brief History,* James drew together two strategies and set them in harmony. By allying the Sacred Harp tradition, at the front and back of the book, with primitive beginnings, James located it close to the center of a boundless history of sacred music, as a fundamental facet of the human condition. So conceived, Sacred Harp was a music whose significance was so vast and so powerful that it stood far above the fray of regional difference, rural-urban conflict, and other barbs of modernism to which it was vulnerable. At the same time, between these conceptual pillars, stood the biographies of its many singers and leaders who, in relentless succession, personified the ideals of a noble endeavor. In effect, James *resisted* the notion of a transcendent, objectified tradition that might have provided an easy target for modernizers. Instead, by using history to project the singing tradition onto individual singers, he enlisted an entire army of followers, each obliged to re-create and embody it.

The James Revision

B. F. White's call in 1869 for attention to the "old paths" would prove to be a fortuitous epithet after 1900. Indeed, just as the new century was rung in, the Sacred Harp tradition was approaching its most perilous hour. Surely the *Organ* had registered dissent in its pages, but this controversy never penetrated the core of the singing tradition—the *Sacred Harp* book itself. It had not been revised since 1869, yet from 1902 to 1911, *five* competing editions of the book appeared, each offering a different response to a widely popular innovation, the gospel song.

In the gospel song, what was encountered in the *Organ* as mere theory had metamorphosed into a widely reproducible and popular new form. Indeed, if nineteenth-century "better music" reform had an elite social base, the gospel song was thoroughly populist. Where elite reformers looked to quasi-civic institutions, the gospel movement employed many of the same institutions as the "old system" (e.g., singing schools, conventions, and shape notes). But the gospel movement made these institutions far more profitable and reproducible by such techniques as quartet performances, singing competitions, and a cheap, expendable book format. Where elite reform was nourished culturally by exclusivity and segregation, the cultural economy of gospel music depended on an ever expanding audience. So, more easily than "better music" reform, the gospel song penetrated traditional Sacred Harp areas. In western Georgia, for example, prolific composer A. J. Showalter of Dalton was luring many Sacred Harp singers to this new type of song (Thurman 1952, 92). Today, even though both gospel institutions and European-style choirs are widespread, it is the gospel movement that most Sacred Harp singers remember as having challenged their "old system."

The gospel song seemed to embody all that the old Sacred Harp songs did not: close harmony, the use of accidentals, and in some cases the concentration of melodic interest into a single part. Nonetheless, in traditional singing areas, gospel songs were popular enough that *Sacred Harp* book revisers thought it necessary at this juncture to accommodate their appeal. They could not be written off as mere misguided innovation. So, a variety of compromises were struck in the editions that appeared soon after 1900, none achieving universal support (see appendix 3).

The edition that most satisfied the faithful in traditional singing areas—the James Revision of 1911—offered the fewest concessions to the gospel movement. Buell Cobb has described this period in detail, noting that before the James Revision was published, some singing conventions even drafted resolutions urging revisers to prepare a more conservative edition (Cobb 1978, 89–110). The 1911 revisers clearly had this audience in mind, explicitly declaring their book free from "the twisted rills and frills of the unnatural snaking of the voice, in unbounded proportions, which have in the last decade so demoralized and disturbed the church music of the present age" (quoted in Jackson 1933, 97).[7] When the book appeared, preserving almost intact the contents of the 1869 edition, it met with widespread acceptance.[8]

What it did not do—alter the content and style of nineteenth-century editions—is well known. What is of interest here, however, is that James included two innovations—new to *The Sacred Harp* and to tunebooks generally—that *enhanced* rather than compromised the book's peculiar antimodernist stance. New, on almost every page, there appeared (1) a scriptural quotation just under the song title and (2) a historical footnote below the song text.[9] Although historians have not attached great significance to this, perhaps deservedly so, these innovations nonetheless distinguished *The Sacred Harp* from other tunebooks for most of the twentieth century. What is important to examine here is how, grounded by the book's traditional approach to musical content, these devices in the James Revision complemented the rhetorical strategy of his *Brief History* and gave his approach to the tradition a much wider base of appeal.

It may be of some significance that James actually tested the popularity of both of these ideas in the *Union Harp and History of Songs,* published in 1909, two years before the James Revision. In the two books, scriptural quotations appeared to be identical and footnotes closely so. Some footnotes even appeared to be set in exactly the same type. Of course, singers rejected the *Union Harp,* it is presumed, because it compromised too much of the musical content and style of the preceding *Sacred Harp* edition (Cobb 1978, 97–98). But both notes and scriptural quotations were retained from the *Union Harp,* indicating that they were not among those features to which singers objected.

Scriptural Quotations

Scriptural quotations were not exactly new to *The Sacred Harp.* For their source, one looks first to psalmody, the poetic translation of the Psalms, sung as music for use in worship and often with an explicit printed reference to a biblical source. But with the development by Protestant reformers of hymnody—religious poetry *based on* Scripture—scriptural references became less obvious and citations more important. Watts, for example, used scriptural headings, somewhat deliberately, to indicate the source of "translation" of his poetry. For his "spiritual songs," which corresponded not to biblical text but to religious experience, he provided a heading summarizing that experience.

These practices were preserved in American hymnbook compilations. For example, in *The Psalmist,* a hymnbook used as a source for *The Sacred Harp,* Samuel Stennett's hymn "On Jordan's Stormy Banks I Stand" was summarized as "Heaven in Prospect"; "Hark, the Glad Sound! The Saviour Comes" as "Design of Christ's Advent"; and "Come Thou Fount of Every Blessing" as "Grateful Recollection."[10] Some hymnbooks were even indexed by scriptural reference. In hymnbooks produced by compilers, citations also appeared, partly to aid preachers in choosing hymns to accompany a sermon on a particular biblical passage or theme.

It should be said that, according to some historians, Watts's citations were not entirely genuine. Watts wrote in an atmosphere of extreme prejudice, when congregational singing was restricted to the Psalms of David and other scriptural canticles. It was this custom which Watts took as his mission to undermine. An important vehicle for this was his own "translation" of the Psalms, "Imitated in the Language of the New Testament."

In it, he infused the texts with his own New Testament biases, for example, by omitting or altering images of the vengeful God. The citations for the Psalms, though not to be called inappropriate, nonetheless serve to reinforce the very scriptural influence that Watts sought to replace (Davie 1993, 71–86; Stevenson 1949). Later, as is well known, hymnbook compilers' radical editing rendered psalm and hymn texts even less recognizable as source Scripture, and tunebook compilers went even further, using only a few of the stanzas of the complete hymn or even mixing stanzas from different hymns (Hitchcock 1882). It is less well known that Watts actually encouraged editing by bracketing text that he thought might be controversial (Arnold 1990).

In short, for the James Revision, whereas there is considerable precedent for recognizing scriptural authority, there is also considerable precedent, as a generic feature of the hymn, for adjusting hymn texts to suit theology. Of course, early tunebooks such as *The Sacred Harp* were not a part of liturgical contexts. They arose from the singing school tradition as part of an interdenominational effort to improve singing—few, if any, featured scriptural citations. For this reason, we might ordinarily attribute to the James revisers a desire to placate clergy. But there is little evidence in nineteenth-century writings (e.g., the *Organ*) that Sacred Harp was viewed by clergy as secular—as singing schools were, for example, in Cincinnati. Instead, to explain his inspiration for including scriptural quotations, we can justly look to James's view, echoing earlier writers, that primitive theology was a cornerstone of Sacred Harp tradition. If any "point" is suggested by the context surrounding the James Revision, it was the need to establish for the Sacred Harp a more fundamental theological and historical grounding than was evidenced in competing forms of sacred music, such as gospel songs. The Sacred Harp's ideas were permanent and basic, the added Scripture indicated; the gospel song, in contrast, was ephemeral, momentary.

In many cases, the James revisers reinforced the original source. To "Babel's Streams" ("By Babel's streams we sat and wept"), for example, was attached Ps. 137:2, and we are thus reminded that the text was a poetic "translation" of the Psalm itself. But the revisers were not fundamentally guided by the principle of direct derivation. "We have quoted the Scripture reference to almost every tune," James wrote in the introduction to the *Union Harp,* "*represented by the sentiment of the words,* and this has been no little task" (v, emphasis mine). In contrast, in his historical foot-notes, James was trying meticulously to establish the author or composer or the source from which B. F. White took the text, even apologizing when he suspected his information was incomplete. But in his use of Scripture—much in keeping with other textual liberties associated with the hymn genre—he treated words as transcendent, as if set loose from their author's voice.

What James did was to attribute a primitive connection of poetic text with quoted Scripture. Scriptural quotation provided a key to original scriptural sentiment, not the author's intent. Ultimately, James even denied that reader "sentiment" had motivated the choices of Scripture. The key passage of the preface was changed in the James Revision to read, "Under the name of the tune is placed the Scripture text upon which the words of the tune are founded, giving citation of book, chapter, and verse of the Bible" (v). This may well have been what justified the distinctive Sacred Harp practice of *quoting,* and not merely *citing,* Scripture. That is, where for Watts the goal was to provide evidence of a scriptural source, the James revisers sought to guide the singer toward sacred sentiments that were associated fundamentally with the text.

Some examples will show the differing consequences of employing authorial intent or attributed sense. The text of "Mear" is a prayer of sup-plication, a plea for an end to distress and to God's apparent silence. The first of the five stanzas in *The Sacred Harp* (49) reads:

> Will God forever cast us off?
> His wrath forever smoke
> Against the people of His love
> His little chosen flock?

For the sentiment of this, we are directed to Romans 9:22, "What if God, willing to show his wrath, and to make his power known, endured with much long-suffering?" This seems an apt match, but for Watts, who "translated" these lines, the source was Psalm 74. It would be less apt were the compilers to have included many omitted verses, some of which refer precisely to the destruction of the Temple, the event that Psalm 74 reports so vividly. Instead, the five quatrains in *The Sacred Harp* depict a more general, though no less authentic, desperation. Its outcome—believers' clinging to faith in the worst of circumstances—shines through still.

The chosen passage from Romans 9 depicts distress in equal measure. But, on closer inspection, it is hypothetical: "What if . . . ?" the passage begins. And the Pauline reassurance, close behind, is that God will "call them my people, which were not my people" (Rom. 9:25). The Psalm, in contrast, addresses God directly and desperately: "O God, why hast thou cast us off . . . ?" (74:1). Watts, it seems, did not exactly favor the form of the Psalm—in this beginning quatrain, he addressed the congregation directly and addressed God only in third person. And there are other differences. "Remember thy congregation," the Psalm pleads, loosely inferring that the speaker is among its number; Watts draws the speaker back to observe many congregations, again not clearly addressing the Creator, saying instead, "Think of the tribes." In the Psalm, God's anger "smokes" with bitter irony "against the sheep of thy pasture"; in Watts the passage was patently contradictory ("against the people of his love"), and we are reminded that in Romans 9:22, God also "endured with much long suffering." If Watts softened God's wrath, which he so often did, we may look for an explanation in his distaste for the vengeful God, necessitating his "imitating" the Psalms in the "language of the New Testament." We may even look to Pauline thinking for Watts's turning "sheep of thy pasture" into "chosen flock," suggesting the nonconformist minority of the "elect." [11]

All of this is only to suggest that the James revisers might easily have been led by Watts's poetry to other destinations than Psalm 74, and that Romans 9:22 was not an unlikely choice. And there is plenty of justification, even in Watts, for the revisers not to have been bound by original intent. This fact is most demonstrably true in the case of secular poetry, such as the nineteenth-century parlor song "The Bride's Farewell," where there is simply no possibility of relating the scriptural quotation to original intent. [12] Two stanzas are included in *The Sacred Harp* (359):

Farewell, Mother, tears are streaming
Down thy pale and tender cheek;
I in gems and roses gleaming,
Scarce this sad farewell can speak.

Farewell, Mother, now I leave you,
Griefs and hopes my bosom swell;
One to trust who may deceive me:
Farewell, Mother, fare you well.

For the sentiment of this we are directed to Ruth 1:14, "And they lifted up their voice, and wept again; but Ruth clave unto her." "They" refers to Naomi and her "adopted" daughters-in-law Orpah and Ruth, both recently widowed after the untimely death of Naomi's sons. Desperate after her own husband's death, Naomi has decided to return to her native land where there recently had been prosperous harvests. With considerable grief, she has admonished Orpah and Ruth not to come with her, lest they forgo any chance of a second marriage.

Even with no possibility of original intent, we are again struck by the aptness and intensity of the corresponding sentiments of song text and scriptural quotation, both resulting from impending separation by marriage of a "daughter" from her "mother." But the revisers omitted a key phrase from the quotation (Authorized Version), and in doing so altered its meaning. The complete passage reads, "And they lifted up their voice, and wept again: and Orpah kissed her mother in law, but Ruth clave unto her." Error and conciseness might explain other discrepancies between the quotations and their sources, but here there seems to have been some effort to recognize Ruth and not Orpah. In fact, only Orpah stayed behind to remarry, as in the song; Ruth "clave unto her" and remained profoundly loyal. Nor is this an obscurity: it can be considered the central theme of the Book of Ruth. The Scripture, then, draws the reader from an unhopeful "Bride's Farewell," through its consonance of sentiment, to an opposite outcome.

This is not to say that the James revisers had all of this in mind. But it seems that any consideration of scriptural quotations leads us unavoidably into exegesis, and *this* may well have been central to their intentions.

Scripture and poetic text are set in direct dialogue, visibly, on the page. By calling their relationship primitive, other voices are eliminated. No "dogmas or creeds" intervene. Neither Scripture nor poetic text "addresses" the singer, as a sermon might, nor do singers always attend to them. The reader or singer engages them as solitary experience, personal truth.

Footnotes

In many ways, James's footnotes were an extension of his historical work in *A Brief History of the Sacred Harp*. But here, history was attached to the songs themselves, there on the page with them, not in a separate edition. Composers and hymn writers were presented as vivid personalities; songs came to life as having appeared in the most celebrated tunebooks and hymnbooks, as associated with the greatest names in hymnody, as emerging from the struggles and triumphs of their composers. For example, *every* time "Pleyel's Hymn" (317) was sung, a singer would have encountered the following on the same page:

> Ignaz Joseph Pleyal, author of the foregoing music, was born in 1757 and died in 1831 in Paris. He was the twenty-fourth child of a village school-master. He commenced the study of music when very young. He studied under Haydn, who often spoke of him as his best and dearest pupil. He was reared in Austria, and composed a great deal of music, and stood high as a musician. Pleyel's Hymn is one of the old standard tunes in this and many other countries, it is in many of the tune and song books of this country as well as more recent publications. See Timbrel of Zion by Collins 1853, and earlier edition Boston Academy's Church Music 1836, and later editions, "Music of the Protestant Episcopal Church," 1828, page 105, and many other books. The words are taken from Mason's Zion Songster 1832, page 9, seventh edition.

In the footnotes, James described, one by one, the many sources and contributors for *The Sacred Harp*. In doing so, he was describing a great institution that united all of the tunebooks and hymnbooks, composers, and authors. By implication, *The Sacred Harp* inherited the mantle of this entire canon of shape note tunebooks, and its singers inherited a solemn obligation as their link with destiny.

Some notes commented on the composition process itself, often with a description of the writer's religious commitment or of the circumstances of writing the hymn. Of Helen Maria Williams, author of "While thee I seek, protecting Pow'r" (the text to "Pleyel's Hymn," p. 143; see appendix 4), singers learned that she wrote the hymn while serving six years in prison in France. Of Robert Robinson, who wrote the text to "Olney" (page 135), James suggested a life of spiritual turmoil:

> He was converted under the preaching of Whitfield, and ordained to the Methodist ministry. He later joined the Baptist, then the Independent, and finally became a Unitarian.

The words to "Sawyer's Exit" (page 338), James wrote, were composed by Rev. S. B. Sawyer "on the day of his death, with a request that they be applied to the melody and published, and on completing the words his spirit took its eternal flight into its new life." Or, with no apology, James drew the singers into the historical process itself ("Morgan," 304): "After diligent search, we have been unable to find the author of the above tune."

In other segments of American life, turn-of-the-century antimodernism was concerned with rescuing the fast-disappearing culture from the jaws of progress. From craft guilds to folksong collections, from museums to Wild West shows, the past was being preserved and displayed for the pleasure of those very citizens who were most enjoying the spoils of modernity. Although this was not quite the circumstance of Sacred Harp singing, we can nonetheless appreciate the strategy of the James revisers. Theirs was not the recreation of a lost past, compensating for an embrace of the future. Rather, at the moment of historical imperative, they formulated the present as heir to a sacred inheritance. James articulated a usable past and infused it into the living tradition—without displacing the presence of that living singing tradition. For James, singing did not *represent* the past. Rather, the past—the commitment and labor of the founders of the tradition, the spiritual thoughts of the earliest musicians, the abundant appearance of *Sacred Harp* songs in other tunebooks and hymnbooks—all were the building blocks for a richer and more rewarding present.

A SENSE OF COMMUNITY: EARL THURMAN'S "REAL CHATTAHOOCHEE CONVENTION"

> Through the records we have been able to trace the physical life of the [Chattahoochee Musical] Convention; the location in specific years and the presiding officers and singers active in these sessions. The great host of singers who have taken part in the sessions throughout the century of its existence make up the physical and visible structure of the Convention. Historically, and from an organizational standpoint, this is both interesting and important but does not depict the real-life—one may well say SOUL—of the Chattahoochee Musical Convention. To get this picture we must as best we can, look into the hearts and minds of the vast throngs which have for one hundred years and under conditions not always favorable or easily overcome—faithfully made their annual pilgrimage to the Sacred Harp shrine, erected in the edifice of the Chattahoochee Musical Convention. And we realize that this can be done only in a very limited and imperfect way.
>
> EARL THURMAN,
> *The Chattahoochee Musical Convention, 1852–1952* (1952)

In 1952, when Earl Thurman produced his book-length manuscript, *The Chattahoochee Musical Convention: 1852–1952,* he could look back on an extraordinary century. The Chattahoochee Convention was the second oldest Sacred Harp convention and the oldest that still held meetings. It was also the only remaining convention organized by those in the B. F. White milieu. Thurman's explicit purpose in writing was, then, to celebrate the history of the Chattahoochee Convention at its centennial juncture. In this respect, its significance as an example of a Sacred Harp writing tradition is limited.

Yet, inevitably, Thurman's narrative was bound also to take stock of Sacred Harp singing and of the dramatic cultural changes in the world around it. In fact, we might note that the occasion of this narrative came, coincidentally, as George Pullen Jackson's influential writing career was reaching its end.[13] Thus we can note their distinct approaches: where Jackson most often explicitly generalized, Thurman chose instead to refract the tradition through the lens of a single convention, indeed, one linked directly to B. F. White. Moreover, Thurman was writing during a period of relative wane that he had observed firsthand. Nearly twenty years had passed since the Denson Revision was published.

Given this circumstance, we can better appreciate that in large part Thurman took the approach of J. S. James, steering clear of the sometimes overbearing rhetoric of culture that had flourished in depression-era folklore and regionalist writing. Through most of five chapters—over a hundred pages—he inventoried the many "individuals and family groups," as he called them, who contributed to the convention over the years. More so than James, Thurman was able to assess the significance of the "singing family" as an institution inclined to preserve its members' affection for Sacred Harp singing. In any case, his manuscript was not organized in individual biographies under separate headings, but by chapter, with families discussed collectively, as transcending the individual singers who belonged to them.

Yet, approaching the close of his narrative, he was compelled to offer somewhat of an apology for this technique. Drawing upon convention minutes for information, he had described family by family, name by name, the contributions of singers to the convention. But he felt the need to defend this approach as a necessity, offering a compelling account of the relationship he perceived between writing style and writing world:

Some may think that we have given too much prominence to the many named individuals and family groups appearing in the narrative and unduly stressed [the] importance of their association with the Convention. To this the writer wishes to briefly suggest a few thoughts that may not have occurred to them. First let us ask—what is the Chattahoochee Convention?

In referring to the proceedings of a session we speak in such terms as "actions taken by the body" or "deliberations of the body." But the Chattahoochee Convention has no material body. It is not something that can be seen with the physical eye or held in the physical hand. The "body" we speak of in referring to the Convention is the sum total of all the efforts and labors of all the men and women—

individuals and family groups—who have over a period of one hundred years, gathered each year at designated places, and with mutual understanding and in a spirit of Christian cooperation, have planned the holding of these meetings and harmoniously agreed on the procedure to be followed during the activities of the annual gatherings.

. . . Individuals and family groups have made up the life of the Chattahoochee—they constitute what we term the "body" of the Convention. The personalities of these individuals and family groups and their contribution to the Sacred Harp cause, have been securely and inseparably woven into the fabric of the "body" we know as the Chattahoochee Musical Convention, and around these individuals and family groups revolves the history of this organization. (Thurman 1952, 121–22)[14]

Thurman had departed somewhat from the social principles that grounded James's nearly identical strategy. For James, the collective could only "embody" the individual—it could never break free from the individual and become a corporeal metaphor. This is why enumeration and biography has been so fundamental a principle in Sacred Harp writing. But why adopt the corporeal metaphor and then disclaim it? Who might have thought that he had given individuals and families "too much prominence?" Could Thurman actually have felt compelled—perhaps by the influence of culture writing—to use the corporeal collective to such an extent that he was not comfortable?

Thurman also diverged from the enumerative strategy in addressing one issue that James did not: that Sacred Harp is *rural* music. James had even located the headquarters of the United Convention, the "central organization of all local conventions, singings, teachers, and leaders," in Atlanta (Cobb 1978, 138). From the outset, Thurman depicted an organic relationship between Sacred Harp and rural life:

It is significant that Sacred Harp singing has always been indulged in, almost exclusively, by people living in the rural communities. The Sacred Harp is not a *city* book. The type of songs dominating the compositions embodied in the book belong to natural surroundings. The music is not *city* music. . . . There was a quietness and tranquility existing in that environment which was conducive to calm, clear and sound ways of thinking that created a profound knowledge of the fundamental values in life. (34)

Later Thurman spelled out a different source: that in the early years of the convention, there was in those rural areas an atmosphere of "almost complete isolation"—there were "no telephones, radios, or motor vehicles" (126). For this reason, Sacred Harp took on extraordinary importance in singers' lives, so much so that they routinely made long journeys to reach singings. For example:

> The writer recalls one specific instance when a journey of this type was made. It occurred in 1898 when the Convention was held at Flat Rock Church, Carroll County. This journey was made by the J. O. Blair family who lived in Winston County, Alabama. They travelled in a covered wagon and the distance was more than two hundred miles. Including the time spent going and returning, and the four days of the session the Blair family was absent from their home not less than ten days in order to be present at the 1898 session of the Chattahoochee Convention. (129)

For Thurman, an account such as this was exemplary of a kind of attitude, idealized in the early years of the convention when this atmosphere of isolation prevailed. When, for example, a four-day session was assigned to a community, this ideal attitude was the natural consequence of the effort and commitment in getting to the convention, the extensive effort required for a small community to feed and house sometimes a hundred visitors over four days, and deep happiness, lifelong friendships, and even marriages that emerged over the years from "four days of delightful singing of Sacred Harp music and brotherly association" (128).

Throughout Thurman's narrative, in fact, ideals seemed to lurk restlessly beneath his written descriptions, as if also beneath Sacred Harp itself. On the one hand, the Convention founders imbued it with "musical strength and spiritual sturdiness" that is the *"true spirit of traditional Sacred Harp Singing"* (8). Or, conversely, the strength of character of its founders, such as N. Mark Wynn, was formed by the ideals of the early conventions, "the fundamental structure underlying the existence of the institution we know as *Sacred Harp Singing*" (20). His final chapter, in fact, seemed to undermine the descriptive capacity of earlier chapters. In "The Real Chattahoochee Convention," Thurman sought to identify elements—such as singers' efforts to get to the convention—not expressible in the enumerative style he used earlier.

Although there might be cause to speculate otherwise, Thurman's uneasiness appears to have arisen from his belief that the "true spirit" was a fundamental element infused into the structure of a convention and thereby also into the singers as a consequence of their efforts. The singing convention and its association, he believed, were the preeminent means of "spreading and prolonging the general life of Sacred Harp singing throughout all the areas of its activities" (141). Its structure was, necessarily, dispersed so extensively among the singers who constituted a convention that enumeration was wholly inadequate for representing it.

So Thurman invented a version of "culture" to redress the inadequacy of the prevailing enumerative style. But in Thurman's troubled narrative, "culture" never broke free from its mooring in individual human effort. In terms of his own metaphors, none of which seem to have been influenced by post-1920s culture writers, the convention was an "edifice" (125) built by singers "laying the foundation and creating and erecting the structure" (34), or it was a "body," the "sum total of all the efforts and labors" (121). But it was never free of the "*personal touch and handiwork*" of its creators (8). Its foundation, "the everlasting principle of the spiritual brotherhood of all mankind" (33), was a structure created by and visible to the singers and, at the same time, immanent *within* the singers as a consequence of their work.

It is worth noting that, quite by accident, Thurman wrote at a time of relative wane in the prosperity of Sacred Harp. Sixteen years had passed since the last revision; during that interim, World War II had taken a heavy toll on the ranks of younger singers. For many Americans, the postwar climate that followed brought prosperity and ease of travel, as well as a widespread fascination with all things modern. It is not clear how these might have affected Thurman's writing. But the fact remains that he set out to write what might have been a straightforward centennial history, and in it turned urgently to a set of issues and a form of writing that seemed designed to achieve some cognitive resolution. If the underlying impulse was to assimilate into traditional discourse the notion of Sacred Harp as cultural object, then Thurman can only be said to have made crucial connections, too often neglected in culture writing, between the objectified collective and individual sentiment and effort. Genuine resolution was yet to come.

"OUR AMERICAN HERITAGE": RUTH DENSON EDWARDS AND THE RHETORIC OF CULTURE

During the span of time from James to Thurman, covering the first half of the twentieth century, the depiction of Sacred Harp tradition within American cultural taxonomy underwent considerable change. From accounts of "white-haired fathers" in southern newspapers in the early decades, to the discovery of Sacred Harp as folksong in the 1920s, to the generous attention given it by George Pullen Jackson, to its emergence in travel and regionalist literature, it would seem that Sacred Harp was cemented into American musical culture as folksong. Images drawn from this perspective were derived from direct observation of singing events by outsiders and took shape most prominently in the form of culture writing. Given this, we can appreciate the consistency with which James articulated and Thurman maintained their uniquely alternative antimodernist discourse.

Curiously, this practice would come to an abrupt end in the late 1960s. Only then would culture writing style be accepted into official writings— evidenced most prominently in the writings of Ruth Denson Edwards (1893–1978), daughter of T. J. Denson. An honors graduate of Peabody College and later a Cullman, Alabama, schoolteacher, Edwards served on the music committee that oversaw the 1960, 1966, and 1971 revisions of *The Sacred Harp*. It was during the period of these revisions that she contributed several short historical essays on the singing tradition, to some degree inheriting from J. S. James the role of official historian. In one, "Sacred Harp Singings in the Southland," she described a "typical" singing:

> On any Sunday in many rural sections of the Southland, a familiar sight is a country church, located in a grove of trees, with cars parked all around. The occasion—a Sacred Harp Singing.

Every community sponsors at least one annual Sacred Harp Singing and sometimes two or three. Singers in many neighborhoods gather in large, more centrally located areas, and hold longer conventions—two and sometimes three days. These conventions are always well-attended. (Edwards ca. 1969)

Some of these appeared as liner notes in a series of six LP recordings produced between 1965 and 1976 by the Sacred Harp Publishing Company in part to help new singers learn songs more easily. For all but one of them, a select group of singers assembled in a studio, favoring a controlled environment so that listeners could be assured of hearing all the parts evenly.[15] These recordings were designed to represent singing as a whole to new singers. In such a context, rhetorical devices used by Edwards in the notes were the means to convey to these new singers the complexities of Sacred Harp performance practice. "Great crowds gather . . . ," she might well have written.

In her writing, she generously drew in voices of other writers, often George Pullen Jackson, crafting a composite whole by which readers engaged Sacred Harp as culture. For instance, to establish the integrity and antiquity of Sacred Harp tradition, she made an initial ethnographic observation, authenticated it in terms of J. S. James's enumerative historicism, and established its origin in a well-known quote from B. F. White:

In conducting a Sacred Harp Singing, present-day singers follow the pattern used by the illustrious and venerable forefathers who, more than a hundred years ago, established the Traditional Style of Sacred Harp Singing and admonished their followers to "seek the old paths and walk therein." (Edwards [1969])

To defend the unique sound of Sacred Harp against complaints raised in the name of conventional choral aesthetics, she turned to a section of George Pullen Jackson's *The Story of the Sacred Harp* (1944) entitled "Some Hearers Don't Like It. Why?":

At this time perhaps I should remind the reader that Sacred Harp (Fa-Sol-La) music is singers' music and not listeners' music. The casual listener claims that "It all sounds just alike" or "I can't hear any tune to it." This is because it is four-part music and has been composed in such a manner that each voice-part is equally balanced. The tune part is submerged more deeply because each part except bass is sung by both men and women. This gives "Sacred Harp" music distinctive qualities which differentiates it from all other types of music, and it is known as dispersed harmony. (Edwards [1969]; Jackson 1944a, xiii–xvii)

To explain the social basis of Sacred Harp, she borrowed without reference from Jackson's section, "The Singers," and then linked this to a quoted passage that set Sacred Harp against a capricious world:

A strong invisible tie binds the singers together, and they feel that they belong to one great family. This feeling is deepened by the consciousness that they stand alone in their undertaking—"Keeping the old songs resounding in a world which has either gone over to lighter, more 'entertaining' and frivolous types of song or has given up all community singing." (Edwards [1969]; Jackson 1944a, xvii)

To summarize the cosmology of the tradition, she borrowed the insightful and sweeping opening line of Jackson's essay:

Aside from the Holy Bible, the book found oftenest in the homes of rural southern people is the big oblong volume of song called the Sacred Harp." (Edwards 1965; Jackson 1944a, v)

More so than any other Sacred Harp writer, Edwards grasped the essential features of the popular concept of culture and used them to describe a distinctive tradition, "different" in fundamental ways from other American musical traditions. Appropriating ethnographic voices, she could draw effortless conclusions about "they, the singers"—that would have been more burdensome and less effective addressed as "we, the singers." Using the rhetoric of folk culture that would come to prevail in 1960s and 1970s America, she could highlight features that reflected core values of the tradition and assign to them a moral priority over popular society.

What must have been her most important writing was her "Introduction and History of the Original Sacred Harp," which appeared in the 1971 revision of *The Sacred Harp* and in subsequent reprints until 1991.

Although it repeated Jackson's "book found oftenest" opening, it was the least ethnographic of her writings. It moved quickly to Shakespeare's mention of four-note music, then to the recreational singing of the Pilgrims, and, in little more than a breath, arrived at B. F. White. From this point on, the "history" of the book became, as it had been in part for James and Thurman, the biographies of its revisers and prominent leaders. Here, in a work not at all designed for the public, there was less justification for ethnographic discourse and more for traditional rhetoric. So she made only brief and cautious reference to other discourses, and then followed the course set by James and Thurman, depicting the tradition and the book as the object not of antiquarian fascination but of the affection of its most prestigious custodians.

The overall effect of Edwards's writing on the tradition seems unmistakable. At the time, singers were beginning to receive requests for folk festival appearances, and Hugh McGraw, executive secretary of the Sacred Harp Publishing Company, was beginning to receive book orders and letters from folksong enthusiasts around the world. Perhaps anticipating both the onslaught of attention from the folksong world and also an opportunity to expand the reach of the singing tradition, Edwards took up the task of resolving cultural and cosmological issues that had lingered since the 1920s. By judiciously weaving the voices of ethnography and cultural history into those of the tradition's own writers, she created a new rhetorical direction that would carry Sacred Harp through the nostalgic U.S. bicentennial and beyond.

Edwards was clearly optimistic about the possibilities that the Sacred Harp revival presented. In 1973 she emphatically concluded:

No, Sacred Harp Music is not dying out! It is more popular now than ever before. Interest in this type of music is increasing and spreading far and wide. More singing schools are being taught and more young people are presently participating in the singing. Musicians in colleges and universities realize the beauty and potentialities of this type of music, and books and albums are in great demand. Therefore, the music departments are ordering these books and albums, not singly but by the dozens. Some of these institutions have included a course in Sacred Harp music in their curriculum.

Sacred Harp music has already retained its popularity for 129 years! Long live Sacred Harp Music—Our American Heritage! (Edwards 1973)

But her work was clearly of a transitional nature, juxtaposing and recontextualizing discourses without disturbing the integrity of their content. Perhaps in the spirit by which James's footnotes were removed to establish a "cleaner page," the 1991 revisers removed her essay from the book.[16]

SACRED HARP MINUTES AS NATIVE ETHNOGRAPHIES

Friday afternoon at one o'clock the convention was called to order by President W. H. Champion, who sang, Sweet Day, Adoration, Concord.

Eighth lesson by A. L. Culvert, Route 3, Warrior, Ala. Songs, Return Again, Mutual Love, Over Jordan, Eternal Home.

J. E. CREEL, Minutes of the Alabama State Sacred Harp
Musical Association, Birmingham, Alabama, 20–22 July 1928

In part through Edwards's writings, Sacred Harp singers were able to adapt the existential implications of ethnographic consensus to the musical performance practices of the tradition. But this did not mean that ethnographic conventions were adopted wholesale. Indeed, since the mid-nineteenth century, Sacred Harp has had its own documentary writing style, which has consistently increased in significance as ethnographic accounts have proliferated. It is of supreme significance that during the entire period of historical, theological, and culture writing, an alternative form of writing prevailed as the authoritative means to describe a Sacred Harp singing event.

Outright objections to culture writing have been rare, but one instance of disagreement suggests its formal limitations. A nostalgic account of "Alabama's Disappearing Singers" appeared in the *Birmingham News Monthly Magazine* (10 January 1954, 20–21), written by journalist Kathryn Windham. On the following February 10, the editor published a reply by singer J. W. Bassett of Troy, Alabama, attaching a title, "Voice of the People." Bassett's letter objected to Windham's claim that "it has been predicted that this type of singing will disappear entirely within the next decade, a victim of the failure to keep abreast with modern musical tastes." In response, Bassett wrote, "I have minutes on hand now listing 237 annual singings and conventions during 1954 in Alabama and Tennessee alone, and I have no record at present of the singings which will be held in Georgia, Florida, Mississippi and other states."

In his reply, Bassett could draw upon "hard evidence," the written accounts of individual singings that are recorded as a part of traditional performance practice. Whereas cultural accounts are general, extending a single circumstance to many others, these "minutes" are particular, presuming no authority beyond the event from which they arise. In this sense, they multiply, many times over, the descriptive authority that arises from ethnographic presence and, when taken collectively, can muster considerable documentary power over ethnography, as Bassett demonstrated. Naturally, this is not the purpose of the writing style of the minutes, but its documentary authority nonetheless arises from the fundamental formal relationship that exists between written minutes and Sacred Harp singing events. With the minutes, the writing and singing emanate from the same communicative context, in turn inscribing onto the event, the singers, the book, and the songs a particular ontological harmony that singers know and love.

Whereas cultural or ethnographic descriptions of a single event may vary because they are the work of an "observer," the minutes of an event formally exclude multiple accounts of the same event. This is not to say, however, that minutes have any kind of formal referential certainty. There are always questions about what and what not to record. But in a peculiar yet real sense, what is not recorded does not really "happen." Recording a circumstance in the minutes is a way of endorsing that circumstance as acceptable to the body of singers—of bringing it into the written world that both writer and singers inhabit. Circumstances that are out of the ordinary are often not recorded.

Similarly, an entire event is thought to have more certainly "happened" if minutes are taken at all. Informal gatherings are not usually recorded. But if minutes are recorded and submitted, there is some obligation that the minutes and thus the proceedings of the event conform to the protocol of singings in general. In recent years new singings have been started in northern cities, and with them, minutes are sometimes submitted as a means to be "included" in the nationwide community of singers. In turn, traditional singers read these minutes and can measure in them the extent and type of support in various areas. In this way, minutes are a means by which the conservative influences of traditional performance practice are exerted from great distances. Even where singings in new areas imitate traditional performance practice observed or described in ethnographic accounts, it is by submitting recorded minutes that they genuinely "submit" to traditional authority.

The procedure for recording minutes is relatively simple. In the early moments of a singing, officers are elected (or appointed with the presumption of elected authority) to preside over the singing. At larger singings and conventions a parliamentary-style structure may include various offices and committees; at smaller ones the slate may be limited to chairman and secretary. In practice, particularly at older singings, these officers have far less influence over the proceedings than do consensus and habit. Calling singings to order, dismissing for breaks or dinner, and even taking minutes are handled skillfully and with little disruption of routine. But it is important that authority is derived from democratic process and not from ascribed status of any sort.

Writing the Minutes

The genre conventions by which minutes are understood differ considerably from those for culture writing texts. The most fundamental difference is that they are seen as emerging from the singing and not as an observation of it. Consequently, the basic unit of description is not the narrative text but the song performance. Before he had ever seen a Sacred Harp singing, George Pullen Jackson received a copy of the minutes of the 1923 United Convention from Joe S. James and observed that they were "recordings of every little happening during the three days' sessions—and all that happened, apparently, was singing, nothing but singing" (Jackson 1926, 6). Before the 1940s, song performances were indicated in the minutes by recording the name of the leader who conducted an instructional "lesson," occasionally adding the song titles or the length of time allotted the leader. Since then the practice has been to record each leader's name and the page numbers of the songs led. In these and other respects, minutes record "just the facts": time and place, names of officers, names of leaders and page numbers of songs they lead, names of those called on to recite prayers, and occurrence of recesses and the noon meal.

Frequently there is an easily textualized event to record, but it is omitted. A group of siblings might lead together in honor of a parent. A beginner might overcome apprehension and lead his or her first song. In the minutes, if they were mentioned at all, their assigned significance would be highly individual, whereas culture writers would no doubt allude through them to the culture as a whole. But more often such events are inscribed only with name and number, stripping away the symbolic component of the song performance, leaving only an indexical component, a trace, with ties to memory and experience. Truly, a song performance can have considerable significance, sometimes noted in a brief testimonial. But this is a personal matter, and the minutes are designed to preserve the various boundaries of significance that partition individual memory from written record.

Occasionally, when speeches are made, the minutes make note of this. Yet, again, a rigid rhetorical contour is observed. Sometimes the exact text of a talk is included; if so, the speaker will probably have provided a written copy, thus avoiding the representation of oral speech. Dialect is never represented in minutes, as is and was the case in some culture writing accounts. Thus, even though singers are accustomed to testimonial speaking and in some cases can deliver eloquent discourses on familiar subjects, the texture of speech is not preserved in minutes. Whereas in ethnographic writing the speech occasion is inscribed by contextual description into the written textualized event, in the minutes they are not, remaining accessible instead only to those present.

Thus speeches are never reported as extensive indirect discourse, which employs second-order description of speech, although occasionally the subject of a talk is indicated. For example, on June 16, 1990, at the National Convention in Birmingham, Alabama, the minutes report: "A vase containing a rose was brought into the hollow square, and Shelbie Sheppard commented on its meaning." At a singing on September 3, 1990, Joe Jones made a "short talk on the history of Shoals Creek Church." Sometimes no subject is mentioned, as on April 15, when, after a prayer, Elder Neal Prichard of Old Harmony Church, Cleburne County, "made a short talk and welcomed everyone." Even in such cases, there is almost certainly a textualized event to record, and the writer seems to have made an effort to avoid it.

The most common example of this pattern is the "memorial lesson." The term *lesson* refers to the once common practice in which song leaders actually held the floor for instructional sessions; the *memorial lesson* is the period devoted to recently deceased members of the singing community and the congregation. In its most succinct form, the memorial lesson consists of reading aloud the names of the deceased and the songs sung in their honor. But it is a solemn occasion, and often a testimonial talk is given that describes vivid memories of dear friends and family members. It is in such a case that the exact text (if prepared ahead), a description of the salient themes of the talk, or the names of those recognized might be included in the minutes (for example, see appendix 5).

If something out of the ordinary occurs at a singing, it is occasionally mentioned, most often in only a sentence. On January 7, 1990, the minutes report that at the singing at Shady Grove Church, a business session was held to provide for a Sacred Harp radio program broadcast in Houston, Mississippi. For the Burritt Museum singing on May 12, the minutes noted that the site was the second highest elevation in the state of Alabama. But, again, the rule is succinctness and restraint, and many noteworthy occasions go unrecorded.

Perhaps the most cogent example of the emergent quality of minutes is when they employ not quoted speech but direct address to both singers and readers. For example, the minutes of the February 25, 1990, Bethlehem Baptist Church singing in Gallant, Alabama, close with the following:

> The singing will no longer be held with this church on this date. We would like to thank you for supporting this singing for many years and our desire and prayer is that the Lord will bless each and everyone.

In this passage, the writer gives us a clue as to the transcendent writing world that has spanned all meetings of this singing through the years. Where internal references address those present at the singing, a direct address to readers is meant for all those who have supported the singing. This is the "writing world" of the minutes.

The "Minute Book"

In recent decades, possibly anticipating the spread of Sacred Harp far outside its traditional domain of influence, singers have produced an annual compilation of "all" singings, presuming a universal "association" of singers without geographical limit or doctrinal affiliation. As the appropriating power of culture writing has spread to the feature page, to recordings and films, and to television, Sacred Harp singers have in turn condensed the minutes into their own authoritative document. As a direct and immediate consequence of this, they have secured control over what counts as a Sacred Harp singing. This has been a fundamental means by which new singers, many of whom come to the tradition through ethnography, are inscribed into the tradition through a more authoritative native discourse.

With the title *Directory and Minutes of Sacred Harp Singings,* the most comprehensive compilation of minutes for contemporary singings appears annually in January or February in paperbound book form. There are also compilations for regional conventions (e.g., "The Proceedings of the South Georgia Sacred Harp Singing Convention") and for associations that use other songbooks (e.g., "Minutes of the Alabama State Christian Harmony Singing Convention"). In fact, the current form, with its appearance of comprehensiveness, has emerged only in recent decades. It may be that its usefulness has been bolstered by the ease of travel since World War II and perhaps also by the increased acceptance of Sacred Harp singing as a cultural entity. In any case, it has become invaluable as Sacred Harp singing has taken on a national scope.

In Buell Cobb's discussion of the minutes, he was justifiably impressed by the logistics of this publication:

There are many separate publications of minutes today, but the most comprehensive is the one produced each year by the Denson revision folk. This compilation is the work of no central organization other than a general secretary, for several years now Mr. W. A. Parker of Birmingham, to whom the secretaries of most of the singings in this region of the Sacred Harp send (along with a small fee for printing costs and labor) the minutes of their singings. The network behind this publication was probably left over from one of the big conventions, but the subsequent merging of sister conventions has now obscured whatever skeletal organization was originally there. (Cobb 1978, 134)

Originally written in 1969 (Cobb 1969, 151–52), Cobb's description is just as apt today. The "minute book" was for several decades edited by Mrs. Parker and was recently turned over to Mrs. Shelbie Sheppard. Either would have been sent by mail, with a modest fee to cover expenses, handwritten minutes from the secretaries of all singings that are to be included. The general secretary then types the minutes and organizes them into the annual minute book publication. In it, singings are listed in order of occurrence. Early in the following year, the books are printed and sent to convention secretaries for distribution at their singings. This extraordinary and tedious process, by which the minutes of so many singings are compiled each year into a book nearly two hundred pages in length, surely ranks the editor of the minute book as one of the most influential custodians of traditional Sacred Harp writing.

As an example, the 1991 minute book opened with a personal letter from the secretary, Mrs. Parker, including a customary report and eulogy on singings which had been discontinued during the previous year. Then, running twelve pages was the directory of singings throughout the United States, arranged chronologically by month and numbered Sunday (e.g., "second Sunday in February"), with directions for driving to the singings. At the end of the book, an appended alphabetical listing of singers' names, addresses, and phone numbers ran thirty-four pages. On the final page was information for ordering Sacred Harp books and other materials from the publishing company in Bremen, Georgia. From pages 14 to 188, one finds the collected minutes recorded at singings, arranged chronologically.

Formulaically, each account follows the official protocol of the singing itself—beginning when a singing is "called to order" by the chair, pausing (spacing in the text) for recess or lunch, and ending when the singing is dismissed. Names and titles of officers appear after the indication of the singing's dismissal. The bulk of the text consists of the names of song leaders and the page numbers of the songs led, sometimes numbering over one hundred songs. The entire account is titled or subtitled according to the exact location (name of church or courthouse, etc.) or the occasion (memorial singing, family singing, or state convention, etc.).

To readers accustomed to cultural or historical accounts of singings, the most striking thing about the minutes is that they seem so uninformative as *cultural* documents. Even during Sacred Harp's most turbulent periods, the minutes reflected considerably less of the turmoil than did other forms. But this is partly because this information is accessible only to insiders. Much can be gleaned by an experienced singer by observing who came to a singing, not only the names of individuals but the overall "territorial spread of the participants at all the singings" (Cobb 1978, 135). And singers do indeed read them. The book appears early in the year, as soon as it is printed. Singers peruse the minutes, looking for their own or other familiar names. Singers might notice which singings have been discontinued, which are new, and which had good or poor attendance. Thus the minute book is a way to take stock of the tradition as a whole. Some editions even included a count of the number of times each song in the *Sacred Harp* was sung during the preceding year—as a measure of songs' relative popularity.

Singers might note the names of those who came to a new singing and might even anticipate the quality and style of an upcoming singing by looking at the list of those who attended the previous year. A singer might, by noting the leader, the occasion, and the song chosen, recall a particular performance and release a flood of memories. The operative principle in reading Sacred Harp minutes seems to be similar to that of its histories— one knows the singings by knowing its people. Thus minutes are not at all uninformative, but they are highly elliptical. They are an index, almost purely so, to experience and memory, and reading them is as individual as experience and memory can be. In this way, they are ethnography's antithesis. If culture writing attempts to bring experience to a distant reader by replacing it with description, the minutes privilege experience by providing only indexical pointers to it.

It is as if the two—ethnography and the minutes—operate in parallel rhetorical modes, neither acknowledging the other, perhaps because of the investment each has in a particular version of reality. For example, when Alan Lomax recorded the United Convention in 1959, the minutes for the convention did not mention his presence nor did they list the songs he asked singers to perform for his recording during the dinner hour (see appendix 5). Likewise, his liner notes did not mention the minutes, and he listed those songs sung at his request as if they were a part of the singing. Here is an excerpt from Lomax's version of the singing:

> Promptly at two o'clock, the chairman called the meeting to order. The "school" assembled in the nave of the church—about forty people ranged around four sides of a hollow square—trebles, sopranos, tenors, and basses—both sexes and all ages in each group. The committee had already drawn up a list of song leaders containing the names of every experienced singer present, and the chairman now called someone forward. Everyone had his "Original Sacred Harp" song book in hand and turned to the page number announced by the leader. In a matter of seconds, everyone had found his page and the older heads in the group had established the pitch. The leader launched immediately into a sol-fa interpretation of the song with the whole group joining in. Thus, every song is rehearsed once with its notes and then one or two verses are sung; another song is announced, found, pitched, sol-faed and performed and another leader is called. Matters proceed so briskly and efficiently that sometimes a hundred songs are sung in one day and before the weekend singing is over, most of the favorites in the book have been sung. (Lomax 1960)

Minutes exert authority over reality by selectively recording discrete traditional "facts" (the songs requested by Lomax were omitted); ethnography controls reality by generalizing (by *not* excluding the requested songs from the description of traditional performance practice).

It should be said that a third written account of the 1959 United Convention, a relatively lengthy newspaper article by reporter Ted Strongin, appeared a few weeks after the event in the *Chattanooga Times* (20 September 1959). As was the case with Alan Lomax's notes, the article did not mention the minutes nor did the minutes mention the presence of the *Times* reporter and photographer. It was an unusual account, depicting the event as a whole in terms of the writer's own response, yet projecting little of this onto the singers themselves. The key image was power: the singing "rolled and thundered," it was "leathery and intense" and "deep and moving," it was "not like opera-singing," it "gripped the stomach," the harmonies were "rough and open." There was a minor historical thread that attributed Sacred Harp's "sturdy and independent" qualities to the "hardy stock" of Colonial American composers. Alan Lomax was not mentioned, but the writer did observe that tape recorders were rescuing Sacred Harp "from the threat of oblivion due to radio and TV."

Equal attention, however, was given to quoted commentary about Sacred Harp by singers themselves. Most of the commentary comes from two singers that the writer met outside the building—one of them T. C. Bailey, of Arab, Alabama—who were keeping up a running commentary about what was going on inside. "There's a song in this book for every human idea," Bailey said of the texts. Of extreme efforts to attend the singing, he commented, "One singer flew in here today from Texas, a doctor." And of the sound of a particular song, "Listen to that high note there." Bailey then introduced the writer to Leman Brown, retiring president of the Convention, who reminded him again, "Sacred Harp is non-sectarian and non-denominational." Toward the end of the narrative sequence, the *Times* photographer was invited to lead. *Had he accepted,* his name would have been included in the minutes; as it was, his presence went unrecorded. Overall, the dual pattern of a writer depicting singing with quoted commentary and tracking his or her own involvement with experiential metaphor would not become prominent until later, as an accessory to folksong revival participation in singing.

In contrast to ethnographic style, the function of the enumerative or nominative style of the minutes seems to be to preserve the integrity of the content or substance of the speech or singing performance. Where the writer omits or obscures reference to this content, she or he provides for considerable dogmatic leeway without the critical scrutiny of the readers.

Matters of considerable significance and emotional import go undocumented. In this way, by preserving the autonomy and sanctity of the separate domains of the said and the unsaid, singing accumulates highly personal and often unexpressed significance. It is public worship but private faith.

Yet, just as written minutes preserve the integrity of content by constructing clear-cut external contours in their manner of reporting, they also deflect any consideration of texture. Singing is never recorded by singers as "astonishing and ludicrous" or in any other textural or stylistic manner. Evolving in a context in which outsiders *have* used such devices—sometimes as a means to deliberately stigmatize shape note traditions—Sacred Harp minutes deflect attention away from texture and thus also deflect authorial penetration of the writer into experience.

The Origins and Social Contexts of Sacred Harp Minutes

Sacred Harp minutes seem to date to the earliest conventions and thus to the first edition of the book. What, then, was their source? Why organize singings and conventions around parliamentary-style public meetings?

Nineteenth-century Sacred Harp singers would not have had to go far for models for recorded minutes. Newspapers commonly printed reports of public meetings in this form. The *Organ,* for example, was more likely to give complete coverage to Sacred Harp singings than other events, but on some occasions—for example, the public meeting on the routing of the railroad—a complete and authorized report was printed in the form of minutes. In such a case, because the report would have been submitted by a secretary, the newspaper editor could avoid taking any stance and would not even have had to attend the meeting. Generally, then, minutes were a reliable and easy way to report on public assemblies of all sorts that might be of importance to citizens.

By recording singings in the form of minutes, B. F. White likened them to public meetings and thus observed conventional documentary restraints designed around democratic discourse. He might well have employed narrative or pictorial styles, diverting documentary authority through his own voice. By recording Sacred Harp singings in the form of minutes, however, White gave emphasis and public recognition to its democratic techniques. And just as, through writing, he constructed singings as public events, he also constructed his audience as citizens of the singing community, not as uninvolved readers whom he might entertain.

Let us dwell briefly on this point. The relationship between experience and written observation has come under severe critical scrutiny in recent years over the habit, inherited from Romanticists, of "logocentrism." Writing, as opposed to direct human interaction, was presumed by the Romanticists to be afflicted with a kind of "disease of modernity," leading to the widespread social alienation that unlettered primitive peoples were observed to have avoided. It cannot be insignificant that, just as the effects of Romanticist thinking were being so widely felt, traditional forms of writing appeared that featured striking and countervailing stylistic tendencies. In these traditional forms, the stylistic features that most affected the realm of experience—for example, the extent and quality of the author, the domain of the describable, the development of techniques of indexicality—accumulated and matured around a coherent style. Just as "logocentric" ethnographers were celebrating the absence of writing, Sacred Harp singers were developing a form of writing, or antiwriting, that undermined the existential conditions that animated the ethnographic style. It was a form that emerged within its own presence, under the same enabling circumstance of speech, and thereby could have inscribed no desire for that presence from which it was never estranged. "Vain discourse"—writing authored outside the divine logos, of which Christian tradition has held such suspicion—was impossible.

This makes all the more compelling the fact that in the twentieth century, minutes disappeared from newspapers while retaining their importance in the singing community. Twentieth-century newspapers were increasingly viewed as instruments of modernism, so journalists sought devices to represent and translate events such as rural singings to readers not presumed to be a part of those events. Sacred Harp had to be reinvented as "culture" just as readers of newspapers were reinvented as "the public." In recent decades, Sacred Harp singing has found its most likely place in the feature section, where ethnographic realism is accepted rhetorical practice, where Sacred Harp singing can be made to appear or disappear at will.

Perhaps because twentieth-century culture-writing journalists aban doned the nominative style in reporting on Sacred Harp, the publication and distribution of minutes by singers themselves has prospered. The minutes have prevailed as functional even where other aspects of singing protocol have become somewhat perfunctory (e.g., the election of officers or the drafting of association bylaws). The practice of "spreading the minutes"—which once included newspapers as an outlet—was consolidated so that minutes from several singings in a certain region were combined in a single publication. The implied social collectivity is not new, however, and it derives from two nineteenth-century social forms that seem to have converged since World War II. Because the writing style of minutes emerges directly from the social structure of singings, we need to give ample attention to those two fundamental forms.

The first of these is the *singing convention*, the event structure. The first Sacred Harp convention was the Southern Musical Convention, organized by B. F. White in 1845 "after talking with a large number of friends" (James 1904, 57). It met annually and encompassed several counties in west central Georgia, including Crawford, Fayette, Henry, Lamar, Meriwether, Pike, Randolph, Troup, and Upson. The convention seems not to have been an evolving idea, however, for records indicate that the political structure of elected officers was consistent from the beginning, as was the practice of adopting a particular book.

Several scholars have noted that shape note singing conventions (from oblong books) coincided with gospel singing conventions in areas where both are established. For example, David Stanley traced the social configuration of the singing convention to the nineteenth-century camp meeting, noting particularly that the founding of several south Georgia gospel singing conventions coincided with the decline of the camp meeting following Civil War (Stanley 1982, 11). This would not account for the Southern Musical Convention, however, which was earlier than these dates. Likewise, in south central Kentucky, Lynwood Montell reported that gospel singing conventions have prospered for many years. There, singers and singing teachers recall that shape note conventions emerged from competition among singing schools and their students (Montell 1991, 30). There is no evidence, however, that the Southern Musical Convention or later Sacred Harp conventions were ever designed around competition among singing schools. In short, the facts surrounding the consistent organizational structure emerging from the Southern Musical Convention would seem to contradict both these accounts of the evolution of singing conventions.

Another possible source for Sacred Harp conventions was the nineteenth-century musical conventions held in northeastern U.S. cities. As early as 1829, a convention of singing schools was held in Concord, New Hampshire, for students of Lowell Mason. Partly as a result of Mason's continued promotion, the convention became an important outlet for music education in normal schools and eventually in music academies and university departments (Loessel 1959, 95; Lucas 1844). It is difficult to imagine that widely publicized public music gatherings in northern cities would have gone unnoticed, particular by journalists such as B. F. White. The interdenominational Richmond [Virginia] Sacred Music Society, for example, engaged George F. Root of the Normal Musical Institute of New York for their first civic Musical Convention in 1855 with the hope of improving public taste in choral and congregational singing (Stoutamire 1972, 216–18). A second convention that year featured Lowell Mason. And in his *Brief History of the Sacred Harp,* J. S. James cited the grand chorus at the Peace Jubilees of Boston in 1866 and other years (James 1904, 8).

None of these examples of northern conventions, however, would have employed the cluster of political and social features that has distinguished southern Sacred Harp conventions from the beginning: elected officers, an adopted songbook, designated geographic domain, independence from civic and religious institutions, for example. Thus it seems likely that, although B. F. White may have gotten the idea of holding annual conventions from northern models, the design of the southern Sacred Harp singing convention was his own. One wonders what he might have learned from his experiences with *Southern Harmony* (1835), compiled by his brother-in-law, William Walker, but Walker's biographers have not turned up convention minutes from the Spartanburg, South Carolina, area where Walker and White then lived.

Singing conventions were events and did not fundamentally feature enduring institutional structures as is common in Sacred Harp. For this, there was a second source social form, the *singing association,* which contributed to the political underpinning of the minutes. In Sacred Harp tradition, a singing association was an organization of singers, usually naming a particular geographic area, within which the convention would always be held. Its members elected officers and organized and conducted conventions according to adopted bylaws (see appendix 6). In this way, behavior at singings could be regulated according to local tastes, and the singing could adopt an official book for exclusive use. In practice, the words *association* and *convention* cover considerable mutual semantic ground and are often used interchangeably. A convention implied an enduring political structure, and an association would have been largely meaningless without an annual meeting.

Primarily because their chief purpose was to sing, associations were uncomplicated structures.[17] Bylaws usually consisted of no more than a dozen items, establishing the name of the association, its geographical range, the roles of officers, and perhaps one or two constraints on behavior. Most often, they regulated the form and not the content of behavior. For example, only one leader might be allowed on the floor at a time, or queries for discussion might have to be presented to the chair in writing before consideration, or the convention might be required to begin and end with prayer. But bylaws did not customarily regulate the content of speech, nor specify any ideological stance for the association, nor address the behavior of individuals outside the context of the convention.

Because of their simplicity and lack of ideological intrusion, associations were important social institutions in the persistence of traditional singing. Where singing schools had served the cause of a teacher or book compiler, singing associations could ultimately outlive the influence of a single individual. Perhaps more significantly, they could absorb the ideologies of a diverse and potentially divisive singing population. To understand how this worked, we need to examine the likely religious origins of the singing association.

Among several nineteenth-century American religious patterns that William Warren Sweet has called "frontier techniques," associationism lent strength to the rapidly expanding Christian movement of the Second Great Awakening. Developed by English Baptists, the association served on the frontier to link diverse congregations. Theologically, the Baptists derived the form from the fluidity of the primitive church as given in the New Testament. This was not a static organizational form but one that was able to express "the diverse forms in which the early community of faith expressed its life in Christ" (Bennett 1974, 53). "The letter destroys," Paul says in 2 Corinthians 3:6, "but the spirit makes alive." Whereas the Bible is a fundamental truth, a church must establish a living tradition adequate to the heterogeneous community of the world.[18]

English Baptists, following the lead of Congregational Separatists, took this to mean that "Christ had given authority to each distinct congregation to direct its own affairs" (Shurden 1967, 2). On the American frontier, associationism was one means by which individual churches could share resources and *discover* a unifying sense of purpose. Minutes taken at local and annual association meetings were printed and distributed even to other associations, reporting on and thus also affirming the value of their spiritual states of affairs. As a general rule, all written correspondence between associations was "predicated upon doctrinal agreement." If doubts about doctrinal agreement appeared possible, correspondence was postponed; if differences surfaced later, correspondence was terminated (Shurden 1967, 63). On the whole, associationism and written association minutes reflected their dissentist origins by retaining local doctrinal authority.

It seems incontrovertible that singing associations drew upon religious associationism as a model. In Georgia, theological writer Jesse Mercer, whose hymnbook, *Mercer's Cluster,* had been used as a prominent source for texts in *The Sacred Harp*, was an ardent proponent of Baptist associations. His *History of the Georgia Association* (1836) indicates the presence of Baptist associations in Georgia well before Sacred Harp singing reached the area. Among the several instances of nineteenth-century associationism, the frontier Baptist model most resembles Sacred Harp singing associations, particularly in the way autonomy was granted to member organizations.

Of course, associationism had a much broader presence in the early nineteenth century due, it is said, to the social consequences of free democracy.[19] Prominent in Alexis de Tocqueville's observations made in

1831–32, voluntary associations echoed the civil administration in their political structure and provided a means whereby "the independence of each individual is recognized," while "as in society, all the members advance at the same time towards the same end" (Tocqueville [1835] 1994, 1:198). According to Tocqueville's theory, voluntary associations arose rapidly as a stabilizing force in the absence of the monarchy or a theocracy.[20] They were a significant means by which Americans of the early national period resolved conflicts between society and the individual.

Tocqueville observed the extraordinary moral power generated in a free society by voluntary associations. Frequently, these institutions enhanced the authority of the oral over the written. In face-to-face meetings, he said, "Opinions are maintained with a warmth and energy that written language can never attain," and we understand him to mean that kind of writing which has sought to supplant spoken presence (1994, 1:192). We also understand him not to be describing the interdenominational moral associations that sought precisely to exert moral influence from great distances through the iterative and mediating properties of the written word in tracts (Foster 1960). Structurally and theologically, these top-heavy bureaucracies had little in common with Sacred Harp singing associations or, for that matter, with many Baptist associations in the South. The spirited antimission backlash they produced, particularly strong in the South, was related to objections to various Arminian techniques and accompanying bureaucracies, but at its core was the sanctity of the divine logos (see Wyatt-Brown 1970). Sacred Harp singing associations, by necessity, avoided affiliating with any creed or dogma, especially the divisive issue of missions.

Yet, far more so than the absence of the monarchy, it has been the rise of cultural America that has motivated traditional Sacred Harp writing. Over the course of its sesquicentury, traditional writing practices have tracked the meticulous development of Sacred Harp as a distinct musical tradition and a self-conceived musicoreligious practice. If any single trait has distinguished Sacred Harp writing from competing discourses, it has been this avoidance of symbolic representation, the enduring sense that the cumulative contributions and experiences of individual singers is the only meaningful map of traditional practice.

Surely it has been significant in the emergence of Sacred Harp as the preeminent representative of the nineteenth-century shape note movement that the tradition has, at almost every point in its history, fostered active writing traditions. Certainly the extent of these writing practices distinguishes Sacred Harp from other tunebooks. From the beginning, Sacred Harp was conceived as a noble cause and sacred obligation, derived directly from Scripture. As the tradition approached the postmodern age, its writers had already begun to assimilate those features of culture writing that echoed its basic principles. The tradition lay poised to accept in its number a slowly expanding—and then exploding—population of new singers who identified it in terms of culture. This "Sacred Harp revival" would precipitate an extraordinary confrontation of discourses, with consequences that few would have expected. Yet, observing the ways that the custodians of Sacred Harp have constructed singing as a tradition—through its writing practices, for example—we can be far less surprised by these results. It is only with such an understanding that we should proceed to an assessment of that "revival."

Chapter 4

"OUR SPIRITUAL MAINTENANCE HAS BEEN PERFORMED": SACRED HARP REVIVAL

In 1969, a decade before he published the current authoritative account of the Sacred Harp singing tradition, Buell Cobb made a brief but unprecedented observation about the state of Sacred Harp singing: "External influence of Sacred Harp is just beginning to be felt. Folk-song proponents have begun to seek out the Sacred Harp movement as a source of folk ways yet untapped" (Cobb 1969, 3).

What is notable about this remark is that by "folk-song proponents," Cobb meant *not* to include the promotional efforts of George Pullen Jackson or the literary salutes of the Agrarians, both of which occurred long before he wrote this passage. Rather, something else had just "begun."

What had begun was the practice by "folk-song proponents" of singing Sacred Harp as folk music. This folk music "revival"—meaning that traditional practices thought to be in decline were being "revived" as quasi-recreational activities—had been going on for quite some time. As a popular movement in America, it reached its apex, some say, in the early 1960s when it commanded considerable attention in the popular media. Arguably, its basic tenets have been assimilated into the pluralist atmosphere of contemporary mainstream culture. At the time, however, it featured its own array of institutions and motivations, often at odds with a more homogeneous mainstream culture, with "folksong" as an organizing principle. Under the folksong rubric, a variety of institutions were contrived to bring together a variety of traditional musical forms, often in a single venue, such as a folk festival variety concert. Whereas the musical forms were consistently traditional, the performance venues were contemporary. The consequence of this was that discrete texts from an increasingly stable canon of genres and master texts were elevated to representational status and then recontextualized as folksong revival performances. Compared with other forms in this canon (e.g., ballads), Sacred Harp music was not among those most frequently adopted by folksong enthusiasts.

The relative unimportance of Sacred Harp today seems hard to imagine. One finds an extraordinary "revival" of Sacred Harp institutions themselves, most of which trace their origins to initial contact with Sacred Harp as revived folksong. Sacred Harp conventions in northern and western cities, which submit minutes and operate with traditional procedures, can attract as many as four hundred singers! The magnitude and quality of this revival is a valid concern in its own right. But more important is the way traditional singers and their folk revival allies have successfully replicated Sacred Harp institutions.

In recent decades, folklore scholarship has brought to the folksong revival process an uncharitable scrutiny. The term *cultural intervention* has been coined as a label that includes well-meaning fascination with a cultural Other, a relationship that is facilitated, systematically so, by latent structural inequities. With this as a backdrop, it would be remarkable enough to describe a process by which singers have employed traditional forms and institutions to retain some measure of influence over the revival process. But, by so many accounts, an even more remarkable consequence is the degree to which these institutions have been reenergized by transforming antiquarian fascination into traditional practices and sentiments. Today, "folksong" recedes into the background as the central interpretive device for Sacred Harp revival. "Spiritual maintenance," one singer has called it—and this in an age where so many traditions are subjected in popular culture to postmodern detachment or are enlisted in dogmatic confrontation. This is what warrants our attention.

THE SACRED HARP REVIVAL

However singers conceive of the music nowadays—as "folksong" or "spiritual maintenance" or whatever—the influence of the folksong schema in the early revival years at *some* level is simply undeniable. Folksong as a "discourse" has provided at key moments an initial and widely available understanding of Sacred Harp to those who have had no prior contact with Sacred Harp singing. Over the relatively short period that this chapter addresses, this discourse has been refined and transformed, in large part to bring it in line with traditional practice. Although there is substantial variety in Sacred Harp practice, these discursive shifts have enabled a highly visible and widely available strain of practice that traditional singers have wholeheartedly endorsed.

An indication of the early influence of folksong regionally and locally was documented in a 1987 thesis by Wesleyan University music student Susan Garber on "The Sacred Harp Revival in New England." To determine, for instance, how singers came to the music, she submitted questionnaires to various New England singers. One responded that she "first heard 'Wondrous Love' in Israel, soon after reading George Pullen Jackson's book in a U.S.I.S. library in India" (Garber 1987, 234). This account is extraordinary, of course, but it is echoed by numerous less remarkable introductions to the tradition, even outside New England. These are the so-called folksong proponents that Buell Cobb recognized in 1969. They have in common an exposure to the singing tradition through some institutional component of folksong revival—recordings, folklore or early music courses, folk festivals, or even George Pullen Jackson's books—and a sense that what is being discovered is indicative of cultural difference.

Garber examined the earliest years of revival of Sacred Harp and identified several key sites of singing activity. There was sporadic interest among old-left folkies in 1950s New York City. It is possible that the stream of influence among the Populist Left originated at the Highlander Folk School in Monteagle, Tennessee, where Zilphia Horton introduced singing from *New Harp of Columbia* as early as 1939.[1] At the Berea, Kentucky, Christmas Country Dance School, a weeklong folk music and dance school that began in the late 1940s, Sacred Harp was featured in some form as early as 1959.[2] In the 1960s, Arthur Schrader, former music director at Old Sturbridge Village, examined the 1967 Sacred Harp minutes looking for old New England tunes that were popular in southern tradition. That same year, Neely Bruce, a graduate student at the University of Illinois, ran across *Southern Harmony* and *The Sacred Harp* while researching songs for a Christmas concert. Sacred Harp singers also performed at the Newport Folk Festival in Rhode Island in 1964. Linda Fannin was among the thirty-three singers who made the week-long bus trip to Newport. Her written report, reprinted in the *National Sacred Harp Newsletter* (March 1989), called the trip a "dream come true." Of the performances, she wrote: "At the festival our group sang three times before an enthusiastic crowd of twelve to fourteen thousand. Some of the songs we sang were 36b, 137, 192, 159, 143, and 200. The crowd really seemed to enjoy it and its response was wonderful. Other performers were: Johnny Cash, Dewey Shepard, the Doc Watson family, the Cajun group, and Jimmy Driftwood." At the time, this festival was the most influential event for a nationwide folksong revival movement.

In the 1970s, the character of folksong revival as a whole changed. Whereas the 1960s had witnessed media figures who reached large audiences through recordings and concerts, the next decade featured less celebrated but more numerous venues—local folk societies, small festivals, folk camps, and acoustic instrument specialty stores—many with a local populace more interested in participating than listening. Garber cites several New England settings, indicating in the 1970s a higher concentration in that region than elsewhere. But there were stirrings outside New England as well. There was informal singing throughout the early 1970s at the Ark Coffeehouse in Ann Arbor, Michigan; an all-day singing was held there in 1974. Group singing at the Fox Hollow Festival in Petersburg, New York, included Sacred Harp; participants there were linked to local singing in Chicago, Washington, and perhaps other localities. In the early 1970s a group was started in Bloomington, Indiana, by two singers who had participated in the Vermont-based Bread and Puppet Theater's performance of "Stations of the Cross," with Sacred Harp music led by Larry Gordon. Each deserves to have its story told; each would echo in varying degrees the general pattern outlined by Garber.

Some of these groups were choral performing ensembles, featuring rehearsed performances, set membership, and a formal director. It should be said that the most prominent of these—the Word of Mouth Chorus (Plainfield, Vermont), Norumbega Harmony (organized at Wellesley College, Boston), and the American Music Group (University of Illinois,

Urbana-Champaign)—were organized not so much around the folk music canon but around Early American choral music. Other groups were informal and might struggle through as few as one or two dozen songs in a single living-room session. There were also college courses that in some way revolved around Sacred Harp, offered by Neely Bruce at the University of Illinois and later at Wesleyan University and by Anthony Barrand at Marlboro College. Sometimes these courses led afterward to the formation of informal singing groups or choirs. In most of these settings, there was little interest in and sometimes little knowledge of southern traditional practice. Later, during the 1970s there was newfound awareness and occasional contact with southern tradition. For the northern singers, it almost always left a big impression.

"RIVERS OF DELIGHT": THE REVIVAL "GOES SOUTH"

Possibly no event was more pivotal in setting this process in motion than the 1976 bus tour of Larry Gordon's Word of Mouth Chorus. Based on a Vermont commune, the group was thoroughly steeped in counterculture values. It had coalesced loosely as a choral ensemble around several early 1970s performances of Early American music (Garber 1987, 210ff.). Some had been recruited from Goddard College and from the Bread and Puppet Theater. In one performance, a production of "Stations of the Cross" that drew upon the life of Jesus as a populist comment on contemporary politics, Gordon directed the music using selections from *The Sacred Harp*. In 1976, the Word of Mouth Chorus even compiled a songbook, *The Word of Mouth Early American Songbook,* that included many Sacred Harp songs, printed in round notes! Curious about the presence of an active southern singing tradition, Gordon contacted Hugh McGraw, then executive secretary of the Sacred Harp Publishing Company, and arranged to attend the 1976 Georgia State Convention as one of several performing and singing stops. Their transportation was a bus, painted in psychedelic designs.

By their own account, they were drawn to Sacred Harp by its "strength and spirit, and its raw Americanness of expression," but they were apprehensive about the "religiosity" of southern singers (Garber 1987, 212;

Gordon 1979). Indeed, Gordon's own assessment of the group's cultural background vis-à-vis the southern singers, as detailed in the liner notes to the recording they would later make, was that of "vast boundaries of age, culture, politics, and religion":

> In April 1976, a group of Word of Mouth singers traveled to the Georgia State Singing Convention and were profoundly impressed by this and several subsequent direct experiences with the ongoing southern shape-note tradition. We were moved by the deep fellowship among the participants, a fellowship that reached out to include us, bridging vast boundaries of age, culture, politics, and religion. Moreover, the singing itself—the rhythmic drive, the unrestrained quality of the voices, the sheer power of the sound—permanently altered our approach to Sacred Harp music. We like to regard Sacred Harp as a live tradition which can be the vehicle for a very special sharing among singers of all ages and abilities. In our area, people have begun once again to create new songs using this idiom, as well as new texts reflecting some of the concerns of our present-day lives. (Gordon 1979)

I mean not to suggest that these "vast boundaries" did not exist but that a discourse of irreconcilable difference had long prevailed, largely in culture writing, over a discourse of possible sameness. The minutes of the singing, in contrast to these notes, indicate that the chorus "sang several songs" as a group, some of which came from sources other than *The Sacred Harp* (see appendix 7). Some from the group also led on their own. The minutes make no assessments related to cultural differences, nor did the convention structure provide for such difference to be noticed.

At the convention, Gordon mentioned to Hugh McGraw that the New England singers were planning a performance at Wesleyan University in Middletown, Connecticut, organized by Neely Bruce. As Susan Garber reports (Garber 1987, 226): "He [McGraw] in turn announced that the singing in Middletown would be a first annual regional *convention,* and on the spot, according to Neely Bruce, some forty Southerners agreed to travel to Connecticut to attend it."

This event, then, was a kind of social drama, accumulating incremental and imperceptible historical change into a single, deeply felt ritual action. Had the southerners not elected to attend the New England singing, this event might have been just another adventure, fueled by ethnographic curiosity. But these visitors were singers, and the southerners undoubtedly saw an opportunity to extend the singing tradition as it was practiced in the South. In fact, Hugh McGraw had already been working very hard to ensure that the Sacred Harp would survive in future generations. Just two years before this, in 1974, he had sent out an impassioned letter to southern singers, urging them to organize singing schools for him to teach. For the summer of 1976, he received funding from the National Endowment for the Arts to organize fifteen two-week singing schools, conducted by various teachers, in Alabama, Georgia, Tennessee, and Mississippi. This monumental effort achieved modest success at best, so one can imagine the impact Gordon's group must have had at the Georgia Convention, having had enough interest to drive all the way from Vermont to sing.

Moreover, through his correspondence with singers throughout the country, McGraw had already come in contact with early Sacred Harp revival sites as they first emerged. He was aware of the extent of book sales throughout the country and the extent of organized groups of singers. Bulging files in his office with dates beginning around 1970 contain correspondence from throughout the country ordering books and records, requesting that he teach singing schools, or reporting on new singing groups. During the nostalgic bicentennial period, requests for festival appearances increased. Later, in 1978, royalty checks began appearing in unprecedented quantities for the use of two copyrighted songs on the Word of Mouth Chorus's popular Nonesuch recording, *Rivers of Delight*. In 1982, McGraw was awarded a National Heritage Fellowship. Thus there was good reason for him to believe that conventions might someday be organized in areas where folk revival singers were meeting.

Ultimately, as McGraw might have hoped, the traditional singing convention would serve as a medium that would supplant the manifestations of ethnographic consciousness—culture writing, informal singing gatherings, and folk festival and stage performances—as the authoritative Sacred Harp experience in folk revival contexts. Moreover, the convention system and all its trappings—hollow square seating, opening and closing prayer, elected officers, equitable distribution of opportunities to lead, recorded minutes, dinner-on-the-grounds, the practice of singing the shapes with each song, and the fellowship that attends all of this—provided minimal ground rules for the conduct of singings. Through the convention system, southern singers could adequately communicate the tradition's core values without the bracketing that folksong discourse customarily imposes. All of these influences seemed to converge at the 1976 Georgia State Convention. It may be too much to say that this was Sacred Harp's postmodern moment, but surely none has qualified more so.

Yet, if ethnographic imagination lost its foothold that day, it was, at least in part, accidental. Reciprocity in attending Sacred Harp singing conventions is a long-revered facet of traditional protocol. So the proposed trip might well have emerged not so much as an effort to impose practices or values on northern groups as from a traditional sense of obligation. McGraw later reflected on the motivation for early trips to this and other northern conventions:

> The main reason I've been to a lot of these places and helped organize their state convention is to get them sitting in parts in the hollow square, opening and closing with a prayer, having dinner on the table for the group, and always singing the notes. I know that after we learn the tune, there's no purpose in singing the notes, but it's a tradition. When we went to singing school, they taught us first the notes. And that's what I want to do—"seek the old paths and walk therein." And all these traditions—the memorial lesson, the election of officers, and having chairmen and an arranging committee—that's part of our tradition, too. That's what I've tried to instill in all these people.[3]

Yet, in reports of early northern conventions, there is never evidence of any pedagogical urgency. If anything, southern singers, again in keeping with traditional practice, took up the role of guests at distant conventions, making suggestions only when uncertainties arose. So the overall effect of this was not to replace one set of calculated practices with another, but to gradually reduce the role that cultural consciousness played in singing practice.

Minutes for the Middletown singing indicate an occasion uneventfully conducted according to traditional practice (see appendix 8).[4] Northern singers who were there, however, recall an atmosphere with some tension.

Some fondly remember a heartfelt testimonial by one southerner who announced that no one from his family had crossed the Mason-Dixon line since the Civil War, and he was proud that he had done so to attend a Sacred Harp singing. But surely the most enduring legacy was the beginning of a meaningful dialogue between southern traditional and northern folk revival singers and the establishment of a means of spreading Sacred Harp among folk revival singers in a way suitable to the singing tradition.

In years to follow, a chartered bus from the South has made regular appearances at each new northern convention, most frequently organized by retired Oxford, Alabama, schoolteacher Ruth Brown. It is difficult to overstate the extent to which this gesture has influenced local singing in northern areas. Not only did it demonstrate the extraordinary commitment of southern singers but, by lifting the quality of singing to unimaginable heights, it left on local groups a considerable burden to continue meeting these raised expectations. Because northern singers were not yet routinely traveling to southern singings, the northern state convention became the chief means by which many new singers grasped the vast spiritual potential of Sacred Harp singing in each new area.

Although the influence of the New England singing was unmistakable, it would not be realized until several years later when conventions and state singings began to spread to other areas (see appendix 9). More immediate in its impact on folk revival singing was the recording that Gordon's group would make, partly inspired by their trip south. Titled *Rivers of Delight* after a phrase from Samuel Stennett's hymn "On Jordan's Stormy Banks I Stand," the recording was released in 1979 by Nonesuch Records, a company at that time exceptional in its wide distribution and modest prices. Between 1979 and 1987, royalty payments to the Sacred Harp Publishing Company reflected sales of nearly 6,000 copies. This figure can be compared to the sale of less than 1,800, over approximately the same period, of New World Records' *White Spirituals from the Sacred Harp*, the field recording by Alan Lomax of the 1959 United Sacred Harp Singing Convention.

During this period, the recording had considerable impact on the repertoire and style of singers in revival areas. This is partly an observation of my own of informal singings in the Midwest. Sometimes it seemed an obligation to reproduce the *Rivers of Delight* repertoire in performances, even more so in informal settings. By the time the convention system came to the Midwest in the mid-1980s, folk revival singers had expanded their repertoire considerably but still favored these songs (see appendix 10).[5] More important, the recording was made in a studio with premeditated arrangements and a set group of singers. Whereas the recording was sometimes touted as rough-hewn in the manner of southern singing, in truth it reproduced little of the self-satisfied informality and sheer power of numbers that live convention recordings would later evoke. But *all* singers know that live convention recordings are notoriously inaccessible to those unfamiliar with the austere traditional sound.[6] So it may be that *Rivers of Delight* filled a specific need during an interim when the population of folk revival singers was just beginning to expand.

"WE'LL TREAT YOU SO MANY DIFFERENT WAYS": BUELL COBB'S RHETORIC OF INVOLVEMENT

Just as the Vermont singers were transcending "vast boundaries of age, culture, politics, and religion," an influential account of the Sacred Harp tradition was set to emerge that would bring the population of singers much closer. Published in 1978, Buell E. Cobb Jr.'s *The Sacred Harp: A Tradition and Its Music* was a long-overdue update of the historical record of Sacred Harp written decades earlier by George Pullen Jackson. Cobb's book has remained in print throughout the pivotal years of the revival and is now available in paperback. It is still the authoritative historical account of Sacred Harp singing, but it is also a cogent statement of Sacred Harp core values. Indeed, its most significant improvement over previous works was to present the tradition more as a viable system of cultural values and social institutions than as a holdover from the past.

Cobb's impeccable prose reflects conscientious handling of many difficult issues. Still within the general romantic framework that guided Jackson, Cobb overhauled the descriptive language, borrowing generously from informal speech to depict a tradition wholly at ease with itself. For instance, in discussing "Attitudes and Values," he observed:

> Altogether, the tradition is a curious blend of the sacred and the secular: from the hybrid origin of many of the songs themselves to the

actual singing, whether in the "meeting house" or at a county court-house. Noticeably, every session is opened and closed with prayer. For some of the singers this may be only a token gesture; for others the prayer is a meaningful moment, serving to tie all the individual expressions of song together and proffer them as a tribute to God.

But there is sense of pleasure for its own sake here too. This is foot-tapping music. And the singers grin or nudge their neighbors when the singing is particularly good. The tenors eye the "tribble" admir-ingly when they can clip along at ease on a tune that runs high. Or both commend the bass class when it hits the fuging songs with heft. Sometimes a leader, after finishing one song, will mop his brow with his hankerchief, then look across the page and say, "Now let's get that other one." And even though Sacred Harp singers are known for vo-calizing the shape-note sounds, one of their number will occasionally insist that they sing not so much by note as "by letter." "We just open our mouths," the explanation goes, "and let 'er fly." (17)

Cobb's style was friendly and accessible, as if his writing itself emerged from the amusement and satisfaction of the singers. Significantly, when Cobb used quoted speech, even dialect, it was as if the speakers shared with the readers in the self-consciousness of quotation, as if the quotation was a mutually acknowledged breakthrough into performance of regional stereotype. Gone from Jackson's style was the sense that something ob-scure and antique has been discovered; gone from the regionalists was the voyeuristic point of view. Without ever actually disputing these ap-proaches, Cobb refracted them through the lens not of a circumstantial encounter with Sacred Harp but of his own continued involvement with singing. Without the fanfare of a scholarly dispute, a new imagery was evolved.

In this respect, particularly in the impact of the book on the emerging Sacred Harp revival, Cobb's status as a writer and singer is of considerable significance. Cobb grew up in Cullman, Alabama—situated in a Sacred Harp stronghold—but discovered Sacred Harp, while in college, through such regionalist writers as Donald Davidson and Carl Carmer. His book had its earliest incarnation as an English department master's thesis at Au-burn University (Cobb 1969). Cobb's attention to such matters as spoken language and attitudes and values—to the tradition as a whole—came from the descriptive apparatus of literary regionalism. His first publication on the subject, "The Sacred Harp of the South" (Cobb 1968), in fact, derived the significance of the tradition largely from the Southern Agrarian movement. Yet, in his thesis, completed a year later, Cobb's dependence on literature had apparently decreased, and his work instead reflected and even facilitated his own expanding involvement with singing. His book, published more than a decade later, bears the mark of many deep and enduring friendships gained during the course of its writing. As reviewers noted, this was one of its greatest assets.

Thus the account of Sacred Harp in Cobb's book was punctuated with traditional devices by which singers customarily engaged their public, particularly visitors or new singers. On the subject of guests or beginners, one singer says, "We'll treat you so many different ways, you're bound to like some of 'em" (18); another, on the tendency for young people who have neglected singing to return to it later in life, explains that "they could see the beauty, feel the power in it" (156). With the regionalists, dialogue was internal to the narrative; with Cobb, it reached outward to the reader. Cobb looked to Carmer's "slim brown-eyed girl," for example, to measure the restless excitement of a singing. But he ended his account just one sentence short of Carmer's narrative subplot, which had her courting by the spring after the dinner hour ended (155–56).

Even more influential were the occasions where he translated observation into motivation. For example, the participants "may sing, before they finish, upward of a hundred songs from the over five hundred entries in their stout, oblong book. And they do not go until they are drained, their voices hoarse—until they simply are not up to anymore of a good thing" (3). Whether "anymore of a good thing" or "pleasure for its own sake," Cobb's version of the tradition was an accessible one, one where traditional attitudes and values were set free from historical bonds. As his writing tracked his own involvement in singing, it could increasingly provide a model for the viable experiences of other newcomers. His basic devices of unpretentious humor, spiritual fulfillment, and emotional power are to be found repeatedly today in the encounter narratives of contemporary new singers.

The influence of the book, it should not go without saying, has been amplified considerably by his continued involvement as a singer. Throughout traditional singing areas, Cobb has thrown his support behind singing conventions, often in uncelebrated roles, all in the spirit of keeping singing alive in places where its roots are deepest. In no small way, this has served to validate his account for a singing tradition that holds such efforts far more dear than written words.

"WE LAID ASIDE OUR GUITARS": CHICAGO AND BEYOND

Although both Cobb's book and *Rivers of Delight* contributed essential elements, the Sacred Harp revival is ultimately to be measured in terms of the new conventions it spawned and the singers who attended them. In this respect, no site has been more influential than Chicago. From its origins in eclectic folksinging and the Old Town School of Folk Music to its relentless support of southern tradition, from its humble living-room gatherings to the magnificence of its present-day Midwest Convention, Chicago has set much of the tone of contemporary Sacred Harp revival.

Its beginnings were unassuming enough. Most of the early principals, says singer Ted Johnson, had roots in folk music and were interested in various forms of vernacular singing.[7] As his wife, Marcia Johnson, put it, only partly facetiously, one night in 1983 they "laid aside their guitars." (The guitar, of course, figured prominently in many folksong revival "re-contextualizations.") Singings, such as they were, were informal, consisting of ten or so friends meeting in the living room trying out various parts from a repertoire of only a few songs. They did not sing the shapes.

There was a marked shift in the size and nature of the group on the occasion in 1983 of an afternoon of music, including Sacred Harp, at the Old Town School of Folk Music. The Old Town School is an institution surviving from the 1960s folksong revival that has served continuously as a gathering place for folk musicians. It still offers concerts, dances, music lessons, and sales of books, recordings, instruments, and other folk music materials. Ted Johnson recalls that for many, it wasn't clear what was going to happen: "And when the people arrived at the Old Town School they thought that they were just going to be treated to a concert, but instead, Phil Trier, who was the person who had done this before, got the audience there involved in singing—said, 'You people sit here; here's music'—so instead of just being an audience people found themselves singing the music." For some of the singers, the Old Town event was the first *public* singing, where Sacred Harp, and not preestablished friendships, was the basis for convening. Without friendship habits, the event needed a more palpable structure. Phil Trier was able to provide that.

Because he had sung Sacred Harp elsewhere, Trier had considerable influence over the group's early performance practices. His experience had come from the Fox Hollow Folk Festival, in Petersburg, New York, where Sacred Harp was presented along with various other vernacular song forms.[8] In Chicago, he became the only song leader and took a choir director's interest in interpreting each song, giving specific instructions, for instance, in the use of vocal dynamics. This practice changed only when some from the group contacted Hugh McGraw and began "going South"—attending southern singings. For some, a crucial trip to the Holly Springs, Georgia, singing served as a kind of personal epiphany. Awakened to the traditional preference for and experiential advantages of turn-taking and perhaps also emboldened by a more authentic link to the traditions associated with the book, singers began to insist on more democratic involvement.

These impulses were given a considerable boost on the occasion of the first Illinois State Convention in 1985. The event was organized by the Chicagoans and by singers in Charleston, Illinois, a group then steeped in choral performance practice. It was held "half-way between," in Paxton, Illinois. By this time the Chicago singers were communicating regularly with Hugh McGraw. Just as with Middletown, when southern singers heard that a convention was being planned, they made plans to bring a group of singers. Ted Johnson recalls one pivotal telephone conversation during which McGraw inquired about the convention:

When we were getting ready for this Paxton thing, Hugh McGraw said, "You *do* sing the notes?" And we said, on the phone, "Why, no, we don't." And there was this silence, and he said, "Well, you'll learn." And so for months before the Paxton First Illinois Convention we were trying to learn to sing the notes. Some of us, in fact, myself included, resisted it, saying that it seemed like just another level of difficulty.

The convention was unremarkable save for the effect of solidifying existing ties between Chicago and southern tradition. On the occasion of the
tenth anniversary of the singing, Ted Mercer wrote a brief retrospective,
calling it "by today's standards . . . a rather odd event."[9] Each of the spon-
soring groups presented short performances; when called to lead, Chica-
goan Judy Hauff armed herself with a music stand so she could conduct
with both hands. But history has proven decisively that these were minor
distractions: the midwest singers were already beginning to realize that the
"fountainhead of this tradition," as Ted Johnson would come to call it,
was in the South.

Inspired by this "fountainhead," the Chicagoans set about with almost
evangelical intensity to promote the music in the Midwest. As it turned
out, they were well suited for the task. Ted Johnson was a lucid writer,
with an established interest in American vernacular music. Marcia Johnson, his wife, was a compelling writer and speaker who could manage
with ease the sensitive and emotional matters that concern Sacred Harp
singers. Ted Mercer had extraordinary organizing acumen and seemingly
endless energy. Judy Hauff brought to the group essential musical insights,
and early on was able to grasp the elusive components of Sacred Harp
composition style. Many others, whose names go unmentioned only with
injustice, echoed and complemented the sentiments and skills of these
four. On the whole, the group mustered an impressive array of resources,
talent, and commitment and seemed to work together well. Better than
others, Chicagoans grasped the essential shifts in the relationship between
cultural self and cultural other that were necessary for a genuine coalition.
As their understanding of the complexities of Sacred Harp tradition grew,
so, too, did the daunting task of conveying this to other new singers. For
this, something more was needed.

"COVERING THE COUNTRY LIKE KUDZU":
THE SACRED HARP NEWSLETTERS

Even before the Illinois Convention was held, the Chicagoans were looking to the future. They published the first monthly *Chicago Sacred Harp
Newsletter* in February 1985. Early issues provided essential logistical in-

formation: singing schedules, travel arrangements, even lists of songs the group had practiced. As time passed, however, the newsletter was used increasingly to articulate the experiences of singers: accounts of trips to singings, interviews with longtime singers, debates about style, new songs, short historical articles, and photographs of people at singings. Infused throughout much of this was a mix of reverence for tradition and a kind of self-effacing humor, for example, poking fun at regional cuisine or recounting ludicrous adventures trying to follow sketchy directions to some out-of-the-way singing. Even logistics took on a life of its own when one Chicago singer who worked as a travel agent recommended a particular low-fare "Sacred Harp Shuttle" to and from Chicago and Birmingham.

Writers emerged from all points, some stretching the rhetorical compass of Sacred Harp writing to unforeseen limits. There was, for example, Richard Whatley of Suwannee, Georgia, whose wry humor could easily disarm proprieties or tensions that had crept unacknowledged into the new singings. Or there was Murray Simmons of Hattiesburg, Mississippi, whose confessional style could magically find a strand of pathos dangling from some subject and pull gently until the whole scene unraveled. The effect of these and other writers' commentary was to discover in "tradition" a kind of protocol to be followed by agreement but to disarm the social and cultural barriers that inhibited full involvement.

Essential to this process was the newsletter's systematic informality. Much of the material was submitted from singers from around the country, and it was set in different typefaces, or sometimes even pasted into the layout *without being retyped at all!* This gave the appearance of minimal editorial manipulation and lent at times a kind of postmodern pastiche texture to the newsletter. The following, for example, comprised the contents of a typical newsletter issue, January–February 1992 (vol. 7, no. 5): Occupying two pages were verbatim comments on the 1991 Midwest Convention excerpted from letters written by Lawrence Olszewski of Knoxville, Tennessee. Typically, it was an observation of an extraordinary event, with the writer situated inside the experience and under its spell. It closed with the following passage:

The special sessions for the children, the Woottens and the Iveys leading a song was good for the program. Got a chance to sit back a spell and watch other people sing and lead. One can get wrapped up in the music and forget where one is. Some people looked like they were in the middle of a revival, eyes glazed, heads down, mesmerized in the book and the music. Others, like they were human tuning forks with feet keeping time, eyes smiling and leaning into the tune with voice, heart, mind, and soul. It is good to get out into the big wide world of Harp singing. One can realize the vastness of other folk in the tuning fork world. The goodness, the fellowship, the spirit is with us, hopefully forever more; till next time, our spiritual maintenance has been performed.

This item was sandwiched between recent clippings on Sacred Harp, pasted in, from the *Hyde Park Herald* and the *Atlanta Journal and Constitution;* a photo of the dinner line from the Chicago anniversary singing; and an announcement of Sacred Harp classes at the Augusta Heritage Center in West Virginia. These were punctuated by short excerpts from various letters: from a veteran singer from near Arab, Alabama; from a Sephardic Jewish singer from Chicago; from a Boston singer announcing a singing in William Billings's home church; from a couple from Dallas, Texas; and from a reader from Guam.

Also in the newsletter, in increasing numbers over the years, were photographs—of singers leading or sitting in the hollow square, talking during dinner, posing in front of a favorite church or singing building. And always, in accounts submitted by readers and in the captions to photographs, there were names, juxtaposed with other names, in a gradual but ultimately defiant gesture against the divisive principle of Sacred Harp tradition as an autonomous cultural enclave—as the "fasola folk." One memorable article proclaimed, "Sacred Harp Singers Repair State Line Church," and described in words and photographs how "a work crew made up of singers from Georgia, Alabama, Wisconsin, and Illinois met at State Line Church on June 26th to raise the roof once more" (June/July 1993). Here was the essence of the new revival—an assimilationist discourse that sought out scenes of common experience, common struggle. On the whole, the newsletter managed to celebrate and validate, on a single scale, the proven tenure of members of old southern singing families, the exaggerated devotion of a convert "bitten by the bug," and the enthusiasm of an enchanted beginner.

These scenes were necessarily a portrait of harmony. But, particularly in the early years when singing practices were still taking shape in Chicago, there were debates in the newsletter over variations in performance practice. These debates, in the *Chicago Newsletter* and in newsletters that were founded in other communities, affected much of the folk revival areas, although to widely varying degrees and with different results. In Chicago, much as in the *Organ,* local writers had the upper hand and sometimes took an unequivocal stance on performance issues. Following the second Illinois convention, for example, Ted Johnson took issue with those who would have installed choral performance practice at singings:

> For it is here—when one performs—that the [hollow] square breaks up; this kind of singing turns itself inside out. Instead of what it was it becomes a *choir* again, and you follow a director who is telling you, pianissimo here, fortissimo there. And it's always the same director for every song, rather than a heterogeneous and organic community of directors. And you *rehearse* things; gratification is deferred; salvation is for later if you're good. There's something to be said for this approach, especially if you intend to sing the Bach B Minor Mass, for example. But it's not the tradition of Sacred Harp. I believe I have learned, sometimes instinctively, sometimes with difficulty and resistance, that the rule to follow is: "Trust the tradition." And it's basically not a performing tradition. (vol. 2, no. 1, 1986)

There was some opposition to this, both local and elsewhere, but the southern turn-taking system was adopted for most occasions in Chicago. In 1987 and 1988, Chicago, St. Louis, and Madison, Wisconsin, each issued convention recordings on cassette—the first live convention recordings ever produced from singings outside the South. Taking a form that had once been the exclusive province of folklore fieldwork, these important recordings provided the means for northern singers to become their own ethnographic objects. Above and beyond any other merits, northern convention recordings served to validate both the experience of attending the convention and the aesthetic principles that defined convention musical performance practices. On the whole, during this formative period, the definitive performance issues seemed to coalesce around the two poles of choral and traditional practice. Newsletter writers in favor of traditional practice astutely transformed cultural difference into a kind of procedural formalism. "Trust the tradition" meant: submit to its purity of form.

The style and content of the *Chicago Sacred Harp Newsletter* was of tremendous value in shaping the quality of the Sacred Harp experience for northern singers. But long before these effects were realized, its significance was felt in other areas. In response to the Chicago experiment— indeed, only four months later—Hugh McGraw published the first *National Sacred Harp Newsletter* in June 1985.[10] A southern-based *National Newsletter* would remind new singers that the Sacred Harp tradition was indeed based in the South (a fact not all northern beginners knew) and, by its nature, moderate the effects of folksong revival rhetoric. Surely this was not just a good idea but a healthy respect for the power of postmodern technologies such as photocopying. Sure enough, in April 1986, Susan Garber founded the *Northeast Sacred Harp News* in Connecticut. Others followed, and the floodgates were opened.

In keeping with traditional writing practice (and unlike other Sacred Harp newsletters), the *National Newsletter* was filled with lists, names, and announcements. From the beginning, a central feature was the list of annual singings for the month. In the summer months, this list could fill two pages, and this was sometimes expanded to three with another list, by state and city, of regular group meetings. As the nationwide movement grew, so did the list of group singings—so much so that the *Newsletter* began omitting it in alternating issues. There were also announcements of births, deaths, wedding anniversaries, lectures, performances, and publications. State conventions were boldly announced, with state names in near inch-high type.

A different sort of list was the monthly compilation of singers' birthdays—the purest gesture of democratic recognition—introduced in only the second number. That same issue featured the first recipe: Charlene Wallace's "Good Old-Fashioned Tea Cakes." The third issue introduced the monthly Scripture passage, which was sometimes submitted by singers and identified as a favorite verse. Each of these devices echoed traditional rhetorical practices, such as employed in the minutes, by providing a limited design for the reproduction of experience in print.

Frequently, though not monthly, there was a featured account of a "Citizen of the Month," reminiscent of the biographical writing of J. S. James and Earl Thurman. These columns contain valuable material, in many cases available nowhere else in print, on the most highly esteemed singers. There were also reprints of archival material—for example, old and recent newspaper clippings, quoted passages from William Billings, reprinted obituaries for such figures as J. S. James and William Walker, and a five-part serialized reprint of the first issue of *Sacred Harp Journal* from 1931. There were discourses on "Music" (August 1986), "What Is a Singing?" (May 1987), and a lengthy retrospective of George Pullen Jackson, calling him a "true son of the Sacred Harp" (February 1988). The newsletter listed contemporary Sacred Harp material for sale—books, recordings, T-shirts, and minute books, for example—but generally only included materials produced or distributed by the Sacred Harp Publishing Company.

Like the *Chicago Newsletter*, the *National Newsletter* used humor extensively and effectively, smoothing over serious issues here, providing an innocent chuckle there. Always, an issue ended with the personable question "And how was your month?" At the beginning, along with the oft-quoted Rev. 14:2, "and I heard the voice of harpers harping with their harps," the masthead proclaimed, "Covering the Country like Kudzu." This southern in-joke confirmed the movement's epicenter and suggested a phenomenon so irresistible that it might, like the dauntless kudzu vine, get out of hand. Sometimes jokes and proverbs unrelated to singing were included as "A Little Humor," "Thought for the Month," or even a cartoon clipped from a newspaper. Often the theme was humility: one epithet read, "He who knows and knows he knows, he is wise, follow him. But he who knows not and knows not he knows not, he is a fool, shun him." Sometimes humor reassured readers that no pretense was intended. One issue featured the kind of wildly exaggerated "dieting tips" that circulate in Xeroxlore. In the recipe column, Hugh McGraw, claiming no recipes had been submitted, once provided his own "How to make a bologna sandwich" and threatened to give instructions on instant coffee if no recipes were sent in for the next issue.

In both newsletters, readers submitted testimonials to the music's extraordinary significance. Singers would report on trips to conventions, but encounter narratives, describing Sacred Harp as a new experience, were understandably rare in the *National Newsletter*. There, convention reports often took the form of travel journals, describing tourist activities along the way, unusual travel or hospitality arrangements, or the scenic features of the convention site. In some of these travel accounts, there were antinarrative elements that undermined the significance of the singer's personal experience. One of these generalized the experience as a "Typical Month in the Life of a Sacred Harp Singer," punctuated with mileage tallies, totaling "30 Hours of Singing; 3665 Miles" (July 1985). In the *Chicago Newsletter,* the prevailing thematic element was more often the singer's own experience.

Like the "pastiche" appearance of the *Chicago Newsletter,* the *National Newsletter* had its own means of deflecting editorial authority. Not infrequently, editors would beg readers to send in material—sometimes only half-seriously, as in Hugh McGraw's call for recipes. Although these pleas were surely genuine, they also had the effect of deemphasizing the editorial role, projecting "ownership" of the publication onto the readers. Indeed, this was policy, as the editors, on the occasion of some layout changes, took care to point out:

> To us, the purpose of the *Newsletter* is clear: a source of information for the Sacred Harp singing community. We print lists of almost all singings held throughout the United States. We relay schedule changes and convention updates. We report deaths, births, marriages, anniversaries and other "people news." We print features such as "What Happened at the Singing Convention" and "Citizen of the Month." And we publish recipes, poems and special holiday articles.
>
> Furthermore, we know what the *Newsletter isn't*. This publication is not a forum for heated debates. Sure, we will print articles on various ideas and theories, but we want to steer clear of becoming a bat-

tleground for controversy. For the most part, we believe the *Newslet-ter* should be pleasant and informative. And we think that our readers feel the same way. (October/November 1991)

Although more subscriptions came from traditional areas than from any other area, the *National Newsletter* appealed to readers nationwide.[11] By deliberately steering clear of folksong revival and other "heated debates," it carved a space for traditional forms and traditional voices. But it was, nonetheless, a *national* publication, so, by its example, it could project onto the movement nationwide the traditional structures through which these voices were articulated.

"DIVINE IGNORANCE": SETTLING IN WITH FOLKSONG

When one considers that the association of Sacred Harp with folksong revival institutions—from regional writing to folk festivals to field record-ings—dates from the 1920s, it seems remarkable that not until the 1980s did any substantial revival occur. There are undoubtedly reasons for this that were beyond anyone's control, including the availability of postmod-ern technologies, the varying concept of folksong in public discourse, even the relative ages of the participants. But more important here is to consider which approaches to folksong, within the spectrum of those available, seemed to produce what most have considered satisfying results. This pro-cess is always local, I hasten to add, so that efforts at revival must inevi-tably address first the community of singers close at hand.

Among the new Sacred Harp sites, Chicago has been exceptional in the success it has had establishing singing institutions with a broad support from the traditional singing community. Its Midwest Convention, first held in 1986, has been enthusiastically supported by southern singers. By 1992, it had grown, some said, to more than 400 singers. In 1990, the United Sacred Harp Musical Association, founded in 1904 as a "central organization of local conventions," held its annual convention in Chi-cago—the first time outside the South (on its origin, see Cobb 1978, 138). Three Chicagoans published compositions in the 1991 edition of *The Sa-cred Harp:* Judy Hauff (four songs), Ted Mercer, and Ted Johnson. Ted

Mercer was elected to the board of directors of the Sacred Harp Publishing Company.

So it seems important to consider why such unremarkable beginnings in Chicago should have had such remarkable results. Significantly, none of the core Chicago singers had competing professional interests. They were not performers or choir directors, with an inherent investment in "interpreting" the music, nor were they cultural scholars, whose attention might be diverted by other musical forms or other means of expression, such as writing. Not having any substantial local or regional affiliation with shape note history, they may have been more inclined to "trust the tradition" than to invent themselves as the consequence of regional history. An unseen influence may have been the overall atmosphere of folk-song revival in Chicago, which, particularly after the University of Chicago Folk Festival began in 1961, fostered an established interest in traditional performers, rather than merely promoting local folk-style professional entertainers. This is not to judge alternatives as less authentic. But it does seem that where one seeks to support living traditions, even with the purpose of enhancing one's own experiential authenticity, these are the conditions that are favorable.

Ted Johnson once described the quality of "divine ignorance" that seemed unique to those who found satisfaction in traditional performance practice. Although he was writing particularly about the requisite skills for composing in Sacred Harp style, his comments have implications that are general:

> In the past few years, as we've all been caught up and swept along in the cultural freshet of shapenote singing, we seem to have been rearranging our lives in various ways. Have you noticed? For one thing, quite aside from the wonderful sense of friendship and community that has grown among us, we've been learning some new survival skills: how to carry a tune, to sing, to read music, to sing shapes, to lead songs, to pull a reasonable pitch out of a hat.
>
> . . . The more you sing this music the more you think you might like to put together some of it yourself. Of course you are unencumbered by any kind of training in musical composition—innocent of

any experience in the field—but why let little things like that stop you? After all, that's part of the tradition too, isn't it? Lots of nice tunes in the book were written by people who never graduated from musical conservatories. So in some kind of divine ignorance we just sail right into it.

Sacred Harp tradition, of its own account, is designed precisely to reward those who are "swept along in the cultural freshet of shapenote singing." Therein lay an irony: the authority or esteem that southern tradition held in folk revival areas was derived, at least in these early years, from folk revival discourse. What made things work in Chicago was that this core group of singers "rearranged their lives." They were sufficiently steeped in folk revival discourse to recognize traditional authority, but not so much that they merely reproduced that discourse. They had to make a crucial shift from a Romanticist perspective that derived generalized transcendent features of folksong from the music to a neoformalist one that deferred specifically to the authority of traditional form.

This is not to suggest that folksong revival institutions are inherently sinister or somehow incompatible with Sacred Harp tradition. But they are not the same as the traditional institutions that they presume in part to represent. In the South, for example, singers participate in folk festivals and receive support from public folklore programs. Here is how singer Pearl Guier described an Alabama folk festival performance in the *National Newsletter*:

Folk Festival Held in Oxford, Alabama

Early on a very cold December morning, a group of fourteen hardy Sacred Harp singers arrived at Oxford High School to participate in a Folk Festival. As the students entered the gymnasium, they could observe a lady weaving various useful objects on two looms. Two woodcarvers, a dollmaker and a chair caner were displaying their wares and explaining how the objects were made. One display contained antique clothing. One unusual display was basket-weaving and wreath-making using *kudzu* vines. The last stop for the students was in a section of the gymnasium where a group of Sacred Harp singers waited to sing for them and talk to them. Jeff Sheppard was in charge of the Sacred Harp presentation.

Jeff did a great job of telling each group how Sacred Harp was started in America—the tradition of singing the notes, then the words. He explained the method of teaching by holding singing schools. The fun and fellowship the singers feel toward each other is evident when a singing is attended. All the students showed interest and were attentive to Jeff's information and our singing. Some of them sat with the singers and sang along. Several of the students managed to keep coming back with other groups and expressed a desire to attend a singing.

When the program was completed, the principal invited the singers to go to the school lunch room where they were served a delicious lunch.

There has been a lot of favorable comment about the appearance of the singers, and plans are already underway to invite them back to the high school next year. (March 1989)

Sacred Harp singers are eager to tell the world about their tradition and can display inexhaustible generosity in doing so. Folksong institutions are one way of getting the message out, but never, ever, are they mistaken for traditional singing institutions.

For one thing, special effort must be made to prepare for *any* event that is not on the calendar of traditional events. In such cases, the logistics of convening a performing group of sufficient size is not always easy but is aided considerably by the deep well of traditional skill from which to draw. In Northport, Alabama, leaders arrange for the performance at the annual Kentucky festival by soliciting support at nearby singings in the weeks prior to the festival. Much the same procedure is used to arrange performances at nursing homes. To muster a group to assist Terry Wootten's 1994 singing school in London—part of a conference on southern culture—singers put out a call for help nearly a year in advance that was announced at singings, printed in newsletters, and sent out by e-mail. Where large groups of singers are desired, some festival planners actually plan the performance around the singing convention schedule. For example, the City Stages festival in Birmingham, Alabama, usually coincides with the National Convention in June. Festival planners schedule the performance at a time just after the convention ends, and arrange for a bus to transport singers from the convention site to the festival site.

At festival performances, admission gate personnel, who are accustomed to set ensembles and lists of performer names, must admit an indeterminate number of singers. Sometimes they are told to admit anyone with a *Sacred Harp* book. Thus, both singers and festival organizers have to make adjustments to customary procedures. For singers, this is a pleasant enough thing to do. But never is it self-motivating in the manner of all-day singings. It is always done, for example, as a courtesy to the community, to promote the music, or to raise money. Usually there is the hope that the audience will have "expressed a desire to attend a singing." This is the view not only in the South but wherever advocates of singing convention protocol prevail.

In the North, where more singers come from a folk music or choral background, there is often a greater desire to give performances. When the result of this is a rehearsed ensemble of set membership, an unpleasant tension can arise from competition for attention between the performing ensemble and the local informal singing group. The South has produced its share of Sacred Harp performers, too, but there the aesthetic superiority of public convention-style singing is so deeply rooted that performing groups are generally not seen as threatening. Southern singers seem to take some delight in the fact that what is unquestionably *their* music would be of interest in the worlds of bluegrass, country music, or choral performance. Again, getting the word out is not a bad thing, but it is not the most important thing.

An unusually successful instance of the use of the folksong concept is the "Capital City" singing, held each July in Montgomery, Alabama. One of its chief supporters is Christian Harmony singer Art Deason, who is notable for the historic interest he has in the music. Recently it has been held in the reconstructed historic district, "Alabama Old Town," and is partly sponsored by the Alabama State Council on the Arts. The singing was begun in 1987 in honor of then Alabama governor Guy Hunt, a Primitive Baptist preacher and occasional singer. It is held on a Thursday so as not to conflict with scheduled singings; no Sacred Harp minutes are submitted.

At the Capital City Singing, the distinctive feature that folksong seems, in part, to facilitate is the use of more than one tunebook. This singing features, in equal periods of time, the four tunebooks used in Alabama: the Cooper Revision and the 1991 Revision of *The Sacred Harp,* the *Colored Sacred Harp,* and the *Christian Harmony.* In general practice, the use of more than one book at a singing is discouraged, dating at least to the turbulent decades of the early twentieth century when proponents of various books vied for singers' support. The idea of folksong, allied with the concept of a native state culture, provides the impetus for this practice to be set aside but not challenged. Otherwise, the event is operated as a singing.

In addition to these structural matters, there are also conflicts of value that can intrude on folksong revival events. Sacred Harp singers, Buell Cobb has written, "have never been fond of the term 'folk music' when applied to their singing" (1978:30). As the presence of the revival drew closer to traditional singing in the 1980s, so also did latent unattractive features of the folksong concept. The *National Newsletter* took several occasions to speak out on the subject. One of these was in the *Newsletter*'s first year, in a column on the faithfulness and devotion of singers, "When It's Got You, It's Got You" (December 1985). It was concluded that Sacred Harp singers "do not take part because they are curious or because there is a present-day fad about 'folk music.'" Rather, something powerful has "taken hold" of them.

The most serious issue was not commitment, however. Some believe that folksong revival events are distinguished as secular and shouldn't be associated with Sacred Harp music. This was the suggestion of an unsigned item that appeared in the *National Newsletter* in March 1986:

When you should and when you shouldn't

Recently a young lady telephoned me and asked if I would arrange for a group of Sacred Harp singers to sing at a hootenanny. I told her I would be glad to but before we completed the arrangements there were certain things she would need to understand.

First, that Sacred Harp music is largely based on the words of the Bible and the great hymnists, Watts, Wesley, Cowper, Doddridge and others. This music, therefore, is strictly of a religious nature. Secondly, since this is the case, the singing of this music would have to be done under appropriate circumstances and this would call for an atmosphere of reverence and devout worship. I explained that all Sacred Harp singings are opened and closed with prayer and that for many generations countless thousands of people have found this music to be genuine expression of piety and grace. Under suitable conditions that would meet these requirements, we would be glad to sing.

. . . Sacred Harp music has as great a message for 1986 as it did for 1844. This message, though, will not be improved by conforming to the various fads of the passing years. Let us, therefore, remember a quotation used by the "venerable and intransigent" B. F. White, "Ask for the old paths and walk therein." Many people insist that the mountain should come to Mahomet, but in the natural order of things the reverse is true and Mahomet should come to the mountain. He'll be welcomed gladly.

Surely no one in 1986 was really organizing a "hootenanny." Nonetheless, this carefully constructed parable effectively posited limits, reassurances, and guidelines for participation in what was then a rapidly growing Sacred Harp revival. No one would take offense at this; no specific events would be "off limits." But by clever indirection, *everyone* would understand that there were some things that were not to be compromised.

These diverse reactions to folksong institutions are not so contradictory as they might seem. Folksong media and the representational features they entail are not inherently destructive. It is precisely the capacity to represent that singers expect and want in them. And certainly traditional discourse suggests at least a provisional investment in a sense of self-as-other that has sheltered Sacred Harp from the more progress-minded mainstream. But most often any kind of display is not an end in itself but a practical means to achieve, for example, publicity, prestige, or service to the community. It is when display takes on a life of its own—when the represented cultural object threatens to replace the singing experience, when participation in a folksong event suggests the endorsement of a folk-song ideology, when display no longer leads onlookers to "the mountain"—that traditional singers object. Chicago singers seemed to find their way to the mountain more quickly and in larger numbers than others. Their core singers had the time, the variety of skills, and the financial and other means necessary both for extensive travel and the relentless organizational effort. Whereas other early revival efforts evolved around a central authority, Chicago had a sufficient number of singers, balanced in assertiveness and confidence with the music, so that no single personality prevailed. It may have mattered that they looked to southern tradition somewhat as an alternative to a local authority figure. But, on the whole, local structural advantages weighed far more heavily than did the idea of folksong in establishing commitment and support for the traditional convention system.

Once established in folk revival areas, the convention system proved compelling as an institution imbued with essential qualities of traditional Sacred Harp singing. In fact, by some mysterious facility, the singing convention is often an experience, saturated with significance, by which folk revival singers exact key shifts of motivation and approach. This widely reported "conversion" experience was the subject of a study, beginning around 1990, by Los Angeles singer and folklorist Janet Herman. Herman sought to confirm her observation that convention participants, even those unconvinced by exposure to Sacred Harp in informal gatherings or recorded media, are swayed toward traditional practices after they attend their first convention. She interviewed several first-time convention attendees, most of whom brought to the experience a thorough identification with folksong. On the one hand, the participation of authoritative traditional singers at the convention (Fourth California Sacred Harp Singing Convention, 1992) and the sheer power of the singing itself suggested a unilateral discursive presence of tradition. But, in reality, participants observed a variety of musical practices—even dissent among experienced singers—and were thus able to situate their own actions "within an accepted *range* of singing behavior" without necessarily adopting traditional practice wholesale or giving up their own values, beliefs, and aesthetic preferences (Herman 1992, 28).

"I'VE SUNG WITH HIM, I'VE EATEN WITH HIM": A NEW CONSENSUS

Perhaps there were less tangible factors involved, too. In folk revival areas, a new attitude seemed to be emerging, one which focused more on the singers, on the social aspects of singing, and perhaps less on the music. Out of the intensity of experience, new friendships were forged. New singers began to experience some of the stock traditional sentiments—not only the bitter sadness of losing a beloved singer, but also the ecstasy of a large gathering of singers focused intently on the moment at hand, or the jovial fellowship during trips to conventions. Hugh McGraw explained the process this way:

> One of the main things in going to singings is not the singing, it's that wonderful fellowship. We'll get as close to somebody in Chicago as we will to the next door neighbor in Bremen because of the love they have for our music. I hear in Bremen, Georgia, that a fellow in Texas has died that I sat and sang with. It hurts me when I hear that he's died, because, I remember him, I've sung with him, I've eaten with him.

These experiences and the sentiments that often attended them were a key component of Sacred Harp tradition that was accessible to folksong revival singers. That they were central to Sacred Harp tradition is undeniable—this was as much as any the point Earl Thurman struggled to express, the point that biographies and revisions and lists of names simply could not convey.

In turn, this led to a new appreciation for the song texts—for the vivid depictions of death and struggle, for example. Whereas gallows humor once was common (see Garber 1987), singers after the late 1980s were more likely to testify to a personal significance for the texts. This was in part because of convention protocol, which encourages brief testimonials on the significance of the song or text. But new singers were also increasingly being named as a part of the "memorial lesson," the segment of a singing convention designed to remember singers who had recently died.

Understandably, the events north and south that emerged as pivotal to the expansion movement seemed to mold themselves around these very experiences. The National Sacred Harp Convention became a celebration, a reunion, of the new Sacred Harp family at large. Yet, there remained a vague uneasiness, as if the discourse of expansion had been honed too sharply, as if unseen compromises had been unwillingly granted. This tension was the subject of the most ambitious writers in the newsletters.

Sometimes this uneasiness touched on perceived southern and northern cultural differences. Georgia singer Richard Whatley, commenting in the *Chicago Newsletter* on the 1992 Midwest Convention, the first northern singing he had attended, directed his ineluctable wit toward the dinner-on-the-grounds:

> All the meals were excellent, although I could not identify most of what was served. Sacred Harp purists will be glad to know that someone remembered to bring the traditional "purple dessert with Cool Whip on top." First-timers from the South, like myself, noticed the conspicuous absence of the more traditional fare like collards with hog "parts," and a decided slant towards pasta dishes. I never did figure out how they kept the cadence of the music at such a fast pace on such a low calorie diet. Never-the-less, it all tasted fine and no one died. (March/May 1993)

Or Murray Simmons, in "Loosascoona," took as allegorical an old annual Mississippi singing with deep community roots, juxtaposed it against the fast-paced Sacred Harp revival, and refracted through these his own ambivalence as a southerner and a Christian.

> So that's my story, and some may wonder why I bothered to tell it at all, may even regard it as a religious polemic with which Sacred Harp needn't be troubled. By way of apology for this subjective and possibly pointless tale, I can only plead the case of a great many people who often have the sinking feeling that their inherited concerns for redemption, for life and death and time and eternity, are being relegated to insignificance in a haggle over whether the basses in "Northfield" should be brought in by turning on the ball of the foot or the heel. The technicalities of singing, fascinating as they are and with

their boundless capacity to spark conversation, are an end in themselves to a good many. As none of us walks on water, it's no one's place to disparage. I merely ask a kind of indulgence for those who see technicalities as no more than a perfunctory means toward an altogether specific and deeply rooted spiritual end, yet who would never dream of intruding their personal brand of salvation on folks busily working on their own. (*Chicago Newsletter,* December 1991)

Things, it seemed, had come a long way since "vast boundaries of age, culture, politics, and religion" separated northern and southern singers. As the neo-formalism of the emerging revival diminished the importance of regional difference in conceiving the new Sacred Harp family, these writers had had to reinvent it as personal experience—how the food tasted to Richard Whatley or Murray Simmons's "inherited concerns." The tension that animated their writing had to do with less tangible components of singing that were outside the traditional domain of convention protocol. So they sought not to define or regulate authentic traditional decorum but to *protect personal experience.* Notably, they wrote as native southerners in the *Chicago Newsletter,* employing, respectively, farce and confession to enter otherwise inaccessible experiences into the discursive compass.

They would get assistance from an unexpected corner. A notable transition in the revival was registered in an influential 1990 documentary, *Amazing Grace with Bill Moyers.* The concept, reasonable enough, was to use as a central organizing principle a single hymn widely popular among groups of English-speaking Christians. Characteristically, Moyers used this principle to celebrate, on a single cultural plane, a diverse assembly of hymn-singing traditions. On the one hand, there were folksong luminaries Judy Collins and Jean Ritchie, opera singer Jessye Norman, gospel singer Marion Williams, the Harlem Boys' Choir, inmates and choir members at Huntsville Prison (Texas), and country star Johnny Cash. Alongside these stood the Wiregrass shape note tradition of southeast Alabama and the Sacred Harp tradition. Sacred Harp was represented by Hugh McGraw and others at the Holly Springs (Georgia) Primitive Baptist Church.

Amazing Grace reorganized the hierarchy of ideas enabling the Sacred Harp revival in two important ways. First, Sacred Harp's status as folk music was recognized, but it was demoted from its rank as a central *cultural* principle. In its place stood a master text and the transcendent community of those who, for deeply personal and possibly vastly different reasons, cherished it. This was evident in part because Holly Springs was a favorite contemporary singing venue for folksong revival singers, so that *Amazing Grace* "captured" and by consequence authenticated this new assimilated community as the *object* of documentary scrutiny. They were now, for the world to see, Sacred Harp singers. But it was also evident because, in the post–*Amazing Grace* era, Sacred Harp revivalists could establish unprecedented bonds with singers from other musical traditions on the basis that their music was "like in the program, *Amazing Grace*." They could now, with the help of the same media that enabled Sacred Harp as folksong, reach out to segments of society for which the folksong idea had less influence.

Second, and equally important, the program expanded the moral relevance of hymn texts to include unprecedented segments of contemporary society. There was the story of the hymn's writing—on the occasion of John Newton's celebrated repentance from a life of lurid iniquity—told this time with his renunciation of slavery as a central motif. As for contemporary relevance, Judy Collins described how the hymn strengthened her during her struggle with alcoholism and during voter registration campaigns in Mississippi in the 1960s. And in every case, it was the direct experience of this hymn that provided moral sustenance. If folksong revivalists were ever repelled by the austere morality of eighteenth-century hymn texts, here was reason not to be.

The transition may have been imperceptible. It may seem enough that Moyers provided compelling personal testimony to the significance of the hymn. But he also unleashed a newfound formalism that gave the hymn text and melody a mysterious power over the great unseen collective of singers. Repeatedly, the singers in *Amazing Grace* reported that the song must have emerged directly from Newton's unimaginable adversity as if both—Newton's adversity and the song—were archetypal: "a song with no guile," as Johnny Cash put it. Identifying a verse associated with the song, yet not written by Newton ("We lay our garments by"), Moyers said this indicates how the song "takes on a life of its own." This kind of hyperformalism, where form transcends even text and author, is precisely what motivated the practice among nineteenth-century tunebook compilers of conflating verses, sometimes even from different hymns and authors, that seemed to emerge from a common idea.

Amazing Grace brought new media attention and many new singers into the revival movement. For what by then had become the old guard of the revival, the immediate response was to enjoy the generous affirmation that Sacred Harp had received—the awe of knowing that something so dear and so often misunderstood had been broadcast to the nation. But if the consequence of all this was to bring the movement together around principles all could share, there was a more potent symbol already in the works. Since 1987, a committee had been at work on a revision of *The Sacred Harp* that would incorporate this cadre of new singers into its center.

THE 1991 REVISION

At one time there were forty-three books in print of four-note shapes—and now they're all gone. I just can't bear the thought of ours being gone.

HUGH MCGRAW

It is often noted that *The Sacred Harp* is the most enduring example of the large corpus of nineteenth-century tunebooks printed in shape notes and promoted primarily by their compilers. Other works have outlined the prevailing historical account of this corpus, in which it has become commonplace to speak of the "decline" of tunebooks generally and the relative "durability" of *The Sacred Harp.* "They're all gone," Hugh McGraw says, and we know instinctively what he means. They're not really "gone," of course, but we have come to measure them not as ordinary books but by the extent of "active use" in public singings. As a book, *The Sacred Harp* is most assuredly not simply the object that one holds in one's hands.

Little underscores this more than the process of revision. Revisions are almost endemic to shape-note tunebooks. The *Easy Instructor* went through at least thirty in a span of active publication much shorter than that of *The Sacred Harp* (Lowens and Britton 1953). In *The Sacred Harp*, only 179 of the 554 songs in the 1991 edition have remained in the book throughout its history (see appendix 11). Yet its historical continuity goes unquestioned.

Sacred Harp singers have even likened revision to surgery, a repair of the interior components that restores the outward health of the book. This interior consists of the songs and their presentation on the page, but also their embedded significance to singers. When the book is revised, songs are added and removed and their presentation is changed. The practice of "page tracking," which seems to have begun when J. S. James in 1904 began cataloging the changes each numbered page had undergone, alludes to a permanent structure and a single unbroken lineage and provides continuity when revisers change the book's contents. If the revision goes smoothly, if it is done in such a way that attachments to the singing community are maintained, then the continuity and historicity of an ultimately evolving text is preserved.

Revisions also reaffirm the process by which they reliably occur; in truth, the revision process itself has evolved over the course of the several editions. The three editions published immediately after the 1844 original were promoted, in fact, not explicitly as revisions but as "new and much improved and enlarged" editions. For the 1850 edition, a committee was convened to oversee the editing process, establishing a standard practice singers say has been essential in enlisting widespread emotional investment in the book. Surely this is an institutional advantage *The Sacred Harp* had over other tunebooks that were under the strict control of a single compiler or publisher.[12]

Yet, despite the certain continuity among the four B. F. White editions (1844–1869), the past was not engaged as an anticipatory force until later. White's 1869 book, the last he compiled, was the first to remove songs, establishing a process by which the character of the book might be altered. More important, it was in the preface to this revision that White issued to his followers his immortal appeal: "We scarcely think that we can do better than abide by the advice—'Ask for the old paths, and walk therein.'" Aptly employing quoted language, he assigned to the past a moral authority preeminent to his own.

For developing the contemporary sense of Sacred Harp revision, credit is owed to W. M. Cooper of Dothan, Alabama. His 1902 Cooper Revision was the first to make substantial editorial changes with the idea of appealing to a new generation of singers, even under the presumed auspices of a statement of loyalty in the preface to "old paths." With B. F. White twenty-three years deceased, the direction of the tradition was as unclear as at any time in its history. But Cooper's appeal was primarily outside areas of traditional strength, so the 1911 James Revision, which included on its revision committee key students and followers of B. F. White, emerged as the most popular edition in the older singing areas. An essentially similar procedure—of substantial change protected by core of continuity—guided later revisers who sought to inherit these followers. Detailed assessments of these and other revisions can be found in Cobb (1978, 84–127), and need not be repeated here.

Through the evolving process of *revision,* the editions of the Sacred Harp have been periodically retraditionalized, severing and then reincorporating their ties to the past in specific ways. This rite calls for the normally self-evident book to undergo a period of exposure, temporarily disempowering the text and transferring authority to the tradition-bearers under whose control the process takes place. Consequently, a revision is effective only if in the end it successfully receives its mandate from all relevant historical points. The 1902 Cooper revision is said to have unsuccessfully rallied a majority of supporters partly because it did not include key followers of B. F. White on its editorial committee. In contrast, the 1911 James Revision invoked antimodernist sentiments and enlisted the support of White loyalists. The 1936 Denson Revision incorporated a multitude of new followers into the tradition. But because of a single song among the 176 deleted, a region of Georgia where the author's family lived did not adopt the 1936 book. It is the legacy of these events that provided the historical backdrop to the 1991 edition.

Like most previous major revisions, the 1991 revision came after a considerable period—in this case since 1971—during which the book had gone unchanged. During that interim, the book was reprinted several times to meet the nationwide demand brought on by the growing revival. In the 1980s, sales to faraway states such as California outpaced even the areas of traditional strength. Singers across the country had been composing new songs in the Sacred Harp style and scouring other nineteenth-century tunebooks for interesting songs to resurrect and sing. Most important, a new generation of traditional singers had increasingly inherited the organizational burdens of the singing tradition.

The swell of interest in composition and experimentation with other books had an ironic mix of consequences. In 1980, Anthony Barrand and Carole Moody had published, in four-shape notation, *Northern Harmony: A Collection of Tunes by Early New England Composers.* In Chicago in 1987, singers produced a *Midwest Supplement* to the *Sacred Harp* that included old pieces and new compositions. Yet, if these publications signaled the sincerity of the emerging revival, they also led to some logistical annoyances. Since the days of competing tunebooks, traditional singers were accustomed, with only occasional exception, to the habit of singing only from the book that each singing event had officially adopted. Integrating these activities into the scope of traditional practice may have been a gesture of respect, but it also incorporated momentum that might have carried new singers away from traditional singing. For all these reasons, a new revision that included the new singing areas was in order.

To no one's surprise, the inspiration for the revision came primarily from Hugh McGraw, manager of a Bremen, Georgia, clothing manufacturing plant and, since 1958, executive secretary and treasurer of the Sacred Harp Publishing Company. In 1959, McGraw sat on the revision committee for the 1960 book. Of the six committee members, he was the lone representative of a younger generation of singers that would carry the tradition through the end of the twentieth century. He speaks fondly of this event as where he "got his training" in Sacred Harp, but in this respect it was also an inheritance of a considerable burden that he bore without complaint. When one looks wistfully for instances of Sacred Harp "traditions" being "passed on," this kind of event, which has laid organizational responsibility in new hands on innumerable occasions, should surely be counted.

For the revision, a music committee of Alabama and Georgia singers headed by McGraw was convened by the board of directors in October 1987. McGraw had also chaired a committee in 1971 consisting of venerable singers Ruth Denson Edwards, Elder Elmer Kitchens, Walter A. Parker, Palmer Goodsey, and Foy Frederick, most of whom were deceased or inactive by the time the 1991 revision was under way. In contrast, the 1991 committee was well stocked with youth, ensuring ample leadership into the next century. Its membership was also distributed geographically so as to attempt representation in most of the old singing areas. Included were Hugh McGraw, Bremen, Georgia (chair); Richard DeLong, Carrollton, Georgia; Raymond Hamrick, Macon, Georgia; David Ivey, Huntsville, Alabama; Jeff Sheppard, Glencoe, Alabama; Toney Smith, Tuscaloosa, Alabama; and Terry Wootten, Ider, Alabama.

The Redesign of the Book

One of the chief ambitions of the revisers was to redesign the book to make it more attractive and more accessible to singers. Previous editions were printed from plates produced at various times dating to 1936, so there was considerable inconsistency in the appearance of some of the pages. For the 1991 revision, then, all pages were reset using computer technology. To raise money for the new revision, even before it was finished, Hugh McGraw began selling the printing plates from the previous edition as souvenirs. Once the physical token of ownership of the book, the printing plates became a ritual gesture, affiliating the singing community with the beginning of a transitional status of the book. Without the plates, no physical means to reproduce the old revision existed. Although there was no question that the revision would go forward, releasing the plates meant there was no turning back. For other reasons, however, the dispersal of the old printing plates outside the province of the publishing company was more controversial than it might have seemed: the plates had accumulated value as tokens of allegiance to the singing tradition, the kind of value which could not be protected in an open sale.

Resetting the pages, of course, meant that the hodgepodge of typefaces and layouts could all be redesigned and standardized. Verses of Scripture were added where previously omitted so as to now appear under every song title. The revisers removed Ruth Denson Edwards's introductory essay as well as the biographical footnotes that James added in 1911. Both contained factual errors that had come to light since their first appearance. The footnotes, moreover, at times reduced biography to only the most picturesque events of authors' lives, and it was thought this might detract from an inexperienced singer's understanding of the significance of the music. These were the reasons given for the removal of the footnotes, underscored by the desire for a "cleaner page"—one with ample space for the music and thus easier to read. At the time of the revision, there was some discussion of a separate volume of author biographies, as is the practice with church hymnals, but none has emerged.

The instructional "rudiments of music" were revised by scholar and singer John Garst to correct errors and expand the discussion of harmony. Some of the added passages of the rudiments addressed issues pertinent for organizing singing in new areas. For example, an entire section on the "Organization and Conduct of Singings and Conventions" was added, including a description of such practices as submitting minutes, election of officers, hollow square seating, the memorial lesson, and dinner on the grounds (chap. 9). There was even a discussion of the Dorian mode, a concept familiar in folksong revival circles: "Traditionally, minor music is sung in the Dorian mode, with the sixth degree a half step higher than the natural minor notation indicates" (chap. 3, sec. 15). Whatever the degree of pedagogical intent, these discussions in so authoritative a document as the rudiments had the potential to empower traditional performance practices in settings where they might have to contend with alternatives.

The Songs Removed

For most of this century, the book has teetered near its upper physical size and weight limit, based on singers' comfort holding the book in one hand while leading. Otherwise, revisers might simply have continued adding songs to the end of the book. So the chief purpose in removing songs was to find sufficient space for the new ones, preserving the book's pagination and size. The chief basis for the selection of songs to remove was their relative popularity. In fact, great pains were taken to choose for removal the least popular songs, since this was seen as the most likely cause for possible controversy. Nearly half (twenty of forty-six) of the deleted songs had been composed for and added to the book as recently as the 1960 edition, so there were certainly living friends and relatives of the authors, if not the authors themselves, who might take offense. The entire process, then, if handled successfully, would require a measure of consensus building.

The committee scrutinized song use statistics that were compiled, at no small effort, by counting the number of times each song was recorded in the minutes as having been led in a certain year. In this way, those songs which were the least popular choices at singings could be identified. As the date neared when the list of removals would be final, Hugh McGraw grew increasingly concerned about the impact of deletions. More than once he related with regret the account of the song, omitted from the 1936 Denson book, that provoked a region of faithful singers not to adopt that revision. During the period leading up to December 1990, McGraw seemed to be at every singing, where he would sometimes forgo leading a song so that he could use the time to talk about the new revision.

But he and music committee members always spoke in generalities; the exact list of deletions was not to be divulged. Then, at what McGraw has called "the right moment," the list was revealed. The occasion was a special singing on December 15, 1990, convened so as to showcase the new songs. It was held at Samford University in Birmingham, Alabama, then the site of the National Sacred Harp Convention. A booklet of the new songs was printed and distributed *only* to those who had attended the singing. A brief preface addressed the significance of the occasion:

Never in the history of Sacred Harp have people had the opportunity to participate in singing songs that have been selected to go in a new revision. You will have something to boast about for many years. In this selection of songs there are twenty-one new living composers who wrote thirty-six new songs that have never been published. We are so proud of these people. Since our beloved book was published in 1844, we have always had living authors who had songs in the book, and we feel that it is the reason our book has lasted so long and will continue to survive.

At this "new songs" singing, the new authors were honored and asked to lead their own songs. A few months later, sound recordings were produced on cassette and released so that singers could hear the new songs for a period before the new books were printed. These tapes were a source of considerable satisfaction, particularly since the sixty songs were recorded, unrehearsed, in a period of only four hours!

Although he did not plan in advance to do so, Hugh McGraw chose the evening banquet, just prior to Billy Joe Harris's after-dinner comedy address, as the occasion to *read aloud* the list of page numbers of the songs proposed for deletion. The "moment" almost seemed scripted. There were the new-revision faithful, even more certainly so at the banquet than at the singing as a whole. Those who cared scrambled for pencils and copied down the numbers. This list was later published in the *National Sacred Harp Newsletter* (January 1991), in both cases accompanied by a plea that objections to any choice would be taken seriously.

Soon enough, however, many singers were absorbed with cassettes and booklets of the exciting collection of new songs, and talk of the deletions faded. Of much greater concern, in fact, was the circumstance that the available stock of the old edition had been exhausted, so new singers could not get books at all. When the new books finally were delivered early in 1992, with new songs to sing, handsomely presented and stoutly bound in a maroon cover—yet still modestly priced at $10—they met mostly with excitement. Serious complaints about the new book or the songs that were removed were rare. Within months, most active singers had purchased new books, so that at a singing one was likely to observe a sea of maroon jackets.

With the atmosphere of apparently seamless enthusiasm that greeted the new book, it is too easy to overlook the extraordinary work and judgment of the music committee. If history is any indication, the revision should have been an acrimonious undertaking. It was probably of some benefit that so many of the new singers were associated in some way with folksong and thereby were predisposed to follow "tradition"; in previous editions, a progressive movement had almost always had some influence on the process of revision. But this is not to deny credit to the revisers, who read these potentially treacherous cultural winds precisely. Now, when singers speak of "tradition," they can confidently deploy the shadings of self-evident objectivity that this term, so notoriously fickle in the postmodern age, has customarily conveyed.

The Songs Added

The process of removing songs was a delicate one because it involved the ecology of loyalties that motivated traditional practice. In contrast, the corpus of new songs, even those by living authors that would "breathe new life" into the book and the tradition, apparently did not require such delicate handling. With little discernible fanfare, the committee solicited and reviewed songs and selected sixty, thirty-seven of which were composed or arranged by recent authors (see appendix 12). Of the twenty-one new composers, youth was again amply represented. Only three of the new composers had songs in the previous edition. Also new were songs by composers from folksong revival areas, primarily Boston and Chicago.[13] By most accounts, the atmosphere of the selection process was not at all competitive, and only a few songs, which did not fall within the traditional style, were omitted.

Many of the remaining songs—those not newly composed—were from colonial American composers already familiar to singers: William Billings (1746–1800) of Boston, Daniel Read (1757–1836) of New Haven, Connecticut, and Timothy Swan (1758–1842) of Northfield, Massachusetts. Curiously, there were none from the best-known Sacred Harp composers, such as B. F. White, A. M. Cagle, Paine Denson, or J. P. Reese. There were also no anthems in the new collection. The older songs were taken from other tunebooks or from earlier editions of *The Sacred Harp*, but even many of these were being sung in folksong revival areas from photocopies or from publications such as the *Midwest Supplement* or *Northern Harmony*.[14] In fact, all but two of the sixty songs were composed either before 1844 or after 1961, and compositions from both of these periods demonstrated stock tunebook devices faithfully and tastefully employed: melodic interest in all parts, parallel fourths and fifths, open chords, infrequent use of accidentals, melody in the tenor, straightforward hymn and fugue form, and so on. The revision reaffirmed the contemporary significance of a sound ceaselessly familiar to Sacred Harp singers.

So did the poetic texts used with them. Even among the texts used with the new musical compositions, only six were written by contemporary authors. This is not unusual. In the tunebook idiom, a division of labor has almost always divided tune and hymn text composition. The remaining texts were taken from the familiar stock of hymn and psalm collections that provided texts for nineteenth-century tunebooks. In fact, the new revision actually amplified the role of Isaac Watts (27 of the 60 in the new collection, and a slightly lesser portion, 136 of 560, in the entire 1991 *Sacred Harp*). Nor is this surprising: Watts has always been the preeminent source for texts for American shape note tunebooks. With these numbers as our warrant, let us dwell momentarily on the role Watts might have played in the religious sentiments that were incorporated into the new book.

While the musical features of traditional style are well known and highly regarded by many new singers, a good deal less is said of the poetry. Perhaps, as a reason for this, Watts seems an unlikely poetic voice for the postmodern age and would not attract the attention of new singers whose tastes were shaped by contemporary culture. But this has long been so. All too often, Watts has been dearest to those who stood at odds with prevailing theological and cultural winds. The earliest American editors made decisive alterations to his topical themes (Benson 1903); later editors softened his austere Calvinism, rewording passages and omitting key verses in denominational hymnals and edited reprints, to make it palatable to genteel nineteenth-century mainstream Protestants (Davie 1982, 72–73). Indeed, today there is surely no Watts revival at hand among prevailing contemporary evangelical Christian movements. Yet Sacred Harp and Watts, largely undiluted, have found a curious, if small, niche in contemporary America. Watts's texts resonate throughout *The Sacred Harp* so pervasively that he quickly becomes familiar to a singer who gives any thought at all to the texts. Must we assume that this engagement is entirely passive?

Editors of the *National Newsletter* were concerned enough about this to acknowledge possible difficulties in the contemporary reception of Sacred Harp texts. In an article on "The Theology of the Sacred Harp," they sought to explain the appeal of noncontemporary aspects of some of the texts (January 1988). "Morbid" texts such as "Morning Sun" ("Your sparkling eyes and blooming cheeks must wither like the blasted rose") are a "challenge and delight" when sung with a good tune. The editors also suggested the possibility that in a "vast portion of all music that is sung," singers simply don't pay close enough attention to the words. But such a statement should be taken in perspective: many singers sing the texts entirely from memory and testify to their significance. And surely, in the new *Sacred Harp* revision, contemporary composers "breathed new life" into the old poetry by choosing the texts for their compositions, reengaging the poetic idiom and providing for renewed personal associations with texts that resonated throughout the singing community.

Perhaps Watts's contemporary reception is only antiquarian—a detached curiosity for alternatives to modern life. This posture, a trademark of Depression-era culture writers, has long been familiar in folksong revival circles, where there is surely no precedent for a restoration of Watts's theology. And there is plenty in Watts to satisfy an antiquarian appetite. Still, is it possible that there is a systematic transition from the world of text-as-object, where antiquarianism flourishes, to a world of active involvement with the text? What possible connection is there to the vivid ritual connection—of fellowship, of transition, of ecstacy—that a diverse class of singers experiences?

This is not an easy question to answer, but I would like to sketch a general realm of possibility. Again, the issue is the relation of Watts (and, by extension, other eighteenth-century texts) to the folksong revival—and most decidedly not a general description of how Watts is understood. This transition from antiquarian fascination to spiritual involvement is the kind that has been described by Donald Davie, possibly Watts's most articulate and enthusiastic supporter in literary circles. Davie suggested a process of adopted and then discarded antiquarianism, beginning at a comfortable distance, with what he calls Watts's "anthropological" writing. This mode of Watts's writing drew heavily from Old Testament imagery, articulating the mythos of the eighteenth-century populace (Davie

1993). For example, a contemporary Watts reader or singer might only advance an antiquarian reading of a "morbid" hymn such as this:

> Why should we start and fear to die?
> What tim'rous worms we mortals are!
>
> ("Prospect," *Sacred Harp*, 30)

or the "anthropological" depiction of believers in Watts's Psalm 63:

> Pilgrims on the scorching sand,
> Beneath a burning sky,
> Long for a cooling stream at hand,
> And they must drink or die.
>
> ("Montgomery," *Sacred Harp*, 189)

These represent Watts's typically candid imagery, a style one would be hard-pressed to find in contemporary mainstream denominational hymnals. Davie's suggestion is that for a contemporary reader, it is all too easy to project Watts's sentiments into the past and not apply them to one's own experiences.

In folk revival performance practice, any anthropological distance established around "morbid" themes has sometimes shrunk to unsettling proximity, articulated by spontaneous irony or even gallows humor (see Garber 1987). Perhaps, one might thus be compelled to ask, "Why should we start and fear to die?" was not so easy a question to answer after all. It was made harder with the spread of the traditional convention system, bringing the diverse singing community together for extended fellowship. Consequently, few would question the fact that the death and suffering of beloved singers has brought Watts's candor to bear directly on the circumstance of the living community. It is this course of events that should not have been so unexpected—that Watts has spoken to a folksong revival population whose deep utopian aspirations have been frustrated not only by the fragmentation of postmodern society but also by an increasingly vivid and personal sense of mortality. "The human soul," Harriet Beecher Stowe had put it, "with its awful shadow, makes all things sacred," and she was writing directly to the sense of detachment that had deprived her spiritual community of its capacity for empathy and moral feeling. Still,

Stowe notwithstanding, this only more intensely begs the question of why Watts, in particular, compels such readers.

Davie suggested another contemporary route to Watts: Watts's "axiomatic" writing, which provides for successive generations, even skeptics, an "opening" to his spiritual thinking:

> Religious belief, it has been bluntly said, is irreconcilable with 'the modern mind.' But even if that were so in some general and abstract sense, it is quite clear that the most modern mind, if (perhaps perversely) it chooses to set itself the task, *can* still enter the imaginative world of Watts, the world of the axiom. One way to make that passage is by relishing the literary (aesthetic) pleasures that only the world of the axiom can supply. If this seems like connoisseurship, the murmurous satisfaction of the antiquary, so be it; perhaps connoisseurship and antiquarianism deserve better than the obloquy that is commonly heaped on them. The connoisseur of poetic diction will, if he pursues that preoccupation strenuously enough, break out of the world of 'the aesthetic' into the regions of human experience more liberating, though also more alarming. (Davie 1993, 38)

Again, this appears at first glance to be a trivial stance, for Davie suggests nothing systematic about Watts that propels an outsider from connoisseurship to uninhibited involvement.

To explain this process, Davie examined two distinct classes of Watts's verse that uniquely situated it within the poetics of his age. In his "axiomatic" writing, for example, Watts set in verse the most fundamental tenets of Christian belief. Watts's characteristic stamp was to treat religious tenets—in a setting where rationalism and skepticism were assembling a forceful challenge to religious dogma—as genuinely unassailable truths. To illustrate this, Davie compared a stanza from Watts's "Hosanna to the royal son,"

> Let mortals ne'er refuse to take
>   Th' Hosanna on their tongues;
> Lest rocks and stones should rise, and break
>   Their silence into songs.

with a 1776 "translation" of the same stanza by evangelical poet Augustus
Toplady,

> Should we, dear Lord, refuse to take
> The Hosanna on our tongues,
> The rocks and stones would rise and break
> Their silence into songs.

Davie assesses the difference, minor yet crucial, in this way:

> For Toplady, the supposed behaviour of the stones is hyperbolical,
> allowing him to harangue his readers reproachfully: "You feel so little
> that even stones would feel more." But for Watts, the stones' sup-
> posed behaviour is simply the necessary consequence of the axiom:
> if God is the Creator, then every one of His creatures—stones as
> well as men—responds to Him and moves at his command. (1993,
> 32–33)

Watts views the events, corresponding "faithfully" to Luke's account of
the same episode, as true "whether or not human beings acknowledge it."
It was precisely in this sense, in preserving the indisputable faith both of
scriptural narrators and readers of his poetry, that Watts could successfully claim his radical poetry as "imitation."

A second of Watts's distinctive poetic modes, similarly engaging in different ways to believers and outsiders, is his treatment of atrocities, such
as the Crucifixion. For example, in what has proven to be his best-known
hymn ("When I Survey the Wondrous Cross"), readers "survey" the cross
at a characteristically broad rhetorical distance. Even the couplet that
brings readers closest

> His dying crimson, like a robe
> Spreads o'er his body on the tree

"flagrantly," as Davie put it, deflects us from the bloody sweat and jeering
multitude that comprised the immediate actualities of this, for believers,
the extreme of atrocities (1993, 40). But, again, Watts "imitates" this
stance from Scripture (Gal 6:14), and, like Paul, "glories in" the cross
over a considerable aesthetic and conceptual distance. This, Davie says, is

a poetics that refuses to distrust its readers, one that, by faith, idealizes the Crucifixion in its monstrosity without resorting to the immediacy of evangelical piety.

If atrocity and axiom confront believers at the most profound extreme of religious experience, they should have been particularly ill-suited to those whom Buell Cobb called "folk-song proponents." One can imagine little in a poetic idiom that should further widen the gulf of anthropological distance that outsiders bring to a religious text than for them to be assaulted with axiom and atrocity. Yet this is precisely Davie's suggestion: that because Watts relied on his readers' faith rather than mistrusted and manipulated it, he could present idealized images, acknowledging but not delineating their profound and disturbing implications. Through these ideals, believers called to mind associations from their own unassailable expanse of personal religious experience. Perhaps as a consequence Watts did not foresee, the distinctions between aesthetic distance, anthropological distance, and conceptual distance were constantly blurred, so that "contemporary" readers have supplied their own associations.

This suggests in only a general way how Watts continues to be the prevailing voice in contemporary editions of *The Sacred Harp*. In the texts by Watts in the 1991 revision, twenty-seven in number, the axiomatic style was most prominent. Themes such as God's omnipotence were often depicted in the abstract or in nature imagery, death and grief, and most conspicuously the theme of praise. "Now shall my inward joys arise and burst into a song," begins the text of Billings's compelling "Africa" (1770), which Watts based on Isaiah 49:13, and with it, singers, as so many have testified, have entered those liberating and alarming regions of human experience. In this hymn, characteristically, the act of praise is not even deliberate but erupts from a wellspring of love. It is a paradox where, in the moment of its performance, sentiment and song, self and community, reverberate and escalate uncontrollably, setting free an outpouring of the unspeakable qualities that Sacred Harp singing is all about.

Surely the 1991 revisers had in mind the meaningful encounter of text with music as a fundamental goal of the revision and assembled its more superficial trappings toward this end. Still, let us marvel a bit more that Watts and other classic hymnists and psalmists remain so central a component to Sacred Harp. In Davie's terms, Watts possesses an encoded resistance to modernity. We moderns may erect mediating schemes for engaging Watts, but these schemes only affirm that a more powerful reading lurks beneath them. Sacred Harp singings, which attract so diverse a spectrum of believers, are ritual encounters in which the mediating schemes that might influence reading—"vain discourse," as Watts himself put it—are kept away. Only self-examination stands between singer and text.

This ritual encounter is reinforced by the historical context of textual instability and the unsituated author. We know that Watts composed the texts, but we also know that he merely imitated or reflected upon Scripture, that with his endorsement numerous editors have altered his texts, and that composers have sifted through complete poems and chosen the verses they liked best. Watts's texts are neither entirely canonical, serving as spiritual archetype, nor are they entirely testimonial, reporting confessed spiritual encounter. In contrast, evangelical religious poets have sought to author their readers' faith in the image of their own experience, sometimes in excruciating detail. This may seem to be overstating things: still, in an age when the cult of the self pervades so much of popular culture, Watts's ontology surely offers a refreshing alternative.

As one of its most salient features, the 1991 revision brought into its canonical center a cadre of talented new composers, including some from outside traditional singing areas. But to say no more than this would be to trivialize a revision process that has proved again and again to be both ambitious and astute in engaging the spiritual investment of an expanding singing population. The revision process—and perhaps all traditional Sacred Harp procedures—is designed to liberate the rhetorical power of the hymns and Psalms so that they can operate directly on the consciousness of the individual singers. Since the earliest tunebook and singing school period, this has been a fundamental reason for holding public singings outside ecclesiastical settings.

PUBLIC WORSHIP, PRIVATE FAITH

"Grace, tis a charming sound," the tune runs, "harmonious to the ear. . . ." Few, if any of us, would argue with that truth,

regardless of whether we see it as a truth embedded in theology
or a beautifully nebulous one.

MURRAY SIMMONS, "Loosascoona" (1991)

Since the initial trickle of folksong proponents in the 1960s, Sacred Harp
has enjoyed a remarkable growth in the numbers of new singers across the
country. Urban conventions outside the South have been particularly
prosperous. But this remarkable journey, in part through the rhetorical
channel of folksong, has not merely resulted in large numbers. There have
also been decisive qualitative shifts, marked by such events as the recording of *Rivers of Delight,* the establishment of local singings in folk revival
areas, travels to traditional southern singings, the shift in folk revival performance from choral practice to singing convention protocol, and the
publication of the 1991 revision. These perceptible shifts in the quality of
participation have been fueled not merely by imitation of traditional performance but also by newfound facility with the formal qualities of the
musical idiom and its traditional institutions. In some cases, these shifts
have entailed a more general transformation from antiquarianism to spiritual renewal, from vicarious objectivity to subjective involvement, from
representation to experience.

In general, these shifts have occurred as a result of direct encounter with
traditional practice and have been well received, if not enthusiastically endorsed, by many traditional singers. Consequently, as a paradigm of cultural change, the general outline of the evolving Sacred Harp revival and
the particular transformation of the folksong idea should be of concern to
those who seek to effectively support or promote informal traditional culture. So, initially, it is to be observed that some measure of satisfaction
among the singing population actually has coalesced around the *decline*
of the authority of folksong discourse as an explicit purveyor of the movement. This might be a disturbing irony: that whereas folksong might in
one instance be an effective mediating device, in another it might stand in
conflict with traditional practice. The *Chicago Newsletter* even took to
printing, as the object of mild scorn, specimens of what it called "outsider" or "elitist" commentary on Sacred Harp, such as passages from the
culture writing era. Would the consequence of this not be to authenticate

the new singers' experiential affiliation with Sacred Harp by liberating it from the protective grasp of outsider writing?

In place of culture writing, the most distinctive and authoritative non-traditional narrative form to emerge has been the testimonial account, describing firsthand the singing experience. Examples of this are innumerable; a notable one was Stephen Levine's account of the 1994 Antioch (Ider, Alabama) singing, "Celestial Fruit on Earthly Ground" (*Chicago Newsletter*, September 1994). So moving was this event that, through it, Levine reinterpreted his past, characterizing his extensive knowledge of and performing experience with Sacred Harp as an "unknowing, decade-long apprenticeship" for the Antioch singing. His most intense reaction came in the afternoon session when several leaders dedicated songs to their late fathers. "We sang the song," Levine remarked of one, "with straightforward sincerity; there was not the slightest trace of a maudlin or mawkish sensibility." This "emotional directness" cannot be imitated, Levine surmised, and could only have sprung from the gestalt of the southern traditional singing. He summarized his reaction to the singing in this way: "But still, the singing at Antioch brought me to a level of emotional release that is priceless and rare in my life. As often happens after a good singing, one or two particular hymns remain in my head for days and days—driving me crazy and comforting me at the same time. The voices that have been singing in my head since Sunday afternoon are the Southern voices this time. What is probably more significant than I am willing to admit is the line that I keep hearing: How happy every child of grace."

If Levine had written in the style of the culture writers, the "emotional directness," if it were noticed at all, would have been attributed only to the participants. But Levine, and so many others in recent years, have employed a type of description in which the formal qualities of the musical performance as a whole are inscribed, through writing, onto the subjective experience and identity of the writer.

Accompanying this rhetorical shift has been an influx of new singers who are as likely as not to come to Sacred Harp through friends or families or churches, with little interest in and perhaps little awareness of folksong, even if publicity materials contain explicit appeals to antiquarian sentiments. And antiquarian appeals themselves may be resolved on a personal, family, or religious basis, rather than as the unifying device of a cultural movement. This is surely a factor in the popularity of Sacred Harp among church members from the European Free-Church family of denominations such as Mennonites and the Society of Friends (Quakers), many of whom carry a historical consciousness as a part of their religious practice. Like traditional Sacred Harp singers, many from these denominations have resisted modernizing influences and maintain an intense and personal sense of religious history and a fondness for older hymnody and psalmody. In 1993, Mennonites published a twenty-fifth edition of the *Harmonia Sacra* (orig. 1832), restoring features from nineteenth-century editions that had previously been discarded.[15] This was a Mennonite undertaking, but it has enjoyed the support of Sacred Harp singers. In some ways the rise of localized antiquarianism as a guiding motivation has been inevitable, but it is through core groups with folksong revival origins that many of these new singers have found Sacred Harp singing outlets.

Other new institutional and rhetorical forms have emerged from the new-singer population that mirror or accommodate these shifts. For example, singer Steven Sabol of the Washington, D.C., area has produced a photocopy-format publication, "Sacred Harp and Related Shape-Note Music: Resources," containing many items of interest only to participating singers. The list includes descriptions and information on purchasing shape note tunebooks and hymnbooks, audio and video recordings, critical and historical works, regional newsletters, and even county maps of southern singing areas. There is also an electronic mail conference on issues related to Sacred Harp that was begun by singers Keith Willard of Minneapolis and Warren Steel, a music professor at the University of Mississippi. Like other topical conferences on the Internet, this conference features announcements, reports of events, and lively debates. Despite its inherent bias toward the technologically adept, the conference has attracted a wide range of participants from the singing population. And in 1992 a California singer, Chris Thorman, published a *Sacred Harp Concordance* designed for new singers as a way to find any song with only a single word from the text. In its formal implications, the concordance brings *The Sacred Harp* to a new stage of canonization, reinforcing its textual coherence and inscribing onto it unprecedented continuity as a book. The concordance also provides an arrangement of words, extracted from their syntactical settings in the texts, that facilitates intertextual references among different songs and among diverse contextual worlds of meaning, some deeply personal. Of course, this is precisely the kind of thing that many traditional singers, because they know the book so well, routinely do by rote. In effect, the concordance can act as a kind of hypertextual crutch for new singers, establishing active, personal, "readerly" participation in the text and redistributing its internal components into a "galaxy of signifiers." [16] For the Sacred Harp revival, these forms mark what may be a decisive rupture in the representational and interpretive character of culture writing and a shift toward forms that facilitate, perhaps even demand, involvement. Essentially, they are tools and not pictures.

This shift away from explicit folksong discourse has also eroded some of the cultural barriers that separated Sacred Harp from mainstream churches. Singers whose Sacred Harp careers began, perhaps superficially, in folksong circumstances might now look to Sacred Harp as a lens through which to refract personal and private spiritual struggles. Because Sacred Harp focuses on conviction and not doctrine, it can liberate ideas that are in conflict with one's religious training or, equally as likely, affirm preestablished belief. Some find in Sacred Harp an intensity not common in mainstream liturgy; others discover an atmosphere of candor and support for engaging severe and unknown eternities. If the Sacred Harp revival was ever a secular experience, it has become decreasingly so as folksong has declined as its main purveyor.

This experience has led some singers to expanded expectations of their own churches. Minimally, a Sacred Harp performance might be employed—as a cultural object—to spice up a church service, perhaps providing a glimpse at musical practices no longer in vogue. Such an experience, however, is apt to provide little real satisfaction for churchgoers and singers alike, each of whom is expecting a different experience from the structural qualities of their respective institution. Much as the case with folk festivals, these institutional differences impose their own logistical inertia that makes organizing church performances difficult.

For some, this implicit institutional dissonance raises questions about the relationship between music, liturgy, and belief. In the broader contemporary social climate, at least some religious institutions have become divisive and doctrinaire; in this light, Sacred Harp can be seen to draw from a tradition that strives to maintain difference without confrontation. Other contemporary religious institutions are quite the opposite, resolving difference by compromise, such as by adjusting liturgical forms to accommodate the widest possible array of beliefs; in contrast, Sacred Harp accommodates religious faith at a personal and private level, demanding tolerance but far less compromise. The fact that Sacred Harp events have an overarching musical purpose facilitates this circumstance. Nonetheless, testimony about memorable singings and conventions points also to a communal affirmation of an unlikely collective—to an extraordinary celebration of ritual unity without explicit doctrinal consensus.

At least one singer has taken this case to her church, calling for a great deal more than idle curiosity. "I've found a new music, or it has found me, and now I'm an evangelist," wrote Chicago singer Elizabeth Hoffman in a liturgical publication for the Roman Catholic Church. She identified five characteristics of Sacred Harp that readers would do well to heed: (1) the energy and intensity of the singing, (2) the robust poetry that does not insult or cajole its singers, (3) the design of the music around the enjoyment of its singing, (4) the importance of the acoustical qualities of buildings where singings are held, and (5) the systematic inclusiveness of singings. She concluded with an urgent call for readers to go to a Sacred Harp singing and discover these things for themselves:

> We are searching for the communal attitudes, the words, the music, the performance styles, the buildings that are up to the tasks of liturgical praise and prayer, of expressing and shaping a lively faith. For a sense of what these could be, go to a Sacred Harp singing. The singers and the sound will lift your spirit, and you may get new insight on what "full, active and conscious participation" could mean and how to help it happen (Hoffman 1992, 9).

Consider that this plea has no overt theological substance, that the same feelings about the nature of worship might be directed toward any church, and you have what seems to be the way singers have situated the experience of Sacred Harp vis-à-vis the church.

But if there is a shift away from explicit folksong discourse, this does not mean that folksong principles are no longer operative. It is clear, for example, that, like folksong, the revival has been carved out of the broad cultural space abandoned by the cultural mainstream. What has been discarded is a kind of unilateral approach to folksong, one measured on a single scale of authenticity and articulated by a stock array of folksong institutions and media. In its place, singers have crafted an approach that draws widely from both Sacred Harp tradition and folksong rhetoric. At its heart is the kind of tunebook pluralism that B. F. White inscribed onto the tradition and onto the book at the outset. To this was added the unique brand of antiquarianism developed by J. S. James, one that attributed to music a fundamental religious value and charged the singing tradition with the solemn custodial burden of this heritage. Later, aspects of the folksong idea reinforced these tenets, notably the depiction by George Pullen Jackson of Sacred Harp and other living traditions of the South as the chief cultural sites of a canon of American religious folksong.

Since World War II, there has emerged a heightened awareness of the transcendent community of Sacred Harp singers, articulated so well in the writing of Earl Thurman. As folksong revival took shape, Ruth Denson Edwards described Sacred Harp as American and southern culture, yet in a way that was consistent with traditional singing values. Later, reflecting his own growing participation as a singer, Buell Cobb transformed the descriptive language for Sacred Harp. His 1978 book, *The Sacred Harp: A Tradition and Its Music,* described a singing tradition both generous and hospitable and constructed the definitive image of a more inclusive Sacred Harp family. All of these predisposed a "revival" based in part on traditional singers' own cultural constructions of Sacred Harp and in part on the heightened value of folk traditions that circulated in mainstream America. But the particular revival that emerged from the interaction of these two influences could only have been brought about with the help of a powerful unifying catalyst. This catalyst has been the post–World War II generation of Sacred Harp singers themselves, who have taken on an emerging role as Sacred Harp ambassadors. More than anyone, it was they who best understood that, with their various components acting in concert, traditional forms could prevail, bringing the full experience of Sacred Harp to those who might otherwise have passed through it as a fad.

It should be obvious that these principles draw upon and at the same time reaffirm a fundamental idea: Sacred Harp tradition itself and the viability of its formal qualities, values, and institutions. But this is not an essentialist argument, nor is Sacred Harp a transcendent entity that need merely be recorded or performed, nor is it a matter of the purity of an authentic context. Rather, what is distinctive is its provisional quality, the sheer absence of internal motivation, the necessity of extraordinary human will that, over a considerable span of time, has clung to a peculiar complex of musical and religious ideas and has resisted pressures to conform to progressive ideas again and again. It is at the juncture of its formal qualities and the extraordinary will to persevere that a Sacred Harp singing occurs.

Consequently, it is little surprise that in any of several of its guises the folksong idea has been an effective—possibly the most effective—rhetorical means by which Sacred Harp has spread far outside its areas of traditional strength since World War II ended. Surely no other conceptual apparatus has nurtured such high regard for Sacred Harp's informal performance practices and institutions, for the antiquarian hues that have girded its traditional historical consciousness, for its propensity to depict music as a complex event inextricably tied to customs and values, for the cosmopolitan spirit that has embraced the revival of tunebook culture as a whole, and perhaps most important, for the deep-rooted sense of the importance of living tradition. But there have been disadvantages as well. Understandably, Sacred Harp has not fared well as a cultural object, particularly in outsider writing. In the prevailing forms of folksong revival performance media, such as festivals, concerts, and recordings by practiced choirs, the effectiveness of Sacred Harp's own performance practices has been sorely underestimated. And the sometimes outspoken idealism of the transcendent folksong revival "movement" has set an imposing obstacle in the way of any kind of shared experience. It has taken considerable negotiation from several sides for a usable coalition to emerge, but in the end it has been a successful one.

It should also be said, of course, that these merits are relative and these efforts are meager compared with the singing tradition itself. Foremost, it has Sacred Harp's capacity to relentlessly attract committed and skillful singers, to produce engaging musical events and institutions, and to provide music that is satisfying and resilient that have given it an appeal that has transcended generations of singers. Traditions, if they are to successfully endure, must construct a cultural face, and folksong has well served that purpose.

Appendix 1

MINUTES OF THE UNION SINGING AS THEY APPEARED IN THE *ORGAN,* FEBRUARY 14, 1855

Even at the session held on Christmas Eve night, the singing was "protracted in consequence of the general excitement and the interest manifested by the citizens." It was resumed on Christmas at 9 A.M. In the early years, both women and men were assigned time as leaders. Sometime during the late nineteenth century, however, women were barred from leading; this practice was reversed sometime in the mid-twentieth century.

UNION SINGING

Held at Society Hill, Crawford County, December 22d, 1854.

Convened on Friday morning—Brother P. Hampton was called to the Chair for the Session.

Commencements—Lesson by P. Hampton 40 minutes.

A Committee of Arrangements was then appointed—consisting of F. M. Ames, Jos. Wright, and T. Hardison—Dr. J. H. Jenkins appointed Secretary.

Lesson by J. Wright 25 min.—Recess 10 min.—Lesson by Dr. E. Sharp 35 min. Adjourned to Saturday 9 A.M.

Saturday, Dec. 23d.

Met pursuant to adjournment—opened with prayer by Judge S. R. Penick.

Lesson by P. Hampton 35 min.—Recess 10 min.—Lesson by A. J. Hardison 35 minutes—Recess 15 min.—Lesson by F. M. Ames 35 min.—Lesson by J. Wright

25 min.—Rec. 40 min.—Lesson by L. B. Walton 35 min.—Lesson by E. Sharp 35 min.—Recess 15 min.

Closing Lesson by Judge S. R. Penick.

Adjourned to Sunday 9 A.M.

Sunday, Dec. 24th.

Met pursuant to Adjournment.

Lesson by Judge Penick 35 min.—Recess 10 min.—Lesson by F. M. Ames 30 min.

Sermon by Rev. T. F. Montgomery.

Recess 30 min.—Lesson by Dr. E. Sharp 15 min.—Recess 10 min.—Lesson by L. B. Walton 45 min. Adjourned to meet at J. W. Hardison's at candle light.

Sunday Evening

Met at Jas. W. Hardison's pursuant to adjournment.

Lesson by Dr. E. Sharp 60 min. Recess 15 min. Lesson by Miss Martha Sharp 35 min. Lesson by Miss M. C. Ames 35 min.

Protracted in consequence of the general excitement and the interest manifested by the citizens. Adjourned to meet at Society Hill on Monday 9 A.M.

Monday, Dec. 25th.

Met pursuant to Adjournment.

Lessons by E. Sharp 35 min., F. M. Ames 35 minutes.—Recess 15 min. Lesson by Miss M. C. Ames 35 min., by Miss Martha Sharp 35 min. Recess 30 min.

Lesson by A. J. Hardison 35 min., by T. Grace 35 min. Recess 18 min. Lesson by J. Hampton 35 min. Closing Lesson by P. Hampton 35 min.

I hope the brethren will excuse me for the delay in sending up the above minutes for publication. Professional engagements have caused the delay.

JOHN H. JENKINS, Sec'y

Appendix 2

ANNOTATED OUTLINE
OF JOE S. JAMES, *A BRIEF HISTORY*
OF THE SACRED HARP (1904)

James's document introduced key elements of native historical discourse at a time when nostalgia was beginning to influence the public reception of the singing tradition.

- *Preface* (3–4). A discussion of James's method [i.e., oral history] and purpose, admitting the likelihood of mistakes. Because the book "does justice to the memory of those who have long since died," James asks for the "generosity of the public in their criticism of the defects and imperfections."
- *Introductory* (5–9). A history of music, echoing the theological view of the *Organ* that posited music as a fundamental means of praise. "God Himself, in the beginning, set all things to music, even before man was made," wrote James, following this with accounts of Jubal (Gen. 4:21), of the invention of harmony by Hayagnis in 1566 B.C., of David's Levitical musical guilds (1 Chron. 15 and 16), of the 1866 Peace Jubilee choruses in Boston, and other milestones of musical history.
- *A Brief History of the Sacred Harp* (11–14). Here James gives an account of B. F. White's life in Hamilton, Georgia, and introduces the practice of chronologizing the history of Sacred Harp by listing the book's revisions. He quotes verbatim the prefaces *only* of those which B. F. White had a direct hand in compiling.
- *The Government or Rules* (15–16). An outline of the sections of the "Rudiments of Music" that appeared at the beginning of *The Sacred Harp*, as well as the names of the "three parts" of early revisions (i.e., pieces used for worship, pieces for singing schools and societies, and odes and anthems).

- *Revision of the Sacred Harp* (17–27). This section echoes the chronology in the "Brief History" section, but details the sanctioning institutions and the revision committees rather than the prefaces. Following this, James discusses the recent use of the book and explains why its adherence to fundamental principles will ensure its endurance. As evidence, he lists (22–27) the sources from which early compilers took the old songs, e.g., the names of songs from *Baptist Harmony*.
- *Prof. B. F. White* (27–37). Biography of White, depicting a man of impeccable character.
- *B. F. White's Children and Grandchildren* (39–53). Discussion of eleven of White's descendants, from short genealogical accounts to longer biographies, such as that of his son, Prof. J. L. White.
- *Southern Musical and Chattahoochee Conventions* (55–70). The origins, chronology of officers and sites, and significance of these, the earliest, Sacred Harp conventions.
- *Stone Mountain and Other Musical Conventions* (71–82). A brief description of thirteen Georgia and Alabama conventions, with a list of Fourth of July singings.
- *Changes Made in the Sacred Harp* (83–88). This extraordinary section introduced the practice of tracking the changes made to each page of *The Sacred Harp,* grounding in discrete facts the sanctity of the pagination of the B. F. White editions. For the 1869 edition, for example, he wrote: "Page 75. 'Paradise' removed, 'I Would See Jesus' inserted."
- *The Composers of the Sacred Harp* (89–118). This section contains biographies of twenty-two composers, mostly southerners (e.g., J. P. Reese), but also including New Englanders (e.g., William Billings) and Europeans (e.g., Ignaz Pleyel).
- *Additional Composers of Tunes in the Sacred Harp* (119–24). The main distinction between this section and the preceding one is the lack of information available to James (in some cases he only lists the songs composed) and the small number of songs in the book by each composer (for many, only one).
- *Prominent Leaders in the Sacred Harp* (125–44). Short biographies of prominent leaders, many James's contemporaries, who were not composers of songs in the book.
- *Leaders of Music in the Sacred Harp* (145–52). Lists, by county (Georgia), the names of notable leaders.
- *The History of Four-Shape Notes* (153–57). Returning to the subject of the general history of music, this section locates the origin of the four-shape system in the four syllables that the ancient Greeks assigned to the tetrachord.

Appendix 3

TURN-OF-THE-CENTURY EDITIONS OF
THE SACRED HARP

The first decade of the twentieth century was perhaps the most tumultuous in Sacred Harp singing, as evidenced by the number of revisions that vied for the singers' support. The list below is derived from Buell Cobb's *The Sacred Harp: A Tradition and Its Music* (1978, 89–110). "Torn between 'the good old way' and the demands of progress," Cobb concluded, "the Sacred Harp of the time was in a frustrated state" (1978, 105).

1902 *Cooper Revision.* This edition was supported largely in southeast Alabama, outside the areas of traditional strength. For the most part, its sphere of influence did not include students of B. F. White. The book appealed to the "old paths," but, in spite of this, it transposed many songs to lower keys, introduced alto parts throughout the book, substituted descriptive titles for traditional tune titles, and added popular gospel songs.

1909 *J. L. White Revision.* This book was revised by a committee appointed by the United Sacred Harp Musical Association and headed by J. L. White, B. F. White's son. It consisted of two sections, with separate rudiments and pagination, the latter completely given over to modern harmony—including songs from the first section reharmonized and repeated in the second. It met with disapproval in traditional singing areas.

1909 *Union Harp and History of Songs.* Commissioned by the United Sacred Harp Musical Association, this edition introduced footnotes and Scripture quotations, both of which would be retained in the 1911 James Revision. It included many of the old songs but added many popular gospel songs in explicit response to demand.

1911   *Fourth Edition, with Supplement.* This book was edited by J. L. White and printed using the plates of the 1870 edition. The 1870 book had been a reprint of the 1869 edition with the title page redone, removing reference to sponsorship by the Southern Musical Convention. This 1911 revision included new hymns and gospel songs and the rudiments from J. L. White's 1909 book, but it eliminated the reharmonized old songs from 1909.

1911   *The Original Sacred Harp, James Revision.* The revision committee for this book was appointed by the United Sacred Harp Musical Association, chaired by Joe S. James. Its membership was almost identical to the Union Harp Committee of 1909. The James Revision included, with only slight alteration, the contents of the 1869 edition and restored some older songs. It also added new songs by Alabama and Georgia Sacred Harp composers. It kept the biographical footnotes and Scripture verses that had been introduced in 1909 and added the word *Original* to the title. The book was widely supported in traditional areas.

Appendix 4

FOOTNOTES FROM
THE 1911 JAMES REVISION

Excerpts from J. S. James's footnotes in the 1911 James Revision of *The Sacred Harp.* James's footnotes provided vivid reminders of the role of Sacred Harp singing as the primary custodian of a tradition of religious music that seemed to have boundless scope. They also provided evidence of the circumstances from which the songs emerged, giving singers easy access to a kind of personal familiarity with the songs and their authors.

Lowell Mason, "Missionary Hymn" (Sacred Harp, *page 133)*

Lowell Mason wrote the music to this hymn in Savannah, Ga., when he was a clerk in a bank, in 1823. It is claimed that the joining of the hymn and tune together was providential. A lady, having received and greatly admired one of Heber's lyrics from England, knew no music that would fit the meter, sent them to Lowell Mason, and in half an hour he wrote the music and returned them to the lady. It came to him naturally on reading the poetry. The song flashed through his mind like lightning, and he wrote and composed the music as if by magic. Mr. Mason said that he made no effort at all in the composition. It was the natural impulse flowing through his mind that dictated it. He was born in 1792 and died 1872. He was an American composer, wrote many valuable books, and was the most able composer of sacred music of his time. He was a Doctor of Music, and stood high the world over as a musician.

Helen Maria Williams, "While thee I seek, protecting Pow'r" (143)

The author of this hymn wrote two volumes of poetry in 1786, which were published about that time. Miss Williams was born in England in 1762. Her poems were published when she was twenty-one years old. She visited Paris in

1788, at a period of great trouble, war being waged between England and France at that time. She was arrested on suspicion of being a foreigner, and an advocate of the Girondist cause, and imprisoned. She was not released until 1794. From this time until her death she lived partly in England, but mostly in France, and died in 1831 in Paris. She composed this hymn while in prison.

Jeremiah Ingalls, "Northfield" (155)

Jeremiah Ingalls was born in Massachusetts 1764 and died 1828. Between his thirtieth and fortieth year he composed a number of tunes. In 1804 he published a book, *Christian Harmony,* a collection of his own and other tunes, and among two of his best were "Northfield" and "New Jerusalem." Both of these tunes are set to the same hymn, "Lo, What a Glorious Sight Appears." "New Jerusalem" set to the first verse, and "Northfield" to "How Long, Dear Saviour?" These two great tunes and hymns have been in most of the choice selections since they were composed. Ingalls was self-taught in music. He taught for a long time in the states of New Hampshire, Vermont, and Massachusetts. The origin of "Northfield" is: During his travels as a singing teacher, he stopped at a tavern in the town of Northfield for dinner. His dinner was very slow coming. He kept thinking, "How long?" He fell into the rhythm of Watts's sacred lines and the tune came with it. He named the tune "Northfield." He also compiled several other volumes in music.

William Hauser, "Carmarthen" (316)

William Walker in his *Christian Harmony,* page 294, credited the foregoing tune to the *Hesperian Harp* composed by William Hauser. He first published the *Hesperian Harp* in 1837, and finally completed it in 1848. Mr. Hauser's book consisted of 576 pages, and the author says he had diligently labored for twelve years in preparing the work for publication. Hauser was a Georgian, but of German descent. He resided for a long time in Jefferson County. His book was printed in four notes, fa, sol, la, me. He had a strong treatise in his book in favor of the use of these syllables, in which he stated they are fully adequate, "To the expression of every musical sound in a scale;" and that four shapes the glorious patent notes of William Smith and William Little are just the thing indeed." The words of this tune appear in *Mercer's Cluster,* page 95, *Presbyterian Psalmist,* 238, *Timble of Zion,* 171, and *Temple Harp,* 155.

Appendix 5

♩ ♩
♩ ♪

MINUTES OF THE FIFTY-SIXTH
UNITED CONVENTION

This convention was recorded by Alan Lomax and later released as *All Day Singing from "The Sacred Harp"* (Prestige/International Records, 1960) and later as *White Spirituals from the Sacred Harp* (New World Records, 1977). Although minutes are considered a definitive account of a singing, there are traditional genre conventions that guide the writer in selecting which aspects of the event to record. These minutes do not mention Lomax or the recording. They also do not mention the songs, included on the recording as part of the singing, that he asked the group to sing for him during the dinner hour. The Prestige recording included 132, 38, 159, 361, 85, and 112, which were not in the minutes, and 208, 290, 84, and 189, which were attributed to different leaders than those indicated in the minutes.

Minutes of the Fifty-sixth Session
of the United Sacred Harp Music Association
Held at Fyffe, Alabama—September 12–13, 1959

The United Sacred Harp Musical Association met at Corinth at Fyffe on the 12th of September at 9:00 A.M. and was called to order by Leman Brown, President, singing 32, after which the morning devotion was conducted by R. E. Denson. The singing was resumed as is the custom by the various officers directing the class. First leader: W. N. Hamrick 47t, 371; E. E. Pipkin 36b, 217; Preston Warren 319, 446; Inez Bentley 142, 432; Coy Putnam 337, 434; Carl Hughes 202, 396; Leonard Morris 192, 268; Hugh McGraw 87; George Phillips 28; M. O. Slaughter 327, 183.

Rest 10 minutes.

Called to order by Leman Brown singing 56. Leaders: M. E. Bowen 73, 106t; Mary Johnson 411, 283; M. W. Light 302, 419; Mary Wood 69t, 77t; Max Golden 100, 89; Lois Sticher 290, 402; Reece Hughes 403, 92; Sally Gilliland 456, 304; Jim Ayers 263, 193; Leman Brown 365.

Rest 10 minutes.

Called to order by Preston Warren singing 114. Leaders: Dewey McCullar 397, 216; Buford King 405, 146. The regular business period was held at this time which resulted in the following officers being elected: Leonard Lacy, President; Jim Ayers, Vice President; Leonard Morris, Secretary and Treasurer; Carl Hughes, Chaplain. Arranging Committee: Leman Brown, M. F. McWhorter, Lloyd Redding, and Reece Hughes. Memorial Committee: A. M. Cagle, W. N. Hamrick, Inez Bentley, Hugh McGraw, and A. A. Blocker. Resolutions Committee: Foy Frederick, Coy Putnam, R. E. Denson, and M. O. Kelley. Location Committee: Leonard Lacy, Jim Ayers, Leonard Morris, Preston Warren, and Dewey McCullar. The new committees were announced and the location committee announced that Bowden, Georgia, had been selected for the 1960 session of the Association at Eva Hall. Leaders: H. N. McGraw 316, 422; Mrs. L. C. Crider 330b, 349.

One hour for lunch.

Called to order by Jim Ayers singing 45t. Leaders: Ruth Denson Edwards 197, 455; M. O. Kelley 200, 220; Irene Parker 430, 355; L. P. Odem 428, 429; Whitt Denson 222, 224; Ellie McDowell 328, 400; Arthur Windham 196, 378; J. W. Laminack 269, 204; Martha Frederick 416, 375; A. A. Blocker 203, 186; Willie Mae Latham 442, 436; R. H. Burnham 208, 460; Marvin Brothers 310, 215.

Rest 10 minutes.

Called to order by M. F. McWhorter singing 135. Leaders: Andrew Steifel, 74; Mrs. A. J. Webb 439, 293; Butch White 126, 299; Rose Hughes 155, 189; Jesse Dryden 181, 296; Willie Mae Driscoll 141, 426; Bill Jordan 78, 383; Clelan Cobb 172, 336; Clarence Oliver 348; Sue Holley 93, 84; A. J. Buttram 39b; Rebadell Lacy 273, 182; J. T. Pruitt 124, 318; Leonard Lacy 345b; and Carl Hughes dismissed the class with prayer to meet the next morning at 9:00 o'clock.

Sunday, Sept. 13, 1959

Called to order at 9:00 A.M. by Leonard Lacy singing 176b. Prayer by Carl Hughes. First leader: A. M. Cagle 171; Noah Lacy 297, 172; L. E. Hopper 326, 286; Gilbert Pope 379, 349; Mrs. O. H. Handley 168, 377; Jasper Harper 422; Lola Jenkins 434, 456; W. D. Chappell 216, 217; Eloise Ivey 426, 318; Mr. Lasseter 383, 283; Mrs. Tom Hyatt 306, 348; Mr. Dawson 186, 155; Valera Jo McCullar 336, 460; Bill Matthews 232, 250.

Rest 10 minutes.

Called to order by Leman Brown singing 147t. Leaders: Homer Murphree 245; B. W. Ashley 280, 324; Bob Leeth 298; Mrs. Woodie Walker 138b. The committee on deceased members made the following report: We your committee on deceased members find that since our last meeting that God in his divine wisdom has seen fit to call from our midst the following members: Mrs. Mollie Morris, Mrs. Lena Cagle, Mrs. Mollie Blocker, Mrs. William Tipton, Mrs. Era Snow, Mrs. Mildred White, Mrs. Della Hilton, Oscar Putnam, Rev. A. J. Snider, Rev. C. E. Dean, Newton Blackmon, Tom Nunnelley, Henry Campbell, D. G. Hughes, W. A. Butler, and T. C. Jackson. We recommend that a lesson be sung in their memory and that this report be made a part of the minutes of this meeting. The memorial lesson was directed by Martin Blackmon singing 73t, 45t; J. D. Reed 203, 376; Carl Hughes 342, 122. The lesson closed with prayer by Carl Hughes.

One hour for lunch.

Called to order by Leonard Lacy singing 166b. Leaders: Joe Daniel 119, 127; Roy Avery 337, 254; J. H. Laminack 419, 402; Faye Allen 89, 75; Odus Parker 207, 176t; Syble Wooten 176b, 300; J. W. Webb 272, 328; [redundant entries omitted] Mrs. J. H. Carter 151, 389; L. L. Welborn 128, 442; Mrs. Foy Frederick 386, 395; A. J. Webb 302, 304.

Rest 10 minutes.

Called to order by Lloyd Redding singing 236. Leaders: C. H. Gilliland 340, 211; Joyce Smith 369, 320. A short business session after which singing was resumed by Marion Holley singing 269, 273; B. B. Steifel 220, 420b; Lee Phillips 454, 438; I. S. West 390; M. O. Slaughter, 178, 271; R. I. Lasseter 378, 168. The association was closed by the traditional taking of the parting hand and prayer by Carl Hughes.

LEONARD LACY, President, Henegar, Ala.

JIM AYERS, Vice President

LEONARD MORRIS, Secretary, Eastaboga, Ala.

JOYCE SMITH, Asst. Secretary, Pisgah, Ala.

Appendix 6

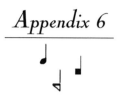

CONSTITUTION OF THE
MULBERRY RIVER CONVENTION

Bylaws of the Mulberry River Convention. The social customs of Sacred Harp singing are profoundly rooted in the institution of the "singing convention." Organized to ensure efficient democratic practice, Sacred Harp singing conventions drafted bylaws, elected officers, established a geographic territory for the convention, collected money for expenses, and adopted an official songbook for exclusive use. Conventions were one of the primary means by which B. F. White established a social base for his book and thus extended to the book an influence that would outlive him. The bylaws excerpted below were adopted by the Mulberry River Singing Convention, Jefferson County, Alabama, in 1905.

At contemporary singings, informal tradition has replaced written rules as the prime motivator of social practice. Officers are still chosen to call the singing to order, call on singers to lead, and record the minutes, but much of this is invisible during the singing itself. In appearance, today's singings give the impression of running, somewhat automatically, on the singers' sheer pleasure in seeing things happen as they do.

Constitution of the Mulberry River Convention
State of Alabama, Jefferson County, November 11, 1905

This convention shall be known as the Mulberry River Sacred Harp Singing Convention.

Its officers shall consist of a President, Vice President, and a Secretary, Arranging Committee, and other committees as the body sees proper to appoint.

This convention shall use the Sacred Harp only during its sessions and the leaders shall use the four shapes; the leaders that are not present at twelve o'clock

Saturday, unless providentially hindered, shall not be allowed to lead.

Its boundaries shall be 25 miles from Partridge beat in Jefferson County. There shall not be but one leader on the floor at a time.

This Convention shall be opened and closed by a prayer.

The Secretary of this Convention shall keep a full list of the names of the members of said convention.

There shall be a memorial lesson conducted at each session in memory of each deceased member, brother or sister, if there should be any.

No convention shall be held in the same community for a second time when there are other petitions asking for it.

In case there is no petition asking for the convention a committee shall be appointed to locate the next term of the convention.

It shall be the duty of the President and Vice President to see there is order kept.

It shall be the duty of the Secretary to keep a full record of the proceedings of each meeting of the convention.

It shall be the duty of the Arranging Committee to select leaders to conduct the music, and the length of time each one shall lead, and to determine what time the convention shall open and close except on Friday.

Appendix 7

EXCERPTS FROM THE MINUTES OF THE
1976 GEORGIA STATE CONVENTION

Larry Gordon and the Word of Mouth Chorus from Vermont attended this convention.

GEORGIA STATE CONVENTION
Oak Grove Church—Roswell, Georgia
March 27, 28 1976

Saturday, March 27

The fifteenth session of the Georgia State Sacred Harp Singing Convention was held at Oak Grove Primitive Baptist Church on the fourth Saturday and Sunday in March. The Convention was called to order by Buell Cobb leading song on page 207. The morning prayer was led by Walter Parker. Officers and members of various committees were called to lead: J. C. Kendrick, 299, 566; Walter Parker, 163, 49b; Charlene Wallace, 277, 439; Preston Warren, 197, 116; Oscar McGuire, 336, 273; Mae Seymour, 436, 316; M. F. McWhorter, 148, 224; Willie Mae Latham, 384, 460; Hugh McGraw, 37b, 276; Leman Brown, 73, 438; Hoyt Cagle, 403, 325; Z. L. Hardin, 32, 314; E. G. Akin, 399, 532.

Recess.

The class resumed singing with Buell Cobb leading song on page 440. A motion was made and seconded to go into a business session. The following officers were elected: Chairman, J. C. Kendrick; Vice Chairman, Kenneth Delong; Secretary, Charlene Wallace; Chaplain, Walter Parker; Arranging Committee, Hugh McGraw, E. G. Akin and Preston Warren; Memorial Committee, Eula Johnson, M. F. McWhorter, and Hoyt Cagle; Resolution Committee, Buell Cobb, Willie Mae Latham, and Kelly Beard; Finance Committee, Z. L. Hardin, Loy Garrison, and Carl

Hughes; Locating Committee, J. C. Kendrick, Kenneth Delong, Lloyd Redding, Oscar McGuire, and Buford McGraw. Leaders called: Henry Kerr, 511, 211; George Woodard, 383, 543; Huey Jones, 47b; Toney Smith, 392; Bob Morrison, 301, 569b; Curtis McLendon, 270, 143; Ralph Heath, 200, 196; John Hollingsworth, 408, 155; Kenneth Delong, 491.

Dismissed for lunch.

The afternoon session was brought to order with J. C. Kendrick leading song on page 496. Leaders: Lloyd Redding, 172, 218; Earnestene Pipkin, 203, 36; Q. A. Barker, 298, 300; Mary Ellen Jones, 196, 498; Kelly Beard, 390, 198; Gertrude Bateman, 297, 157; Doris Delong, 311, 380; The Word of Mouth Chorus from Vermont sang several songs. Members of the choir were: Larry Gordon, Juanita Kyle, Anne Zuckerman, Fred Carlson, Ned Carleton, Cynthia Ross, Heidi Broner, Steve Light, Kathy Munson, Lynn Uretsky, Steve Kelsey, Peter Knbaska, Joanne Schultz, and Ralph Denzer. Songs they used were: Russia, Amonda, Exit, Kittery, Babylon, and Huntington. Wesley Haley, 182, 236; Lovella Warren, 102, 542; Angela Hollingsworth, 145b, 45; John Chessler, 217, 215.

. . . Sunday, March 28

. . . Resolutions report: First, be it resolved that we thank the church and community of Oak Grove for hosting this convention and showing such wonderful hospitality. Second, we express gratitude to the officers of the convention for the efficient manner in which they conducted the affairs of the convention. Third, we appreciate the efforts of the many visitors who traveled long distances to make this one of the best sessions ever held. Respectfully submitted: Willie Mae Latham, Kelly Beard, and Buell Cobb.

Locating Committee report: The convention voted for the 1977 session to be held at Nidrah Plantation, one mile from Leslie, Georgia, on Hwy 280 toward Cordele.

A motion was then made to end the business session. Leaders called were: Elmer Johnson, 77, 74b; Della Reese, 100, 358; Juanita Kyle, 107; Cynthia Ross, 324; Larry Gordon, 188; Steve Light, 114; Ann Zuckerman, 412. The officers of the convention then led song on page 62 (Parting Hand) for the closing song. J. C. Kendrick dismissed with prayer.

Appendix 8

MINUTES OF THE FIRST
NEW ENGLAND CONVENTION (1976)

This was the first northern convention that southern singers attended as a group.

NEW ENGLAND SINGING
Wesleyan University Chapel
Middletown, Conn.
October 2, 1976

The first session of the New England Sacred Harp Singing in over a hundred years was held on the campus of Wesleyan University. About fifty Sacred Harp singers from the South attended with singers from adjoining states. Neely Bruce called the class together leading song on page 63. He was followed by: Talley Kitchens, 36; Terry Wootten, 64, 137; Hugh McGraw, 37b, 49b.

The class was organized for the day by electing the following officers: Chairman, Neely Bruce; Vice Chairman, Hugh McGraw; Secretary, Juanita Kyle; Arranging Committee, Leman Brown and Poppy Gregory. Hugh McGraw then led song on page 61. Neely Bruce led 192 and 302. The morning prayer was led by Z. L. Hardin. Dr. Colin Campbell, president of Wesleyan University, made a short talk and welcomed everyone to the campus. Neely Bruce then led song on page 222. The following leaders were called: Z. L. Hardin, 32; Shelley Posen, 220; Buford McGraw, 145; Larry Gordon, 203; Buell Cobb, 176, 176b; Ann Zuckerman, 294; Daphene Causey, 304.

Recess.

The class resumed singing with Neely Bruce leading songs on pages 260 and 369. Others who led: Hugh McGraw, 361; Tina Calabro, 268; George Woodard, 455; Cindy Ross, 282; Tina Calabro, 156; Faye and Colby Allen, 560, 384; Steve Light, 106; Millard McWhorter, 204; John Camansky, 58; Neely Bruce, 59, 358.

Dismissed for lunch.

The afternoon session resumed with Neely Bruce leading songs on pages 290 and 217. Leaders called: Guy Pugh, 291; Gertrude Bateman, 479; Joanne Schultz, 128; Oscar Ray, 81; Peter Amidon, 123b; Willie Mae Latham, 460; Dave Harmon, 159; Freeman Wootten, 39b, 383; Leonard Spencer, 216; Mary Gardner, 196; Robert Barrett, 186; T. H. Ross, 34; Gordon Lewis, 303; Susan Harcrow, 480; Cindy Burton, 192; Teddy Klaus, 170; Millard Handley, 371; Hugh McGraw, 250.

Recess.

The class reassembled with Neely Bruce leading songs on pages 85 and 277. Leaders called were: Phillis Meckowitz, 189; Juanita Kyle, 193; Lonnie Rogers, 318; Kathy Hains, 155; Carlene Griffin, 224; Moris Kessan, 254; Leonard Lacy, 144; Lynn Uretsky, 327; Eula Johnson, 328; Heidi Brover, 77; Word of Mouth Chorus, 180, 183; Elizabeth Sanders, 476; Sue Kitchens, 182; Kenny Arken, 181; Nancy Husser, 114. The singing next year will go to Christ Church, Montpelier, Vermont, and the following year to Boston, Mass. It will be held on Friday night and Saturday before the first Sunday in October. The third year it will return to Wesleyan University. Neely Bruce led song on page 46. Neely Bruce and Hugh McGraw led song on page 62, "Parting Hand," as the closing song. The class was dismissed with prayer by Talley Kitchens.

> NEELY BRUCE, Chairman
> HUGH MCGRAW, Vice Chairman
> JUANITA KYLE, Secretary

Appendix 9

CONVENTIONS AND STATE SINGINGS IN NEW AREAS, 1976 — 1993

The National Convention is held in Birmingham, Alabama, not in a new area, but appears in the chronology because it reflects the nationwide growth of Sacred Harp singing. Also, Texas is not a new area, although the state convention itself is newly organized.

1976	New England
1980	National Convention
1983	Kentucky State Convention
1984	Connecticut State Convention
1985	Illinois State Convention
1986	Missouri State Convention
1986	Midwest Convention (Chicago)
1987	Wisconsin Singing
1989	North Carolina Convention
1989	All-California Convention
1989	New York State Convention
1990	Potomac River Convention
1990	Louisiana State Convention
1990	Rocky Mountain Convention
1990	Twin Cities Convention (Minneapolis)
1992	Pacific Northwest Convention
1992	James River Convention (Virginia)
1993	Ohio State Convention
1993	Texas State Convention
1993	Garden State Convention (New Jersey)

Appendix 10

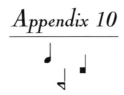

RIVERS OF DELIGHT CORPUS

The *Rivers of Delight* corpus represents only 19 of 560 songs in the book, and it was a part of a folksong revival "core repertory" before the convention system took hold in revival areas.

The headings "1979" and "1984" represent tabulations of how often the song was led at all Sacred Harp singings in the United States that submitted minutes. "Total" is the number of times the song was led; "Rank" indicates its popularity ranking among all songs in the book. For example, since 199 singings submitted minutes in 1979, a singer would have had an almost even chance (102 of 199) of hearing "The Better Land" that year; it ranked thirty-sixth in popularity. For either year, only three songs from this corpus ever ranked in the top fifty, indicating little overall popularity in mostly southern singings. Yet from 1979 to 1985, the years following the release of *Rivers of Delight,* there were eleven improvements and seven declines in the overall use of this corpus.

The heading "1985 Chi/Cha" represents songs listed in the repertory of the Chicago and Charleston, Illinois, singing groups just before the first Illinois State Convention; * means it was designated a favorite. For Chicago, the *Rivers of Delight* corpus comprises 13 of 41 songs on their local list; for Charleston, 12 of 56. In comparison, the corpus from a 1972 recording by Neely Bruce's American Music Group at the University of Illinois, on which several from the local groups performed, contributed only 8 of 56 to the Charleston repertory and 2 of 41 to Chicago. Note that only two *Rivers of Delight* songs appear in neither the Chicago nor the Charleston list.

The remaining columns measure their popularity in the Midwest: "1985 Illinois" is the first annual Illinois State Convention, a one-day event; "1986 Midwest" is the first annual Midwest Convention, a three-day event; "N" and "S" represent songs led by northern and southern (Alabama or Georgia) singers at those events. Summarized below is the percentage of songs from this corpus of all songs led by singers in each group, which adjusts for the differing numbers of singers from each area. These numbers should be compared with the percentage of the entire book that the Word of Mouth corpus represents, which is 3.4 percent.

		1979 Total/Rank	1984 Total/Rank	1985 Chi/Cha	1985 Illinois	1986 Midwest
38b	Windham	14/335	21/267	Chi*	N	SN
47b	Idumea	58/127	77/64	Chi*/Cha	N	
48b	Kedron	10/363	12/340	Chi*		N
65	Sweet Prospect	37/197	29/210			NN
155	Northfield	156/4	149/3	Chi*/Cha	N	NN
159	Wondrous Love	89/61	79/61	Chi*/Cha*	N	NNN
163	Morning	34/210	48/137	Chi*		N
168	Cowper	124/19	28/214	Chi*		
183	Greenwich	65/105	45/146	Chi*	N	N
196	Alabama	56/132	57/112	Cha	N	S
209	Evening Shade	17/306	29/207	Chi*/Cha*	S	
273	Milford	64/110	47/142	Chi/Cha		N
288	White	61/118	62/96	Chi*/Cha		
299	New Jerusalem	88/63	74/72	Cha		
324	Northport	18/301	23/244	Chi/Cha	N	N
383	Eternal Day	69/95	82/54			
454	The Better Land	102/36	78/62	Cha*	S	NN
455	Soar Away	38/195	36/178	Chi*/Cha*	N	N
532	Peace and Joy	36/204	23/245	Cha*		N

% led by northern singers					19%	15%
% led by southern singers					9%	4%

Appendix 11

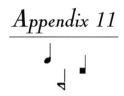

REVISIONS OF
THE SACRED HARP

This chronology is based on editions that are considered direct ancestors of the 1991 edition. Chronologies are selective, emphasizing continuities between various editions and omitting those editions that conflict with the linear sense of history that the chronology is meant to describe. This chronology, for example, leaves out the influential Cooper revision of 1902. Sometimes major revisions are distinguished from minor revisions by such criteria as whether songs are removed. Dates are publication dates.

Major	*Minor*	*Revisions of* The Sacred Harp
1844		Consisted of selections from a stock nineteenth-century repertoire of hymns, anthems, and songs, combined with compositions by B. F. White and other regional authors. (242 songs)
	1850	(344 songs: 102 added as an appendix)
	1859	(418 songs: 74 added as an appendix)
1869		Last B. F. White edition; preface included the oft-cited epithet "Ask for the old paths, and walk therein." (498 songs: 129 added, 49 removed, 1 page change)
1911		James Revision. Historical and biographical footnotes added; Scripture quotations added below titles; alto parts added to 327 songs. Southern authors and composers contributed an unprecedented two-thirds of the texts and tunes in the book. (580 songs: 82 added, 2 page changes, none removed)
1936		Denson Revision. Book purchased by the Sacred Harp Publishing Company in 1933, organized by T. J. Denson. (446 songs: 41 added, 175 removed, 94 page changes)

1960   (549 songs: 103 added)

1966   Undertaken mainly to correct errors introduced in 1960. (539 songs: 12 added; 22 removed, all of which had been added in 1960; 9 page changes)

1971   (539 songs: 1 page change)

1991   1991 Revision. Footnotes removed; Scripture added where previously omitted. (560 songs; 60 added, 46 removed)

Appendix 12

NEW SONGS IN THE 1991 REVISION

Recently composed songs were added to the 1991 revision of *The Sacred Harp*. In addition to these, twenty-three songs from nineteenth-century tunebooks were added, five of which were reintroduced from earlier editions of *The Sacred Harp*. In all, sixty new songs were added and forty-five old ones were removed. In comparison with earlier ones, this revision was characterized by the predominance of composers who had not previously contributed to the book and composers from folk revival areas. Never before had a contemporary composition been added to the book whose composer resided outside Alabama, Georgia, and neighboring states.

New Songs by Alabama Composers

"Rockport" (372)	Jim Carnes	Montgomery
"A Thankful Heart" (475)	John Hocutt	Jasper
"Easter Morn" (415)	David Ivey	Huntsville
"Heavenly Land" (303)	Jeff Sheppard	Glencoe
"Love Shall Never Die" (278)	Toney Smith	Tuscaloosa
"Shining Star" (461)	Terry Wootten	Ider

New Songs by Georgia Composers

"Big Creek" (494)	Richard DeLong	Carrollton
"Corley" (510)	Richard DeLong, arr.	Carrollton
"Lebanon" (354)	J. Monroe Denton	
"Alexander" (393)	Timothy R. Gilmore	Vidalia
"Humility" (50)	David Grant	Macon
"Christian's Farewell" (347)	Raymond C. Hamrick	Macon

"Emmaus" (569)	Raymond C. Hamrick	Macon
"Invocation" (492)	Raymond C. Hamrick	Macon
"Lloyd" (503)	Raymond C. Hamrick	Macon
"Nidrah" (540)	Raymond C. Hamrick	Macon
"Haynes Creek" (466)	Joyce Harrison	Macon
"DeLong" (516)	Hugh W. McGraw	Bremen
"Farewell to All" (570)	Hugh W. McGraw	Bremen
"Phillips' Farewell" (549)	Hugh W. McGraw	Bremen
"Reynolds" (225)	Hugh W. McGraw	Bremen
"Wootten" (548)	Hugh W. McGraw	Bremen
"Holcombe" (77)	Charlene Wallace	Mt. Zion

New Songs by Composers from Other Areas

"Akin" (472)	P. Dan Brittain	Cazenovia, N.Y.
"Cobb" (313)	P. Dan Brittain	Cazenovia, N.Y.
"McGraw" (353)	P. Dan Brittain	Cazenovia, N.Y
"Novakoski" (481)	P. Dan Brittain	Cazenovia, N.Y.
"Heavenly Union" (484)	Neely Bruce	Middletown, Conn.
"Ainslie" (348)	Judy Hauff	Chicago
"Granville" (547)	Judy Hauff	Chicago
"Stony Point" (368)	Judy Hauff	Chicago
"Wood Street" (504)	Judy Hauff	Chicago
"New Agatite" (485)	Ted Johnson	Chicago
"O'Leary" (501)	Theodore Mercer	Chicago
"Sheppard" (464)	Theodore Mercer	Chicago
"Mount Desert" (474)	Bruce Randall	Boston
"Natick" (350)	Glen Wright	Boston

Notes

CHAPTER I.

TIMOTHY MASON IN CINCINNATI:

MUSIC REFORM ON THE URBAN FRONTIER

1. Many sources give the date of publication as 1798, when a copyright was secured in Pennsylvania. But Irving Lowens and Allen P. Britton (1953) found that most evidence suggests the appearance of the genuine first edition in 1802. Most editions of the book were published in Albany, New York.

2. In specifying "wide use," Jackson meant not to include less widespread use of other tunebooks, such as *Southern Harmony*, whose traditions he discussed in *White Spirituals* (64–67); on this basis some contemporary singers might object to his assessment (Loftis 1987). Apparently he meant to recognize both the Denson and Cooper revisions of the *Sacred Harp*, which have always had active singing traditions. *Colored Sacred Harp*, also an offshoot of the *Sacred Harp*, was in 1933 yet unpublished (Dyen 1977).

3. Buechner did not warn readers that Chauncy, a liberal theologian and staunch opponent of revivals, was guided as much by prejudice as by accuracy (see, e.g., Goen 1962, 17). This bias, however, seems irrelevant to Buechner's point that the singing was not regular.

4. Benson, citing the church history, reported that West Church, under Jonathan Mayhew, seated a choir around 1754 ([1915] 1962, 174).

5. Let us recall that a chapter of John Cotton's *Singing of Psalms: A Gospel Ordinance* (1650) was devoted to the question of "Whether Women may sing as well as Men." In the context of a document developing the scriptural grounds for psalm singing, Cotton examined the proscription against women speaking in the church. He found, through Scripture and ecclesiastical history, that biblical law was specific on the matter and allowed for such spoken discourses as singing and also "subjection" (giving account of offenses). Surely this close reading of law chartered a practice and later an institution—inscribed from within by so potent an expressive form as the singing of praise and circumscribed from without by suspicion—that would be distinguished as a site of gendered discourse.

6. Attendance at Cane Ridge is often used as a measure of the significance of camp meetings. At the time it was held, the population of nearby Lexington, the largest settlement, was only 1,795. Attendance estimates vary widely; Finley's 25,000 is probably the largest. The smallest was a count of 147 wagons. But this figure is probably misleading: a different count lists 143 "carriages and wagons" but includes other means of conveyance totaling 1,143 vehicles (Hudson 1981, 138). Various estimates are given in Weisberger (1958, 307n. 68).

7. Other narratives of later activity support this view. Many are included in Ellen Jane Lorenz's *Glory Hallelujah!* (1980), a compilation of descriptions of camp meeting singing.

8. Leavitt was an ardent disciple of Charles Finney, a New York evangelist and adversary of Lyman Beecher. As Buechner noted, Leavitt was a shrewd business-man and, unlike some other tunebook compilers, deliberately established sales of his book far outside his and Finney's immediate spheres of influence. It comes as no surprise that he would have worked through bookstores and newspapers in Cincinnati to expand the influence of his book. Perhaps it also comes as no sur-prise that his interest in shape notes was limited. Volume one of *The Christian Lyre* (New York, 1832) was printed in shape notes in its first edition, but no later editions or parts of the *Lyre* used shape notes. Buechner noted that such features indicate that the *Lyre* was meant to appeal to a revival following and not to the shape note singing population. The use of shape notes in the *Journal* as well as the expansion of the arrangements from two to four parts suggests that the *Journal* did seek to attract this audience.

9. There is no connection other than their coincidentally similar titles between *The Sacred Harp* (1844), which is still popular today, and *Mason's Sacred Harp*, which was published in Cincinnati. Many books of that era were called "Harps," and most contained sacred music.

10. Ministers and musicians often worked together successfully: James Waddel Alexander and Lowell Mason, and Henry Ward Beecher and John Zundel worked in ways similar to Beecher and Timothy Mason (Kraege 1980, 101). Beecher drew directly from his own experiences with Lowell Mason in seeking out Timothy to bring to the West.

11. In a systematic comparison of the pedagogical practices of Mason and Pes-talozzi, Rich (1946) found sufficient difference to credit Mason with considerable modification to Pestalozzi's ideas (see also Stevenson 1966, 78). Also, Mason claimed that pedagogical innovations in his *Manual of the Boston Academy of Music* were derived from the "system of Pestalozzi," when in fact the *Manual* closely followed a translation (that Mason may have commissioned) of G. F.

Kübler's *Anleitung zum Gesang-Unterrichte in Schulen* (Stuttgart, 1826; see Ellis 1955). Nonetheless, the general remark that Pestalozzi inspired a pedagogy of childhood should be well taken.

12. All quoted passages preserve the original emphasis. Holdings of the *Cincinnati Journal,* renamed the *Journal and Western Luminary,* were incomplete; my account is based on installment 5 (18 February 1836) through installment 20 (11 August 1836). A new series on "Church Psalmody" began 3 November 1836—clearly a continuation of the objectives of the "Music" series. Throughout the run of the series, the author was identified only by the initials S.H.C., corresponding to no prominent figure of the period; it was not unusual for those in the Beecher milieu to sign contributions to the *Journal* with obfuscating initials. It may well have been Charles, because at about this time, Harriet wrote in her journal, "Both our pieces have gone to press to-day, with Charles's article on music, and we have had not a little diversion about our *family newspaper*" (C. Stowe 1889, 82). Nonetheless, if Mason did not actually write the series, then he had significant influence over it. Surely no one else would have been in a position to advance the particular constellation of ideas represented in the series.

13. They married in 1836. Calvin Stowe was on the faculty at Lane Seminary when Lyman Beecher arrived in Cincinnati to serve as its director. He was Beecher's faithful and outspoken supporter, even when Beecher opposed a student-led antislavery movement. Beecher's opposition to the movement appears to have been more pragmatic than ideological, although earlier in his life, under no pressures from the citizenry, he had claimed to be both an abolitionist and a colonizationist "without perceiving in myself any inconsistency" (Wyatt-Brown 1969, 127).

14. Charles Hamm's (1958) conclusion is actually stronger: that only one shape note book was introduced at all in Cincinnati after that date. He may not have meant to include seven-shape books, which according to Fetta (1922) were still being printed in Cincinnati in 1922.

15. Gallaher was recruited by Old School stalwart Joshua L. Wilson because of his extraordinary preaching skills, and he subsequently became pastor of the Third Presbyterian Church. As Gallaher veered decisively toward Arminian-tending New School theology, however, Wilson turned against him (Lesick 1980, 23).

16. The Beechers were not actually Presbyterians but Congregationalists. Under the 1801 Plan of Union, Congregationalists and Presbyterians agreed to share clergy, largely because both denominations had adopted the Nicene Creed as theological premise and liturgical practice. The fact that denominational tensions heightened the sense of division in Cincinnati is unmistakable: Wilson proclaimed during the ordination procedure that, on the basis of his denominational affilia-

tion, George Beecher was no Christian and would "never see the gates of eternal bliss." To make matters worse, Lyman Beecher's own Presbyterian credentials had come from the Third Presbyterian Church of New York—a New School church (Nutt 1991, 35; United Presbyterian Synod of Ohio 1968, 127).

Perhaps not ironically, Congregationalists also were dismayed by the consequences of the Plan of Union. Presbyterians, after all, had employed it in the West with such zeal that by midcentury they would be referred to as "Presbyterian opportunists milking Congregationalist cows" (Caskey 1978, 52).

17. It is of passing interest that Dwight composed a poem, "Columbia," in 1777, praising the new nation as the refuge of the oppressed. After 1800, the skeptical Federalist Dwight dramatically reversed his stand, eventually calling for an end to immigration altogether (see Silverman 1969, 139). The full text of the poem was published in *American Museum* 3 (June 1787): 566, and verses from it circulated in shape note tunebooks, including *The Sacred Harp,* set to the tune "Murillo's Lesson."

18. Smith had found the tune as he was "turning over the leaves of several books of music—chiefly music for children's schools—the words being in the German language," unaware that its original source was the English tune "God Save the Queen." Ordinarily this circumstance is considered patently ironic. But Sonneck reckoned that because it was sung in the colonies before the Revolution, the tune belonged as much to Americans as to the British.

19. According to Scholten (1976), shape note teacher and composer Lucius Chapin moved to Cincinnati in 1836 to live with his wife's family. (His father-in-law was Joseph Kemper, one of the early Presbyterian ministers in the area; Kemper's home has been restored and reconstructed at a historical village in the Cincinnati area.) But at the age of 75 he was disillusioned with music teaching. There is no evidence that he mounted a defense of shape notes at this time, nor was this the reason for his coming to Cincinnati.

20. Charles Hamm (1958, 309) identifies the group as Father Kemp's Old Folks, but all indications are that this was not the same group.

21. Henceforth, all references to Stowe's published works will include only the volume and page from *The Writings of Harriet Beecher Stowe,* Riverside edition (1896).

CHAPTER 2. SACRED HARP AS CULTURAL OBJECT

1. Historian Hayden White (1978) discusses irony as a means by which "rational" discourse accommodates genuinely alternative modes of thought. This is precisely the sense in which public musical culture, touted in the nineteenth century

as "scientific," has embraced the shape note tradition without taking it as commensurate with its own conventional forms. Irony in ethnography has been addressed in Webster (1982) and Rabinow (1985).

2. Worthman (1971, 180) reports that in 1890, 28 percent of the males over 21 were foreign-born or sons of immigrants. Of these, many were "Germans from Louisville or Cincinnati who worked in the building trades or as tailors or shoemakers."

3. Visitors to Birmingham from other parts of the state gave reports that were "sharply at odds with the enthusiasm of the developers" (Wiener 1978, 169). One reporter, alluding only partially to the contagious fever he had observed among residents, warned his readers: "When I go to Birmingham again, I intend to tie a piece of asafoetida around my neck to guard against the contagion, and I would advise all visitors to take a similar precaution." Some opponents of industrialization argued that Old South planters held the key to southern culture and that, with industrialization, southerners would "lose their literature, their former habits of thought, their intellectual self-assertion" (Wiener 1978, 196).

4. Joe S. James was perhaps the most important turn-of-the-century figure in the Sacred Harp tradition, if for nothing other than his contribution to the 1911 James Revision of *The Sacred Harp.* Before he moved to Atlanta, James edited *New South,* a Douglasville, Georgia, newspaper. I have not been able to locate surviving copies of the paper, but I suspect that James did foresee some benefit in affiliating Sacred Harp with New South institutions. At the same time, he sought to install other antimodernist features for Sacred Harp; these will be discussed in chapter 3.

5. Birmingham was also chosen as the permanent site of the annual National Sacred Harp Singing Convention, first held in 1980.

6. Dated but otherwise unidentified clippings for these singings are on file in the Sacred Harp Publishing Company headquarters in Carrollton, Georgia.

7. "Carmer Editing Folklore Book," *Crimson White,* University of Alabama, 6 March 1924, p. 3.

8. "Carmer Speaks on 'Harp' Songs as Folk Music in Local Talk," *Crimson White,* University of Alabama, 9 December 1926, pp. 1, 8.

9. It was in 1961 that Carmer tried to reclaim her authority for *Stars.* Carmer submitted a short piece on "My Own Unforgettable Character" to *Reader's Digest,* but it was rejected on the basis that Carmer "had not known [Miss Ruby] long or well enough to have been influenced by her in the way the author should be by this most unforgettable character" (Brown 1993, 184). Tartt, in fact, in a letter to John Lomax, concurred with Lomax's disapproving review of *Stars* (October 1943, printed in Brown 1993, 156).

10. The nineteenth-century editions of *The Sacred Harp* included many three-part harmonies to which the revisers of the 1911 edition added alto lines. While it seems possible that this change would have been controversial, only Carmer's account provides evidence of a dispute (see Cobb 1978, 93; McKenzie 1989). It may well have been an exaggeration, a liberty taken by Carmer to provide dramatic intrigue.

Other errors are easier to identify: few singers would miss the error in Carmer's description (1934, 53) of the beginning chord of "The Bride's Farewell." In it, the character "Perfesser Hinton" sings a "baritone *mi.*" In fact, in no song in *The Sacred Harp* does *mi* appear in the beginning chord since it is not part of the tonic chord of any mode or key. Carmer, unlike Jackson, was probably unconcerned with details of this sort.

11. My preference for the condensed *Reader's Digest* version is again based on its likelihood of having reached a vaster audience and having more thoroughly influenced public perception of Sacred Harp than did the *Virginia Quarterly Review* (Davidson 1934a). In both versions, the basic structure of the narrative was the same. In some ways, the effect of condensing the original was actually to remove some of its more intrusive features—such as his relentless reference to Eden, the name that "ought to be, but is not" given to the area of Middle Georgia where he then resided.

12. Beginning in 1945, Jackson did publish on the subject of Amish music and culture, recognizing in the Amish those admirable qualities that provided for their resistance against elitist impulses in American culture (Jackson 1945a, 1945b, 1945d, 1946a).

13. "Dr. Jackson's Rites Will Be Held Tuesday," *Nashville Banner,* 20 January 1953; "Dr. G. P. Jackson Services: Folk Music Pioneer Was Leading Critic, Author, Organizer," *Nashville Tennessean,* 20 January 1953. These accounts—indicating Walker County, Alabama, in 1920 as Jackson's first singing—are incorrect.

14. Sidney Denson's letter is reproduced fully in Jackson 1926, 10 and 1933, 107–8.

15. The books were *Songs and Pictures* (1928), *Singing America* (1940), *New Music Horizons* (1944), and *Music, the Universal Language* (1941). Jackson's categories and the average percentages for the four books were "Imported Folksongs" (29.75%), "Composed Songs" (45.75%), "British Isles Folksongs" (6%), and "American Folksongs" (13.25%). Apparently, of the 591 songs, there were some in each of the four books that did not belong in any of these categories or that Jackson could not identify.

16. David E. Whisnant's *All That Is Native and Fine* includes a promotional photograph and a brief discussion of the group (1983, 197–98).

17. I am indebted to Charlotte Wolfe for the details of some of the later performances.

18. Obituaries appeared 19 January 1953 in the *Nashville Banner, Birmingham News,* and *New York Times,* and 20 January in the *Nashville Tennessean* that outline his civic contributions. It is worth noting that much of this predates his folk music work.

19. Quotations are taken from undated *Nashville Banner* clippings housed in the Jackson collection at Vanderbilt University.

20. *Vanderbilt Alumnus* 8 (March 1923): 136.

21. The extent to which minstrel shows were debilitating and spirituals were empowering is a complex and inconclusive issue, of course. One salient irony was the fact that the Fisk Jubilee Singers adopted European performance practices and measured their success in part by reactions from white audiences. At the time, however, the prevailing view was that the spiritual was vastly more beneficial than minstrelsy.

22. Du Bois's period of study in Germany and his undergraduate degree from Fisk both preceded *Souls* by only a few years. It should be said that Du Bois himself did not recognize Herder or other German folklorists as mentors.

23. R. Nathaniel Dett, director of the Hampton Institute choir, wrote in 1938 that there had been "three factors outstanding in their influence on the thought of America regarding Negro music development": (1) the world tour of the Fisk Jubilee Singers, (2) the compositions of Stephen Foster, and (3) Dvořák's symphony, *From the New World* (Dett 1938, 1243).

24. Notably, Carl Carmer *had* made the connection between Sacred Harp and Negro spirituals. In 1926, the University of Alabama's *Crimson White* (9 December) reported, "Carmer Speaks on 'Harp' Songs as Folk Music in Local Talk: Negro Music Not Only National Music, Claim." He attributed the "tongue-in-cheek theory" to Thomas W. Palmer, former president of Alabama College, who pointed to the "wailing sadness" of "dour Calvinists forced out of Virginia by Church of England people, to wander southward."

25. The prejudice that Jackson reported in music institutions against vernacular shape note singing has not completely abated. Consider, for example, Fletcher Clark Anderson's 1978 dissertation, "A History of Choral Music in Birmingham, Alabama." It does not mention *The Sacred Harp,* or the prestigious Alabama State Convention, or the influential work of Birmingham singer Paine Denson, who oversaw the completion of the 1936 revision of *The Sacred Harp* and contributed

several popular compositions over the years. It does provide the account of Benjamin Guchenberger's farewell ceremony and quotes George Pullen Jackson's remarks. This may also be the case for other musical histories of cities where singing schools or shape notes were once or still are popular.

CHAPTER 3. WRITING TRADITIONS OF *THE SACRED HARP*

1. The *Organ* began publication in 1852 as a weekly, distributed on Wednesday. Although it frequently featured new songs, Buell Cobb has reminded us (1978, 72) that it was not a means of testing the popularity of songs before the 1844 edition of *The Sacred Harp*.

As for the sparse population of Harris County, the 1850 census recorded (White 1854, 494) the following: Dwellings, 1,175; families, 1,242; white males, 3,391; white females, 3,318; free colored males, 15; free colored females, 15. Total free population, 6,739; slaves 7,982. Farms, 873, manufacturing establishments, 73. The county measured 360 square miles, and total population density was 41 people per square mile (22 slave, 19 free).

The *Organ* was succeeded in 1860 as the local newspaper by the *Harris County Enterprise*. If the issue examined in Louise Barfield's *History of Harris County* (1961, 232) is any indication, it was similar to the *Organ* in most respects (including a distaste for polemics), except that it had no concern at all with music.

2. Massachusetts native Isaac Baker Woodbury (1819–1858) was a prominent figure in American hymnody and an influential music teacher. He succeeded Lowell Mason as director of public school music in Boston (Higginson 1969). His last years were spent in Charleston, South Carolina, where he published the *Harp of the South* (1853). I have not been able to identify Isaac Holcombe, although his absence from Joe S. James's history probably indicates that he was not active as a singer in Georgia. Mason and Hastings are covered in chapter 1.

3. Although initially trained in music by B. F. White, E. T. Pound worked as a Normal School music teacher and published several books in round notes and unconventional seven-shape notation (see Wilcox 1976). It has been suggested that the introduction of competing books at the Southern Musical Convention began in 1852 and that the Chattahoochee Convention was actually formed in reaction to that. If this is true, the founding of the *Organ* in that very year can only be seen as a mustering of forces in service to the conservative cause. But James's *History* indicates nothing of the sort, and Thurman's *Chattahoochee Musical Convention* (1952, 5) records that Oliver Bradfield and his friends met in the fall of 1851 to plan a convention "similar in form and character to the Southern Musical Convention."

4. Apparently, Holcombe had neglected to add a second ending to a passage that was repeated *da capo* and had used the notation "D.C.," according to White, to indicate repeated *text* rather than repeated music.

5. Hereafter in this section, references to James's *Brief History of the Sacred Harp* will include only the page numbers.

6. Biographical accounts in the Sacred Harp literature are abbreviated and rare. The best are by George Pullen Jackson (1933, 81–82), Buell E. Cobb Jr. (1978, passim), and a reprinted obituary in the *National Sacred Harp Newsletter* (March 1987).

7. It is not certain what role James played in the conservative or antimodernist character of the 1911 revision. James was not an unwavering champion of old music; in fact, he engaged in a variety of progressive musical experiments. So it is not clear whether he wholeheartedly endorsed the antimodernist book, merely recognized its need within the singing population, or reluctantly responded to the pressure of the committee. For this reason, I have taken care to credit certain features to "the revisers" in cases where the role of James himself is not known.

8. The word *intact* should be qualified: the James Revision added alto parts to 327 of its 609 tunes, probably taking its cue from the Cooper Revision. Generally this gesture has been called a "*major* concession to modernism" (Cobb 1978, 91). But Wallace McKenzie has analyzed the effects of the alto on overall harmony and concluded that they actually reinforce preexisting harmonic traits: "If it were for the purpose of modernization, one would have to conclude that the composers held rather hazy notions about modern hymn style" (McKenzie 1989, 171). It might well be noted also that the alto part was common in earlier New England tunebooks, but it had not been included, for reasons that remain unclear, in some arrangements in southern tunebooks.

9. Oral history holds that Sidney Burdette Denson was the actual source of the scriptural quotations, although she did not serve on the music committee, as did her husband, Seaborn M. Denson. It is also said that she wrote the numerous alto parts for which her husband is explicitly credited. I have seen no mention of these facts in print, although James did say in a footnote to her composition "The Marriage in the Skies" (*Sacred Harp* 1971, 438) that she "often assists her husband in teaching music schools." With the hope of leaving this uncertainty to others to unravel, I have credited the scriptural quotations to the "James revisers."

10. James listed source hymnbooks and tunebooks for *The Sacred Harp* in his *Brief History* (22–27). Of these sources, *The Psalmist* contributed more songs than any other. Watts's *Hymn Book* had descriptive titles, specific thematic subtitles (indexed), Scripture citations indexed but not given with the hymns, and an author index. *Zion Songster,* a camp meeting songster, indicated no themes or

authors. *Mercer's Cluster* used thematic titles, such as "The Presence of Christ makes all well," for the text "How tedious and tasteless the hours."

11. It should be said that the "chosen flock" came originally from Tate and Brady. Davie (1993) compared the Tate and Brady version and the Watts version of Psalm 74, exploring the theological motivation for the changes Watts exacted on the earlier version. Stevenson (1949, 238) quoted passages from Watts's footnotes, which indicated Watts's distaste for the vengeful God of some of the Psalms.

12. With added stanzas addressing farewells to other family members, "The Bride's Farewell" was written by Miss M. L. Beevor and set to music (not the tune in *The Sacred Harp*) composed by Thomas Williams. The score was published, with no date indicated, in Baltimore by G. Willig Jr. The song was also recorded in the logbook of the whaling ship *Fortune* in 1840 (Huntington 1964, 241–43), and it was also included in J. P. McCaskey's *Franklin Square Song Collection* in 1892 (8:127). Of the known sources, the most likely to have influenced its inclusion in the 1869 edition of *The Sacred Harp* was the *Harmoniad and Sacred Melodist* of 1857.

13. Jackson, in fact, addressed the centennial meeting of the Chattahoochee Musical Convention. Thurman reported this as a kind of afterthought to his discussion of individuals and family groups as the "body" of the convention. The brief mention of Jackson was set off from the chapter as an attached section, immediately preceding the final chapter on "The Real Chattahoochee Convention."

14. Hereafter in this section, references to Earl Thurman's article, "The Chattahoochee Musical Convention: 1852–1952," will include only the page numbers.

15. The studio recordings were as follows: *Original Sacred Harp* SHPC-101, *Presenting Another Fa-Sol-La Music Album* SHPC-102, *Sacred Harp Singing at the Old Country Church* SHPC-103, *Sacred Harp Singing with Dinner on the Ground* SHPC-104, *Fa-Sol-La Is Here to Stay* SHPC-105. The Sacred Harp Publishing Company produced other recordings not for this purpose, such as *The Singing Creel Family* (UMS-105), which was a live recording from singing at the County Line Church. The sixth was an open session held in Birmingham, Alabama, to record songs for the U.S. bicentennial celebration.

16. It may also have concerned revisers that parts of Edwards's account are considered suspicious by some authorities. For example, Edwards gives considerable attention to an account, first reported by J. S. James, of B. F. White's joint authorship, with William Walker, of the *Southern Harmony*. After careful study of Walker's life, Harry L. Eskew has not been able to substantiate this story. His case may have been strengthened by the discovery of a pre–*Southern Harmony* manuscript on which appears Walker's signature but not White's (Price 1978).

17. Buell Cobb (1978, chap. 5) provided a lucid observation of Sacred Harp conventions, so only an abbreviated account is necessary here.

18. Corinth, as Peter Berger recently has reminded us, was a community of the world considerably more diverse than contemporary America, and it was in this setting that the principle of the New Testament church was established (Berger 1992).

19. There was another less likely source that warrants mentioning. Theories of associationism advanced by nineteenth-century American Transcendentalists might have supplied a link between the social collective and musical expression. These writers discovered in music a "harmonious connection between the organic and the inorganic, between man and God, between man and the world, and between the world and the universe" (Lowens 1964, 258). Derived from Fourierism and advanced in America by Albert Brisbane, associationism postulated a "natural" form of human social order:

> God is the Ruler of the moral as well as of the material world. He has not given us faculties and passions at random, and with the chance of their being eternally in conflict; on the contrary, he has created them with infinite wisdom and foresight, and adapted them to a System of Society, pre-existing in his Intelligence, in which they would produce the most beautiful Order and Harmony (Brisbane 1843, 3).

Much of Brisbane's "System of Society" had little in common with Sacred Harp singing associations. But possibly B. F. White embraced those particular Transcendentalist ideas that related God, nature, and music. Their basic principles were certainly familiar to writers in the *Organ*. But it is also likely that these general ideas came to the singers from other sources of romantic thought.

20. In the early decades of the nineteenth century, these associations had the most impact in the religious arena. The revolution had taken its toll on most churches, and adoption of the First Amendment in 1791 indicated that authority was not to be derived from the civil administration. The Congregationalist Church, the largest colonial church, had been disestablished in New Hampshire in 1791, in Connecticut in 1818, and in Massachusetts in 1833.

CHAPTER 4. "OUR SPIRITUAL MAINTENANCE HAS BEEN PERFORMED": SACRED HARP REVIVAL

This chapter is an expansion of two papers, one presented at the meetings of the American Folklore Society, St. John's, Newfoundland, 18 October 1991, and the other published in *Tributaries* (Bealle 1994).

1. California singer Leon Wilson attended the school from around 1939 to 1942 and recalled being exposed to shape note music in Zilphia Horton's music classes. Subsequently, Wilson and a few others from Highlander Folk School sought out Sacred Harp singing, including trips to singings and to Nashville to visit George Pullen Jackson (see Herman 1993).

2. At the time, the Christmas Country Dance School was one of only a few programs that taught folk traditions in an intensive, weeklong format. Today they are numerous, in part because influential performers and organizers across the country were trained at Berea. Sacred Harp classes are still taught there; for several years, Hugh McGraw was employed as the teacher.

3. This and subsequent quoted remarks by Hugh McGraw are from an interview conducted 21 September 1990 in Bremen, Georgia.

4. It should be said that the New England singing was not the first folk revival singing to organize and submit minutes. In the early 1970s, Sacred Harp singings were held at the Ark Coffeehouse in Ann Arbor, Michigan. Through the urging of Warren Steel and Charlotte Wolfe and the advice of traditional singers Pauline Childers and Bill and Reba Dell Windom, convention protocol was gradually established and minutes were submitted. But the Ark singings never attained the stature or the influence of the state singings. By the time groups were organized in Illinois and other midwestern states, Ark singings had been discontinued. I am indebted to Warren Steel and others on the Sacred Harp e-mail conference for supplementing the historical account indicated by the minutes.

5. This is not to suggest that regional preferences in general are exclusive to folksong revival areas. In fact, there are regional repertories in southern singing areas, rather than a homogeneous distribution of the most popular songs. The point is merely that the *Rivers of Delight* corpus was more popular in folksong revival areas.

6. From 1965 to 1973, a series of recordings was produced by the Sacred Harp Publishing Company, partly to aid new singers in learning tunes. They were recorded in a studio by a select group of singers. In the 1980s, two cassettes, *Favorite Songs* and *Amazing Grace,* were produced much for the same reasons and by the same technique. When singing school teacher Richard DeLong was interviewed on a Cincinnati radio station before a 1990 school he was to conduct, he brought along *Favorite Songs* to play on the air.

7. This discussion is based partly on an interview with Ted Johnson 16 December 1990 in Birmingham and on an installment of "Life in the Hollow Square," from the *Chicago Sacred Harp Newsletter* (February/March 1991), where Marcia Johnson recounted significant events in the group's founding.

8. Fox Hollow was more a gathering for self-professed folksingers than, as most folk festivals are today, a presentation of representatives from vernacular traditions. Both recordings by Fox Hollow participants, *Golden Ring* (Folk-Legacy FSI-16, 1964) and *Five Days Singing* (Folk-Legacy FSI-41 and FSI-42, 1971), feature shape note hymns. On the first, Win Strake, cofounder of Chicago's Old Town School of Folk Music, sings bass on "Babe of Bethlehem," from *Southern Harmony*. Notes to the recordings indicate a comprehensive exposure to folklore collections and written sources, including George Pullen Jackson, John Powell, and the tunebooks of William Billings and Daniel Read. In the notes to the second recording, folklorist Joe Hickerson provided the address for ordering Sacred Harp books.

9. "Dueling Concerts, 'Yelping,' and Music Stands in the Square—The First Illinois State Convention Remembered," *Chicago Sacred Harp Newsletter,* December 1994.

10. McGraw acknowledges the *Chicago Newsletter* as his source of inspiration. It should be said, however, that these were not the first Sacred Harp newsletters. Tennessee singer Priestly Miller began publishing the *Harpeth Valley Sacred Harp News* in the 1960s (Cobb 1969, 173). And in 1931, a lavish *Sacred Harp Journal* was begun by singers based in Mineral Wells, Texas—although it was intended, the masthead said, for singers in "Texas, Louisiana, Alabama, Mississippi, Georgia, Oklahoma, and New Mexico," in that order. *Harpeth Valley Sacred Harp News* is still published by Timothy J. Reynolds of Nashville. Richard DeLong became editor of the *National Newsletter* in 1989; in 1991 the masthead listed a committee that included Hugh McGraw, Richard DeLong, Charlene Wallace, and Bill Denny. In July 1993, it ceased publication.

11. A sample of names from the mailing list printed in the 1989 minute book indicated 34.6 percent from Alabama, 16.2 percent from Georgia, and 49.3 percent from all other states. The suggestion that the newsletter appealed disproportionately in new singing areas is supported by a different slant on singing activity: the number of songs led in various areas. I used the minute book for 1995 singings to make such an assessment, with the following results. Songs led, by state (top five): Alabama 8,376; Georgia 2,217; Texas 818; Ohio 515; Illinois 443. Songs led, by county (top five, all in Alabama): Winston 1,255; DeKalb 1,000; Walker 971; Jefferson 886; Cleburne 815. All counties where 200 or more songs were led were in Alabama or Georgia except for Cook County, Illinois, where Chicago is located. Songs led by leader: the highest ranking leader from nontraditional areas was Paula McGray of Massachusetts, ranked number seventy.

12. Sacred Harp singers value their sense of "earned" continuity. In one of the

few excursions into academic debates, editors of the *National Newsletter* (April 1988) took aim at Glenn Wilcox's uncharitable view of Sacred Harp in his introduction to the reprint of the 1854 *Southern Harmony*. Wilcox had concluded, "One need look no further than the *Sacred Harp* to see how 'correction,' 'modernization,' and 'improvement' of its many editions have decimated the original music idiom" (Wilcox 1987, iii).

13. In addition to Boston and Chicago composers there were Neely Bruce, who had directed the American Music Group at the University of Illinois, Urbana-Champaign, and P. Dan Brittain, a church music director living in upstate New York, who had discovered Sacred Harp while stationed at a military base in Georgia.

14. Nine of the forty-three songs in the *Midwest Supplement* were included in the 1991 revision. If its relative prominence at the Midwest Convention is any indication, the *Midwest Supplement* has gone out of use since the appearance of the 1991 revision. In part because of the music's historical ties to New England, *Northern Harmony* was reprinted in 1990 with the support and approval of the Vermont Statehood Bicentennial Commission. This edition was organized by composer, with biographies and a map of New England showing the composers' birthplaces.

15. The most dramatic facets of its antiquarian character were the restoration of the oblong format and the relocation of the melody from the soprano to the tenor. These features had been standard from 1832 until the twenty-fourth edition (1980), when they were replaced with the format of contemporary hymnals. Mennonites have also taken care to recognize the annual singings in the Shenandoah Valley of Virginia, surviving continuously since 1832 (see Nafziger 1994).

16. Hypertext is customarily achieved electronically as computer hypertext— "text composed of blocks of words (or images) linked electronically by multiple paths, chains, or trails in an open-ended, perpetually unfinished textuality" (Landow 1992, 3). But it is also achieved by such means as indexes, bibliographies, and concordances. Ethnomusicologist Jeff Todd Titon (1994) has insisted on a distinction between (1) the kind of hierarchical hypertext composed on computers and (2) weblike hypertext, whose multiple entry points and unsubordinated branches have much more in common with traditional practice.

References

Aaron, Daniel. 1992. *Cincinnati: Queen City of the West, 1819–1838*. Columbus: Ohio State University Press.

Anderson, Fletcher Clark. 1978. A History of Choral Music in Birmingham, Alabama. Ed.D. diss., University of Georgia.

Appiah, Kwame Anthony. 1992. *In My Father's House: Africa in the Philosophy of Culture*. New York: Oxford University Press.

Arnold, Richard. 1990. "Those Damn Sacred Hymns": Some Problems with the Ontology of "Text." In *Man and Nature: Proceedings of the Canadian Society for Eighteenth-Century Studies*, edited by Hans-Gunther Schwarz, David McNeil, and Roland Bonnel, 57–67. Edmonton: Academic.

Bailyn, Bernard. 1960. *Education in the Forming of American Society: Needs and Opportunities for Study*. Chapel Hill: University of North Carolina Press for the Institute of Early American History and Culture, Williamsburg, Va.

Barfield, Louise Calhoun. 1961. *History of Harris County, Georgia, 1827–1961*. Columbus, Ga.: Columbus Office Supply.

Bealle, John. 1994. New Strings on the "Old Harp": The 1991 Revision of *The Sacred Harp. Tributaries: Journal of the Alabama Folklife Association* 1 : 5–23.

Bean, Shirley Ann. 1994. Introduction to *The Missouri Harmony*. Lincoln: University of Nebraska Press.

Beecher, Lyman. 1835. *A Plea for the West*. Cincinnati: Truman and Smith.

———. [1864] 1961. *The Autobiography of Lyman Beecher*. Vol. 2. Edited by Barbara M. Cross. Cambridge: Harvard University Press.

Bell, Bernard W. 1974. *The Folk Roots of Contemporary Afro-American Poetry*. Detroit: Broadside Press.

———. 1985. W. E. B. Du Bois's Struggle to Reconcile Folk and High Art. In *Critical Essays on W. E. B. Du Bois*, edited by William L. Andrews, 106–22. Boston: G. K. Hall.

Bennett, F. Russel Jr. 1974. *The Fellowship of Kindred Minds: A Socio-Theologi-*

cal Study of the Baptist Association. Atlanta: Home Mission Board of the Southern Baptist Convention.

Benson, Louis F. 1903. The American Revisions of Watts's "Psalms." *Journal of the Presbyterian Historical Society* 3 (June/September): 18–34, 75–89.

———. [1915] 1962. *The English Hymn: Its Development and Use in Worship.* Richmond, Va.: John Knox Press.

Bentley, William. 1905. *The Diary of William Bentley, D.D., Pastor of East Church, Salem, Massachusetts (1784–1819).* 4 vols. Salem, Mass.: Essex Institute.

Berger, Peter. 1992. *A Far Glory: The Quest for Faith in an Age of Credulity.* New York: Free Press.

Berk, Stephen E. 1974. *Calvinism versus Democracy: Timothy Dwight and the Origins of American Evangelical Orthodoxy.* Hamden, Conn.: Archon Books.

Boney, F. N. 1977. Part Three: 1820–1865. In *A History of Georgia,* edited by Kenneth Coleman, 127–204. Athens: University of Georgia Press.

Brantley, Rabun Lee. 1929. *Georgia Journalism of the Civil War Period.* Nashville: George Peabody College for Teachers.

Brasher, John Lawrence. 1984. Preface to *Warren's Minstrel,* by J. S. Warren Jr. Athens: Ohio University Press.

Brice, Mark, and Chris Petry. 1984. *Sacred Harp Singers.* Beaconsfield, U.K.: National Film and Television School.

Brisbane, Albert. 1843. *A Concise Exposition of the Doctrine of Association.* New York: J. S. Redfield.

Brown, Alan, ed. 1993. *Dim Roads and Dark Nights: The Collected Folklore of Ruby Pickens Tartt.* Livingston, Ala.: Livingston University Press.

Brown, Virginia Pounds, and Laurella Owens. 1981. *Toting the Lead Row: Ruby Pickens Tartt, Alabama Folklorist.* Tuscaloosa: University of Alabama Press.

Bruce, Dickson D. Jr. 1974. *And They All Sang Hallelujah: Plain-Folk Camp-Meeting Religion, 1800–1845.* Knoxville: University of Tennessee Press.

Buechner, Alan C. 1960. Yankee Singing Schools and the Golden Age of Choral Music in New England, 1760–1800. Ph.D. diss., Harvard University.

———. 1979. Joshua Leavitt's *The Christian Lyre* and the Development of Rural Hymnody in the North. Paper presented at the Symposium on Rural Hymnody, Berea College, Berea, Kentucky, 27–29 April 1979. Housed in the archives of the Hutchins Library, Berea College.

Buell, Lawrence. 1980. Calvinism Romanticized: Harriet Beecher Stowe, Samuel Hopkins, and *The Minister's Wooing.* In *Critical Essays on Harriet Beecher Stowe,* edited by Elizabeth Ammons, 259–75. Boston: G. K. Hall.

————. 1983. Rival Romantic Interpretations of New England Puritanism: Hawthorne versus Stowe. *Texas Studies in Literature and Language* 25(1):77–99.

Carmer, Carl. 1928. The Sacred Harp Singers. *Yale Review* 18:204–7.

————. 1934. *Stars Fell on Alabama.* New York: Farrar and Rinehart.

————. 1993. My Most Unforgettable Character. In *Dim Roads and Dark Nights: The Collected Folklore of Ruby Pickens Tartt,* edited by Alan Brown, 184–90. Livingston, Ala.: Livingston University Press.

Cartwright, Peter. 1856. *Autobiography of Peter Cartwright, the Backwoods Preacher.* Cincinnati: Cranston and Curtis.

Caskey, Marie. 1978. *Chariot of Fire: Religion and the Beecher Family.* New Haven: Yale University Press.

Chase, Gilbert. 1987. *America's Music: From the Pilgrims to the Present.* Rev. 3d ed. Urbana: University of Illinois Press.

Cist, Charles. 1841. *Cincinnati in 1841: Its Early Annals and Future Prospects.* Cincinnati: Privately printed.

Clifford, James, and George E. Marcus. 1986. *Writing Culture: The Poetics and Politics of Ethnography.* Berkeley: University of California Press.

Cobb, Buell E. Jr. 1968. The Sacred Harp of the South: A Study of Origins, Practices, and Present Implications. *Louisiana Studies* 7 (summer): 107–21.

————. 1969. The Sacred Harp: An Overview of a Tradition. M.A. thesis, Auburn University.

————. 1978. *The Sacred Harp: A Tradition and Its Music.* Athens: University of Georgia Press.

Conkin, Paul K. 1988. *The Southern Agrarians.* Knoxville: University of Tennessee Press.

Coulter, E. Merton. 1960. *Georgia: A Short History.* Chapel Hill: University of North Carolina Press.

Crawford, Richard. 1968. *Andrew Law, American Psalmodist.* Evanston, Ill.: Northwestern University Press.

————. 1984. Introduction to *A History of the Old Folks' Concerts,* by "Father" Robert Kemp. New York: Da Capo Press.

————. 1990. "Ancient Music" and the Europeanizing of American Psalmody, 1800–1810. In *A Celebration of American Music: Words and Music in Honor of H. Wiley Hitchcock.* Ann Arbor: University of Michigan Press.

Crozier, Alice C. 1969. *The Novels of Harriet Beecher Stowe.* New York: Oxford University Press.

Davidson, Donald. 1934a. The Sacred Harp in the Land of Eden. *Virginia Quarterly Review* 10:203–17. Reprinted in *Still Rebels, Still Yankees, and Other*

Essays (Baton Rogue: Louisiana State University Press, 1957), 137–56. Second reprint in *Music in Georgia,* edited by Frank W. Hoogerwerf, 1–15 (New York: Da Capo Press, 1984).

————. 1934b. Songs of the Sacred Harp. *Reader's Digest* 24 (May): 83–86.

————. 1935. White Spirituals: The Choral Music of the South. *American Scholar* 4:460–73.

————. 1950. Why the Modern South Has a Great Literature. Presented at the annual meeting of the Southern Literary Festival, Mississippi State College. Reprinted in *Still Rebels, Still Yankees,* 159–79 (Baton Rouge: Louisiana State University Press, 1957).

Davie, Donald. 1982. The Language of the Eighteenth-Century Hymn. In *Dissentient Voice: The Ward-Phillips Lectures for 1980 with Some Related Pieces,* 67–82. Notre Dame, Ind.: University of Notre Dame Press. Originally an address delivered at the William Andrews Clark Memorial Library, Los Angeles, March 5, 1977.

————. 1993. *The Eighteenth-Century Hymn in England.* New York: Cambridge University Press.

Demos, John. 1970. *A Little Commonwealth: Family Life in Plymouth Colony.* New York: Oxford University Press.

Denisoff, R. Serge. 1971. *Great Day Coming: Folk Music and the American Left.* Urbana: University of Illinois Press.

Dett, R. Nathaniel. 1938. Negro Music. In *International Cyclopedia of Music and Musicians,* edited by Oscar Thompson, 1243–46. New York: Dodd, Mead.

Downey, James C. 1986. Joshua Leavitt's *The Christian Lyre* and the Beginning of the Popular Tradition in American Religious Song. *Latin American Music Review/Revista de musica Latino Americana* 7(2):149–61.

Drake, Benjamin, and E. D. Mansfield. 1827. *Cincinnati in 1826.* Cincinnati: Morgan, Lodge, and Fisher.

Du Bois, W. E. B. 1903. *The Souls of Black Folk.* Chicago: A.C. McClurg and Co.

DuBose, John Witherspoon. [1888] 1976. In *Northern Alabama: Historical and Biographical,* 744–58. Spartanburg, S.C.: Reprint.

Dvořák, Antonín. 1895. Music in America. *Harper's New Monthly Magazine* 90: 429–34.

Dyen, Doris J. 1977. The Role of Shape-Note Singing in the Musical Culture of Black Communities in Southeast Alabama. Ph.D. diss., University of Illinois.

Earle, Alice Morse. 1891. *The Sabbath in Puritan New England.* New York: Scribner.

Eddy, Mary O. 1951. Alexander Auld and the Ohio Harmonist. *Midwest Folklore* 1:19–21.

Edwards, Ruth Denson. 1965. "Advancement of Sacred Harp Music" and "History of *The Sacred Harp*." Liner notes to *Original Sacred Harp: Singing in Traditional Style by Sacred Harp Singers*. Bremen, Georgia: Sacred Harp Publishing Company. SHPC-101.

———. [1969]. Sacred Harp Singings in the Southland. Liner notes to *Sacred Harp Singing at the Old Country Church*. Bremen, Georgia: Sacred Harp Publishing Company. SHPC-103.

———. 1973. Liner notes to *Fa-Sol-La Is Here to Stay*. Bremen, Georgia: Sacred Harp Publishing Company. SHPC-105.

Ellis, Howard E. 1955. Lowell Mason and the Manual of the Boston Academy of Music. *Journal of Research in Music Education* 3:3–10.

Epstein, Dena J. 1977. *Sinful Tunes and Spirituals: Black Folk Music to the Civil War*. Urbana: University of Illinois Press.

———. 1983. A White Origin for the Black Spiritual? An Invalid Theory and How It Grew. *American Music* 1(2):53–59.

Fetta, Emma L. 1922. Printing Song Books in Cincinnati. *Cincinnati Enquirer*, October 8.

Finley, James B. 1857. *Autobiography of Rev. James B. Finley; or, Pioneer Life in the West*. Cincinnati: Methodist Book Concern.

Fletcher, William Harold. 1988. Amos Sutton Hayden: Symbol of a Movement. Ph.D. diss., University of Oklahoma.

Flint, Timothy. 1816. *Columbian Harmonist*. Cincinnati: Coleman and Phillips.

Flynt, Wayne. 1989. *Poor but Proud: Alabama's Poor Whites*. Tuscaloosa: University of Alabama Press.

Foster, Charles I. 1960. *An Errand of Mercy: The Evangelical United Front, 1790–1837*. Chapel Hill: University of North Carolina Press.

Fraser, James W. 1985. *Pedagogue for God's Kingdom: Lyman Beecher and the Second Great Awakening*. Lanham, Md.: University Press of America.

Fulling, Katherine Painter. 1939. Singers of the Soil: Including the Fascinating Story of "Buckwheat" or "Shaped" Notes. *Etude* 57 (August): 501–2.

Garber, Susan L. 1987. The Sacred Harp Revival in New England: Its Singers and Its Singings. M.A. thesis, Wesleyan University.

Gary, C. L. 1951. A History of Music Education in the Cincinnati Public Schools. Ed.D. diss., University of Cincinnati.

Gilman, Samuel. [1829] 1984. *Memories of a New England Village Choir*. New York: Da Capo Press.

Goen, C. C. 1962. *Revivalism and Separatism in New England, 1740–1800*. New Haven: Yale University Press.

Gordon, Larry. 1979. Liner notes to Word of Mouth Chorus, *Rivers of Delight:*

American Folk Hymns from the Sacred Harp Tradition. Nonesuch Records H-71360.

Gould, Nathaniel. 1853. *Church Music in America. Comprising Its History and Its Peculiarities at Different Periods, with Cursory Remarks on Its Legitimate Use and Its Abuse.* Boston: A. N. Johnson.

Graham, John R. 1971. Early Twentieth-Century Singing Schools in Kentucky Appalachia. *Journal of Research in Music Education* 19:77–84.

Green, Archie. 1975. Commercial Music Graphics #32: The National Folk Festival Association. *JEMF (John Edward Memorial Foundation) Quarterly* 11:23–32.

Hall, James William Jr. 1968. The Tune-Book in American Culture, 1800–1822. Ph.D. diss., University of Pennsylvania.

Hamm, Charles. 1958. Patent Notes in Cincinnati. *Bulletin of the Historical and Philosophical Society of Ohio* 16:293–310.

———. 1960. The Chapins and the Sacred Music in the South and West. *Journal of Research in Music Education* 8:91–98.

Hatch, Nathan O. 1989. *The Democratization of American Christianity.* New Haven: Yale University Press.

Heafford, Michael. 1967. *Pestalozzi: His Thought and Its Relevance Today.* London: Methuen.

Herman, Janet. 1992. Seekin' the Old Path and Walkin' Therein': The California Sacred Harp Singing Convention and Its Impact on Three First-Time Participants. Presented at the meetings of the American Folklore Society, Jacksonville, Fla., October 15–18.

———. 1993. Interview with Leon Wilson. *California Harp News* 2 (April): 5–12, 2 (July): 4–7.

Henry, Stuart C. 1973. *Unvanquished Puritan: A Portrait of Lyman Beecher.* Grand Rapids: William B. Eerdmans.

Higginson, J. Vincent. 1969. Isaac B. Woodbury (1819–1858). *Hymn* 20:74–80.

Hightower, Raymond Lee. 1934. *Joshua L. Wilson, Frontier Controversialist.* Chicago: University of Chicago Libraries.

Hirsch, Jerrold. 1987. Folklore in the Making: B. A. Botkin. *Journal of American Folklore* 100:3–38.

Hitchcock, A. P. 1882. Hymns and Hymn-Tinkers. *Atlantic Monthly* 49:336–46.

Hoffman, Elizabeth. 1992. Full, Conscious, and Active Singing. *Liturgy* 90 (October): 8–9. Issued by the Office of Divine Worship, Archdiocese of Chicago.

Hudson, Winthrop S. 1961. *American Protestantism.* Chicago: University of Chicago Press.

———. 1981. *Religion in America.* New York: Scribner.

Hulan, Richard Huffman. 1978. Camp-Meeting Spiritual Folksongs: Legacy of the "Great Revival in the West." Ph.D. diss., University of Texas.

Huntington, Gale. 1964. *Songs the Whalemen Sang*. Barre, Mass.: Barre.

Hyman, Stanley Edgar. 1955. Constance Rourke and Folk Criticism. In *The Armed Vision: A Study in the Methods of Modern Literary Criticism*, 114–31. New York: Vintage.

Irwin, Joyce. 1978. The Theology of "Regular Singing." *New England Quarterly* 51:176–92.

Jackson, George Pullen. 1908. German Student Dueling. *World Today* (December): 1241–49.

———. 1911a. From Young Lessing to Percy's "Reliques." Ph.D. diss., University of Chicago.

———. 1911b. Traces of Gleim's Grenadierlieder in 1809. *Modern Language Notes* 26:112–13.

———. 1913. Further Traces of Gleim's Grenadierlieder. *Modern Language Notes* 28:205–8.

———. 1916–17. The Rhythmic Form of German Folksongs. *Modern Philology* 13 (February 1916): 129–49; 14 (June 1916): 1–28; 14 (October 1916): 101–27; 15 (June 1917): 15–38.

———. 1919. American Indifference to the Study of Folklore. *Journal of American Folklore* 32:438–39.

———. 1926. The Fa-Sol-La Folk. *Musical Courier* 93(11):6–7, 10.

———. 1932. The Genesis of the Negro Spiritual. *American Mercury* 26 (June): 243–55.

———. 1933. *White Spirituals in the Southern Uplands: The Story of the Fasola Folk, Their Songs, Singings, and "Buckwheat Notes."* Chapel Hill: University of North Carolina Press.

———. 1936a. America's Folk-Songs. *Virginia Quarterly Review* 12:34–42.

———. 1936b. Stephen Foster's Debt to American Folk-Songs. *Musical Quarterly* 22(2):154–69.

———. 1939. Some Enemies of Folk-Music in America. In *Papers Read at the International Congress of Musicology Held at New York, September 11th to 16th, 1939*, 77–83. New York: American Musicological Society.

———. 1941. Old Time Religion as Folk Religion. *Tennessee Folklore Society Bulletin* 7 (March): 30–39.

———. 1943. *White and Negro Spirituals, Their Life Span and Kinship, Tracing 200 Years of Untrammeled Song Making and Singing among Our Country Folk, with 116 Songs as Sung by Both Races*. New York: Augustin.

————. 1944a. *The Story of the Sacred Harp, 1844–1944.* Nashville: Vanderbilt University Press.

————. 1944b. Review of *A Treasury of American Folklore,* by Benjamin A. Botkin. *Musical Quarterly* 30:496–98.

————. 1945a. Review of *Amische Lieder,* by Joseph Yoder. *California Folklore Quarterly* 4:100–101.

————. 1945b. Review of *Rosanna of the Amish,* by Joseph Yoder. *Tennessee Folklore Society Bulletin* 11 (September): 10.

————. 1945c. Sing Brothers Sing! *Tennessee Folklore Society Bulletin* 11 (May): 1–3.

————. 1945d. The Strange Music of the Old Order Amish. *Musical Quarterly* 31:275–88.

————. 1945e. Why Does American Folk Music Spread So Slowly? *Tennessee Folklore Society Bulletin* 11 (February): 1–3.

————. 1946a. The American Amish Sing Mediaeval Folktunes Today. *Southern Folklore Quarterly* 10:151–57.

————. 1946b. The Folklorist as Apostle of a Broader, Deeper Humanism. *Southern Folklore Quarterly* 10:211–18.

————. 1946c. Revolution in Pittsburgh. *Tennessee Folklore Society Bulletin* 12 (May): 1–6.

————. 1947. Wanted: An American Hans Sachs. *Georgia Review* 1:18–27.

————. 1948. Review of *Fireside Book of Folk Songs,* by Margaret Bradford Boni. *Southern Folklore Quarterly* 12:101–2.

————. 1950. On Knowing Ourselves First (presidential address). *South Atlantic Bulletin* 15 (January): 4–6.

————. 1953. American Folksong and Musical Art. *Southern Folklore Quarterly* 17:140–42.

Jackson, George Pullen, and Charles Faulkner Bryan. 1947. *American Folk Music for High School and Other Choral Groups.* Boston: C. C. Birchard.

James, Joe S. 1904. *Brief History of the Sacred Harp.* Douglasville, Ga.: New South Book and Job Print.

Jedan, Dieter. 1981. *Johann Heinrich Pestalozzi and the Pestalozzian Method of Language Teaching.* Las Vegas: Peter Lang.

Johnson, Charles A. 1955. *The Frontier Camp-Meeting: Religion's Harvest Time.* Dallas: Southern Methodist University Press.

Johnston, Johanna. 1963. *Runaway to Heaven: The Story of Harriet Beecher Stowe.* New York: Doubleday.

Keller, Charles Roy. [1942] 1968. *The Second Great Awakening in Connecticut.* Handen, Conn.: Archon Books, 1968.

Kemp, Father Robert. [1868] 1984. *A History of the Old Folks' Concerts*. New York: Da Capo Press.

Kirkpatrick, John E. [1911] 1968. *Timothy Flint: Pioneer, Missionary, Author, Editor, 1780–1840*. New York: Burt Franklin.

Knott, Sarah Gertrude. 1939. The National Folk Festival—Its Problems and Reasons. *Southern Folklore Quarterly* 3 : 117–24.

Kraege, Elfrieda A. 1980. The Masons and the Beechers: Their Crusade for Congregational Singing in America. *Tracker* 25(1):101–8.

Kübler, G. F. 1826. *Anleitung zum Gesang-Unterrichte in Schulen*. Stuttgart.

Landow, George P. 1992. *Hypertext: The Convergence of Contemporary Critical Theory and Technology*. Baltimore: Johns Hopkins University Press.

Law, Andrew. 1793. *Musical Primer*. Cheshire, Conn.: William Law.

Lesick, Lawrence. 1980. *The Lane Rebels: Evangelicalism and Antislavery in Antebellum America*. Metuchen, N.J.: Scarecrow Press.

Levine, Lawrence W. 1988. *Highbrow/Lowbrow: The Emergence of Cultural Hierarchy in America*. Cambridge: Harvard University Press.

Lindberg, Stanley W. 1976. Introduction to *The Annotated McGuffey: Selections from the McGuffey Eclectic Readers, 1836–1920*, by William Holmes McGuffey. New York: Van Nostrand Reinhold.

Loessel, Earl Oliver. 1959. The Use of Character Notes and Other Unorthodox Notations in Teaching the Reading of Music in Northern United States during the Nineteenth Century. Ed.D. diss., University of Michigan.

Loftis, Deborah C. 1987. Big Singing Day in Benton, Kentucky: A Study of the History, Ethnic Identity and Musical Style of Southern Harmony Singers. Ph.D. diss., University of Kentucky.

Lomax, Alan. 1960. Liner notes to *All Day Singing from "The Sacred Harp."* Recorded at the 1959 United Sacred Harp Singing Convention, Fyffe, Ala. Prestige/International Records 25007.

Lorenz, Ellen Jane. 1980. *Glory Hallelujah! The Story of the Campmeeting Spiritual*. Nashville: Abingdon Press.

Lowens, Irving. 1964. Introduction to *Wyeth's Repository of Sacred Music. Part Second*. New York: Da Capo Press.

Lowens, Irving, and Allen P. Britton. 1953. The Easy Instructor (1798–1831): A History and Bibliography of the First Shape-Note Tune-Book. *Journal of Research in Music Education* 1(1):30–55. Reprinted in Irving Lowens, *Music and Musicians in Early America* (New York: W. W. Norton, 1964), 115–37.

Lucas, G. W. 1844. *Remarks on the Musical Conventions in Boston*. Northampton, Mass.: Privately printed.

Luebke, Frederick C. 1974. *Bonds of Loyalty: German-Americans and World War I*. DeKalb: Northern Illinois University Press.

Lytle, Nelson Andrew. 1930. The Hind Tit. In *I'll Take My Stand: The South and the Agrarian Tradition*, 201–45. New York: Harper and Brothers.

McCaskey, John Piersol. 1881–1892. Franklin Square Song Collection. New York: Harper.

McKay, David, and Richard Crawford. 1975. *William Billings of Boston: Eighteenth-Century Composer*. Princeton: Princeton University Press.

McKenzie, Wallace. 1989. The Alto Parts in the "True Dispersed Harmony" of *The Sacred Harp* Revisions. *Musical Quarterly* 73:153–71.

Marcus, George E., and Dick Cushman. 1982. Ethnographies as Texts. *Annual Review of Anthropology* 11:25–69.

Marini, Stephen A. 1982. The Language of the Soul. In *Radical Sects of Revolutionary New England*, 156–71. Cambridge: Harvard University Press.

Mason, Lowell. 1834. *Manual of the Boston Academy of Music*. Boston: J. H. Wilkins and R. B. Carter.

Mason, Timothy B., and Charles Beecher. 1837. Report on Vocal Music as a Branch of Common School Education. *Western Literary Institute and College of Professional Teachers, Minutes and Transactions* 7:159–78.

Metcalf, Frank J. 1937. The Easy Instructor: A Bibliographical Study. *Musical Quarterly* 23(1):89–97.

Miller, Terry E. 1975. Alexander Auld, 1816–1898: Early Ohio Musician. *Cincinnati Historical Society Bulletin* 33:245–60.

Montell, William Lynwood. 1991. *Singing the Glory Down: Amateur Gospel Music in South Central Kentucky, 1900–1990*. Lexington: University of Kentucky Press.

Mosier, Richard David. 1947. *Making the American Mind: Social and Moral Ideas in the McGuffey Readers*. New York: King's Crown Press.

Nafziger, Jeremy. 1994. Virginia's Tradition of *Harmonia Sacra* Sings: "No Frequency of Use Can Wear Out These Venerable Airs." *Gospel Herald: The Weekly Magazine of the Mennonite Church* 87(31):6–7.

Nutt, Rick. 1991. *Contending for the Faith: The First Two Centuries of the Presbyterian Church in the Cincinnati Area*. Cincinnati: Presbytery of Cincinnati.

Osburn, Mary H. 1942. *Ohio Composers and Musical Authors*. Columbus: F. J. Heer Printing.

Owsley, Frank Lawrence. 1949. *Plain Folk of the Old South*. Baton Rouge: Louisiana State University Press.

Pemberton, Carol Ann. 1985. *Lowell Mason: His Life and Work*. Ann Arbor: UMI Research Press.

Pitzer, Donald Elden. 1966. Professional Revivalism in Nineteenth-Century Ohio. Ph.D. diss., Ohio State University.

Price, Milburn. 1978. Miss Elizabeth Adams' Music Book: A Manuscript Predecessor of William Walker's *Southern Harmony*. *Hymn* 29(2):70–75.

Rabinow, Paul. 1985. Discourse and Power: On the Limits of Ethnographic Texts. *Dialectical Anthropology* 10:1–13.

Raines, Howell. 1990. The "Strange Country." *Virginia Quarterly Review* 66: 294–305.

Rampersand, Arnold. 1976. *The Art and Imagination of W. E. B. Du Bois*. Cambridge: Harvard University Press.

Rankin, Adam. 1802. *A Review of the Noted Revival in Kentucky, 1801*. Lexington: John Bradford.

Rich, Arthur L. 1946. *Lowell Mason: "The Father of Singing among the Children."* Chapel Hill: University of North Carolina Press.

Riley, Rev. B. F. 1888. *Alabama as It Is; or, The Immigrant's and Capitalist's Guide Book to Alabama*. Atlanta: Constitution.

Rogers, William Warren. 1970. *The One-Gallused Rebellion: Agrarianism in Alabama, 1865–1896*. Baton Rouge: Louisiana State University Press.

Rourke, Constance. 1931. *American Humor: A Study of the National Character*. New York: Harcourt Brace.

———. 1942. *The Roots of American Culture*. New York: Harcourt, Brace.

Rubin, Louis D. Jr., ed. 1962. *I'll Take My Stand: The South and the Agrarian Tradition*. New York: Harper and Row.

Scholes, Percy A. 1934. *The Puritans and Music in England and New England: A Contribution to the History of Two Nations*. London: Oxford University Press.

Scholten, James W. 1976. Lucius Chapin: A New England Singing Master on the Frontier. *Contributions to Music Education* 4(4):64–76.

Schultz, Nancy L. 1992. The Artist's Craftiness: Miss Prissy in *The Minister's Wooing*. *Studies in American Fiction* 20 (spring): 33–44.

Seeger, Charles. 1957. Music and Class Structure in the United States. *American Quarterly* 9:281–94.

Shryock, Richard Harrison. 1926. *Georgia and the Union in 1850*. Durham, N.C.: Duke University Press.

Shurden, Walter B. 1967. Associationalism among Baptists in America, 1707–1814. Th.D. diss., New Orleans Baptist Theological Seminary.

Silveri, Louis D. 1988. The Singing Tour of the Fisk Jubilee Singers, 1871–1874. In *Feel the Spirit: Studies in Nineteenth-Century Afro-American Music*, edited by George R. Keck and Sherrill V. Martin, 105–16. Westport, Conn.: Greenwood Press.

Silverman, Kenneth. 1969. *Timothy Dwight*. New York: Twayne.

Simpich, F. 1931. Smoke over Alabama. *National Geographic* 60(6):703–38.

Singin' Billy's Book. 1939. *Time*, June 12, 67.

Smith, O. D. 1947. Joseph Tosso, the Arkansaw Traveler. *Ohio Archaeological and Historical Quarterly* 56:16–45.

Smith, Timothy L. 1967. Protestant Schooling and American Nationality, 1800–1850. *Journal of American History* 53:679–95.

Sonneck, Oscar G. [1909] 1972. *Report on "The Star-Spangled Banner," "Hail Columbia," "America," and "Yankee Doodle."* New York: Dover.

Southern, Eileen. [1972] 1983. An Origin for the Negro Spiritual. In *The Theater of Black Americans: A Collection of Critical Essays*, edited by Errol Hill, 89–98. New York: Applause.

Spencer, Jon Michael. 1994. The Emancipation of the Negro in the Negro Spirituals from the Racialist Legacy of Arthur de Gobineau. *Canadian Review of American Studies* 24(1):1–18.

Stanislaw, Richard John. 1976. Choral Performance Practice in the Four-Shape Literature of American Frontier Singing Schools. D.M.A. diss., University of Illinois at Urbana-Champaign.

Stanley, D. H. 1982. The Gospel-Singing Convention in South Georgia. *Journal of American Folklore* 95:1–32.

Stansbury, Arthur Joseph. 1835. *Trial of the Rev. Lyman Beecher, D.D., before the Presbytery of Cincinnati, on the Charge of Heresy*. New York: New York Observer.

Steinberg, Judith T. 1973. Old Folks Concerts and the Revival of New England Psalmody. *Musical Quarterly* 59:602–19.

Stevens, Harry R. 1943. The Haydn Society of Cincinnati, 1819–1824. *Ohio State Archaeological and Historical Quarterly* 52:95–119.

———. 1947. Adventure in Refinement: Early Concert Life in Cincinnati, 1810–1826. *Bulletin of the Historical and Philosophical Society of Ohio* 5(3):8–22.

———. 1948. Folk Music on the Midwestern Frontier, 1788–1825. *Ohio State Archeological and Historical Quarterly* 57(2):126–46.

———. 1952. New Foundations: Cincinnati Concert Life, 1826–1830. *Bulletin of the Historical and Philosophical Society of Ohio* 10(26):26–38.

Stevenson, Robert. 1949. Dr. Watts' "Flights of Fancy." *Harvard Theological Review* 42(4):235–53.

———. 1966. *Protestant Church Music in America: A Short Survey of Men and Movements from 1564 to the Present*. New York: W. W. Norton.

Stoutamire, Albert. 1972. The Music Conventions. In *Music of the Old South*, 216–18. Rutherford, N.J.: Fairleigh Dickinson University Press.

Stowe, Calvin E. 1838. Report on the Course of Instruction in the Common Schools of Prussia and Wirtemberg. In *Transactions of the Seventh Annual Meeting of the Western Literary Institute and College of Professional Teachers.* Cincinnati: James R. Allbach.

Stowe, Charles Edward. 1889. *Life of Harriet Beecher Stowe, Compiled from her Letters and Journals.* New York: Houghton Mifflin.

Stowe, Harriet Beecher. 1896. *The Writings of Harriet Beecher Stowe.* Riverside edition. New York: Houghton Mifflin.

Sutton, Walter. 1961. *The Western Book Trade: Cincinnati as a Nineteenth-Century Publishing and Book-Trade Center.* Columbus: Ohio State University Press.

Sweet, William Warren, ed. 1923. *Circuit-Rider Days along the Ohio.* Cincinnati: Methodist Book Concern.

———. 1936. *The Baptists, 1783–1830.* Vol. 1 of *Religion on the American Frontier.* New York: Henry Holt.

———. 1946. *The Methodists, 1783–1840.* Vol. 4 of *Religion on the American Frontier.* Chicago: University of Chicago Press.

Thorman, Chris. 1992. *The Sacred Harp Concordance.* San Francisco: Privately printed.

Thurman, Earl. 1952. *The Chattahoochee Musical Convention.* East Point, Ga.: Privately printed.

Titon, Jeff Todd. 1994. Hypertext and Ethnomusicology: Two Scenarios for EF/hm. *Ethnomusicology Research Digest* 5(47): lines 126–202. Electronic file retrievable by anonymous FTP or TELNET or GOPHER as filename ERD 186 (ERD 94–186) from inforM. umd. edu (128. 8. 10. 29), directory /inforM/ Educational Resources/ReadingRoom/ Newsletters/EthnoMusicology/Digest.

Tocqueville, Alexis de. [1835] 1994. *Democracy in America.* New York: Alfred A. Knopf.

Trollope, Frances. [1832] 1949. *Domestic Manners of the Americans.* New York: Alfred A. Knopf.

Tunison, Frank E. 1888. *Presto! From the Singing School to the May Music Festival.* Cincinnati: Criterion.

Turner, Darwin. 1974. W. E. B. Du Bois and the Theory of a Black Aesthetic. *Studies in the Literary Imagination.* 7(2):1–21.

Tyack, David. 1966. The Kingdom of God and the Common School. *Harvard Educational Review* 36 (fall): 447–69.

Tyler, Moses Coit. 1895. *Three Men of Letters.* New York: G.P. Putnam's Sons.

United Presbyterian Synod of Ohio. 1968. *Buckeye Presbyterianism.* Wooster: United Presbyterian Synod of Ohio.

Valeri, Mark. 1994. *Law and Providence in Joseph Bellamy's New England: The Origins of the New Divinity in Revolutionary America*. New York: Oxford University Press.

Wallaschek, Richard. 1893. *Primitive Music: An Inquiry into the Origin and Development of Music, Songs, Instruments, Dances, and Pantomimes of Savage Races*. London: Longman, Green.

Ward, Robert David, and William Warren Rogers. 1965. *Labor Revolt in Alabama: The Great Strike of 1894*. Tuscaloosa: University of Alabama Press.

Webster, Stephen. 1982. Dialogue and Fiction in Ethnography. *Dialectical Anthropology* 7(2):91–114.

Weisberger, Bernard A. 1958. *They Gathered at the River: The Story of the Great Revivalists and Their Impact upon Religion in America*. Boston: Little, Brown.

Westerhoff, John H. 1978. *McGuffey and His Readers: Piety, Morality, and Education in Nineteenth-Century America*. Nashville: Abingdon Press.

Whisnant, David E. 1983. *All That Is Native and Fine: The Politics of Culture in an American Region*. Chapel Hill: University of North Carolina Press.

White, Rev. George. 1854. *Historical Collections of Georgia*. New York: Pudney and Russell.

White, Hayden. 1978. *Tropics of Discourse: Essays in Cultural Criticism*. Baltimore: Johns Hopkins University Press.

Wiener, Jonathan M. 1978. *Social Origins of the New South: Alabama, 1860–1885*. Baton Rouge: Louisiana State University Press.

Wilcox, Glenn C. 1976. E. T. Pound and Unorthodox Musical Notation. In *Festival Essays for Pauline Alderman: A Musicological Tribute*, edited by Burton L. Karson, 195–208. Provo, Utah: Brigham Young University Press.

———. 1987. Introduction to *The Southern Harmony and Musical Companion*, by William Walker (1854 edition). Lexington: University Press of Kentucky.

Williams, Peter W. 1980. *Popular Religion in America: Symbolic Change and the Modernization Process in Historical Perspective*. Englewood Cliffs, N.J.: Prentice Hall.

Wilson, Forrest. 1941. *Crusader in Crinoline: The Life of Harriet Beecher Stowe*. Philadelphia: J. B. Lippincott.

Wilson, Mrs. W. S. 1925. All-Day Singings. In *Musical Alabama*, edited by M. F. Thomas, 27. Montgomery, Ala.: Paragon Press.

Wilson, William A. 1973. Herder, Folklore, and Romantic Nationalism. In *Folk Groups and Folklore Genres*, edited by Elliott Oring, 21–37. Logan: Utah State University Press.

Wittke, Carl. 1936. *German-Americans and the World War*. Columbus: Ohio State Archaeological and Historical Society.

Worthman, Paul B. 1971. Working-Class Mobility in Birmingham, Alabama, 1880–1914. In *Anonymous Americans: Explorations in Nineteenth-Century Social History,* edited by Tamara K. Hareven, 172–213. Englewood Cliffs, N.J.: Prentice Hall.

Wright, Conrad. 1955. *The Beginnings of Unitarianism in America.* Boston: Beacon Press.

Wyatt-Brown, Bertram. 1969. *Lewis Tappan and the Evangelical War against Slavery.* Cleveland: Press of the Case Western Reserve University.

———. 1970. The Antimission Movement in the Jacksonian South: A Study in Regional Folk Culture. *Journal of Southern History* 36:501–29.

Index